UK energy

Structure, prospects and policies

UK energy

Structure, prospects and policies

RICHARD BENDING

and

RICHARD EDEN

*Cambridge University Energy Research Group,
Cavendish Laboratory, University of Cambridge*

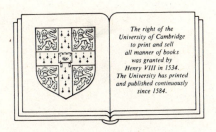

The right of the
University of Cambridge
to print and sell
all manner of books
was granted by
Henry VIII in 1534.
The University has printed
and published continuously
since 1584.

CAMBRIDGE UNIVERSITY PRESS

Cambridge
London   New York   New Rochelle
Melbourne   Sydney

Published by the Press Syndicate of the University of Cambridge
The Pitt Building, Trumpington Street, Cambridge CB2 1RP
32 East 57th Street, New York, NY 10022, USA
296 Beaconsfield Parade, Middle Park, Melbourne 3206, Australia

First published 1984

Printed in Great Britain at The Pitman Press, Bath

Library of Congress catalogue card number: 84–7827

British Library Cataloguing in Publication Data

Bending, Richard
UK energy.
1. Power resources—Great Britain
I. Title   II. Eden, Richard
333.79′0941   TJ163.25.G7

ISBN 0 521 26708 0

PP

Contents

Figures

Tables

Preface

The provision of energy to meet the needs of economic development and general welfare is one of the key issues of our time. In the mid-1980s the United Kingdom has a seeming abundance of energy resources – coal, oil, gas and power stations for electricity generation. But it is widely accepted that oil and gas resources will be depleted so that by the turn of the century the UK will be once again a net importer of energy, and within the lifetime of our children the present flow of oil and gas from the North Sea will have become a distant memory.

The future prosperity of the UK depends not only on the wise planning of energy development and use, but also on the timely execution of those plans so that supply options become realities, and so that the future dependence on energy imports is reduced by improved efficiencies in energy use. Such achievements will depend on understanding and acceptance of both the need for change in energy supply and use, and the long lead-times that separate initial decisions from eventual achievement in energy projects. Difficulties are compounded by uncertainty about the future, which is a crucial ingredient of energy planning and requires diversity and a flexible approach.

There is no simple solution to energy problems – some developments will be more successful than others, some may fail and external circumstances may change. We hope that this book will contribute to a wider understanding of UK energy, and will thereby assist in determining what needs to be done.

The book is designed around three themes: structure, policies and prospects. These are necessarily interwoven: for example, our review of the formulation of energy policy involves also the structure of institutions concerned with energy supply. Similarly, in describing the structure of energy demand we are concerned also with the use of this structure for forecasting possible future energy needs. We begin with introductory chapters on the global energy scene in relation to the UK and on the development of energy policies. Next, we consider in some detail the patterns of energy use in different sectors of final demand, and their relation to economic growth and physical activities. The third part of the book reviews the development of, and prospects for, the energy supply industries. The final part brings together the forecasting element of earlier chapters to give possible scenarios for the future of UK energy demand and supply. These illustrate some of the options, as well as the problems and uncertainties, that must be considered in formulating policies. The final chapter provides a summary of major policy objectives and discusses some of the priorities and difficulties that will need to be resolved if these objectives are to be achieved.

Most of the material presented in this book has benefited from earlier studies carried out over the past twelve years by members of the 'Cambridge Energy Research Group' (CERG). This is an interdisciplinary group of graduate students and research staff based in the Cavendish Laboratory, the Physics Department of the University of Cambridge. We are indebted to our colleagues and former colleagues who have contributed in this way. We wish to express our thanks particularly to Caroline Harper, who provided much of the detailed material and modelling of energy use in households; to Roy Cattell for his contributions on industrial energy use and the services sector; to Colin West, who gave similar help on the transport sector based on earlier work by Ian Bloodworth and Beng Wah Ang; to Nigel Evans for advice and help on electricity supply; and to Tom Kennedy for his valuable comments and suggestions on many aspects of UK energy.

As authors, we take full responsibility for the views expressed in the book, which should in no way be attributed to those whose advice and comments we have sought. With this proviso in mind, we wish to thank friends and associates in the energy industries who have made helpful suggestions and comments during the preparation of the book, particularly including staff of British Petroleum and the National Coal Board.

We also acknowledge past and present financial support to the Cambridge Energy Research Group, which assisted the studies that led up to the book, namely from the University of Cambridge, the Department of Energy, the Science and Engineering Research Council, the Social Science Research Council (now the Economics and Social Research Council), British Petroleum, British Nuclear Fuels, the Electricity Council, the National Coal Board and Shell International.

Finally, we wish to thank the Group's information officer Mrs Cynthia Wilcockson, BA, and secretaries Mrs Gerie Lonzarich, BA, and Mrs Jan Jenkins, for their invaluable assistance in the preparation of the book.

Cambridge 1984   RICHARD BENDING
                                                           RICHARD EDEN

Abbreviations

(See appendix for further abbreviations associated with energy units.)

ACE	Association for the Conservation of Energy
ACEC	Advisory Council on Energy Conservation
AGR	advanced gas-cooled reactor
APRT	advanced payment petroleum revenue tax
ATM	advanced technology mining
BGC	British Gas Corporation
BNFL	British Nuclear Fuels Ltd
BNOC	British National Oil Corporation
CCE	cost of conserving energy
CEGB	Central Electricity Generating Board
CERG	Cambridge Energy Research Group
CHP	combined heat and power
CIBS	Chartered Institute of Building Services
COD	coal/oil dispersion
COM	coal/oil mixture
COP	coefficient of performance (of heat pump)
CPE	centrally planned economies
CPRS	Central Policy Review Staff
CVT	continuously variable transmission
DEVC	developing countries
DIY	do-it-yourself
DNC	declared net capability
EdF	Electricité de France
EEC	European Economic Community
ETSU	Energy Technology Support Unit
FBR	fast breeder reactor
FLAGS	Far-North Liquids and Associated Gas System
GDP	gross domestic product
GTOE	billion (thousand million) tonnes of oil equivalent

IEA	International Energy Agency
kWso	kilowatts sent out (i.e. power station capacity less own use)
LB-HC	lean-burn, high-compression
LBG	low btu gas
LNG	liquefied natural gas
LPG	liquefied petroleum gases
MBD	(or mbd) million barrels per day
MBDOE	(or mbdoe) million barrels per day oil equivalent
MBG	medium btu gas
MIT	Massachusetts Institute of Technology
MLH	minimum list heading (defining a single industry)
MTOE	(or mtoe) million tonnes of oil equivalent
MWso	megawatts sent out (i.e. power station capacity less own use)
NCB	National Coal Board
NDB	net decision benefit
NEC	net effective cost
NEDO	National Economic Development Office
NEL	National Engineering Laboratory
NEPSG	Nuclear Energy Policy Study Group
NGL	natural gas liquids
NHS	National Health Service
NIES	Northern Ireland Electricity Service
NSHEB	North of Scotland Hydro-Electric Board
NUM	National Union of Mineworkers
OECD	Organisation for Economic Cooperation and Development
OPEC	Organisation of Petroleum Exporting Countries
PAYE	pay-as-you-earn
PRT	petroleum revenue tax
PRV	petroleum replacement value
PWR	pressurised water reactor
R&D	research and development
RD&D	research, development and demonstration
SGE	supercritical gas extraction
SGHWR	steam-generating heavy water reactor
SNG	substitute natural gas
SPD	supplementary petroleum duty
SSEB	South of Scotland Electricity Board
TIP	total industrial production
TOE	(or toe) tonne of oil equivalent
TRRL	Transport and Road Research Laboratory
TUC	Trades Union Congress

UCG	underground coal gasification
UKAEA	United Kingdom Atomic Energy Authority
UKCS	United Kingdom Continental Shelf
VAT	value-added tax
WOCA	World outside Communist areas
WOCOL	World Coal Study

1

Introduction

1.1   Policies and uncertainty

Energy policies in the United Kingdom during the past forty years have been numerous and diverse. Their diversity has been matched by the rich variety of the energy landscape and economic climate in which they have been successively formulated and discarded. First there was coal – the post-war need to increase production was transformed into a need for reduction as imported oil replaced coal in many of its traditional markets. By 1973 oil imports provided half of the total energy supplies and the fourfold increase in oil prices that followed the energy crisis in that year led to a serious balance of payments problem. Ten years later oil demand had declined and North Sea oil production had increased so that the UK was a net exporter, insulated from changes in the world oil price but unprotected from competition in international trade and the world economic recession that was due, in part, to the second oil crisis.

The circumstances surrounding electricity planning were no less varied than those for energy. Post-war shortages and blackouts were overcome within a decade, and the industry succeeded in meeting a growth in demand that averaged 7 per cent annually until 1970. This achievement became tarnished after that year, initially through failure to anticipate the impact on electricity markets of the immensely successful marketing of natural gas that accompanied the rapid growth of North Sea production. This initial difficulty was compounded by the recession and subsequent low economic growth that followed the 1973 energy crisis. Difficulties for the electricity supply industry from reduced electricity demand were increased by changes in the relative costs of fuels for generation and by changes in public and political views on environmental issues in general and on nuclear power in particular.

It is no wonder that by the 1980s governments had become reluctant to declare new energy policies, let alone formulate plans. Politicians may well ask – 'What chance is there that energy plans can correctly anticipate the future?' – even supposing the plans are not changed by some succeeding government with different views on social needs or political priorities. However, it may be appropriate here to anticipate our later analysis and to observe that energy is so

1

pervasive throughout the economy that almost all actions by government impinge on energy in some way, and the absence of a positive energy policy means in practice that the policy is determined by default. It would be prudent, at the very least, to examine the energy implications of policies in other areas. But, national needs go well beyond this minimum level: there are critical decisions in the energy arena that only government can make, and, for some of these, procrastination and delay could be harmful to economic needs and national welfare.

Our main objective in this book is to describe the background against which energy policies are formulated and decisions made. We shall describe the energy landscape, to which we referred earlier, and ask what lessons can we learn from the main features of the terrain through which the UK has journeyed in the past. We shall also look towards the future, and ask how one can best plan under uncertainty – and whether there are any features that can reasonably be perceived in advance.

The future, even as far distant as the middle of the next century, cannot be entirely set aside in the decisions that are made today. A power station whose construction is started in, say, 1985, will probably still be in use in 2025. Some energy technologies which will be important in 2050 will depend on research and development in progress today. The middle of the next century is less than a lifetime away – those who are children today will be senior citizens then and their children will be in mid-career, no doubt grappling with difficulties that have been, in part, bequeathed to them by those responsible today.

We are not primarily concerned with forecasting energy futures, though we do use illustrative scenarios to discuss problems that need to be considered. If one is to plan for an uncertain future, it is necessary to examine some of the possibilities or outcomes from particular actions or events. This would reveal some of the risks that it might be prudent to reduce or avoid, and some of the opportunities that could lead to benefits. It would help to identify what options are available, and what courses of action could maintain or close particular options.

We shall discuss later the objectives of energy policy and the problems posed by conflicts between some objectives. However, before we turn to future objectives and options for the UK, we shall examine the past and the present. Thus a major part of the book is concerned with the structure of energy demand and supply, the way in which they have changed in the past and the mechanisms that underlie these changes.

1.2   Fuel demand and supply

Prior to 1950, for more than two hundred years, the demand for energy in the UK had been met almost entirely by indigenous coal production. During the nineteenth and into the early decades of the twentieth centuries, there had been

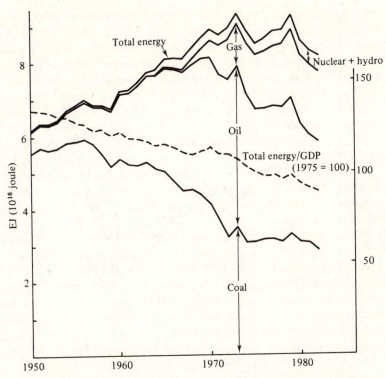

1.1 UK energy use and energy/GDP ratio, 1950–82. Non-energy uses of oil are excluded

a substantial surplus of coal production over demand and UK coal exports were an important factor in the balance of payments. The second world war left the coal industry with reduced capacity and for some years it was unable to meet the increasing demand generated by the post-war recovery. Then, during the 1950s, the availability of cheap oil in world markets encouraged substitution from coal to oil in the UK as elsewhere. The resulting decline in the demand for coal and the complementary growth in oil use are illustrated in figure 1.1.

In the late 1960s, following the discovery of natural gas in the North Sea, there was a rapid expansion in production, and its use soon became widespread in most sectors of final energy demand, with the obvious exception of transport. Whereas in 1950, 90 per cent of total primary energy consumption was met by coal, in 1972 this figure had fallen to 36 per cent, and oil and gas accounted for 48 per cent and 12 per cent, respectively (Department of Energy, 1983a and earlier editions). Thus the sudden fourfold increase in world oil prices in 1973/4 found the UK substantially dependent on oil.

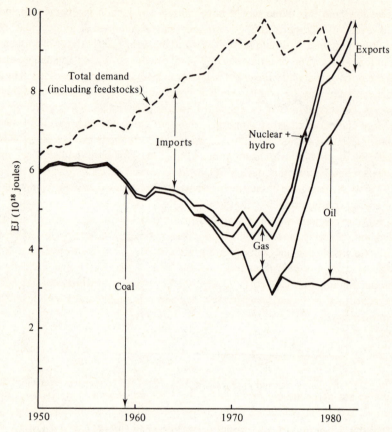

1.2 UK energy production and imports, 1950–82

The decline in coal demand was matched by a decline in coal production, as the size of the industry was reduced, and by an increase in imports of oil (figure 1.2). However, after 1973, following the development of natural gas fields in the southern part of the North Sea, there were major discoveries of oil in the northern part. Their development, together with increased gas production, resulted in the UK becoming a net energy exporter by 1982.

This move towards UK energy self-sufficiency was enhanced by events following the world energy crises of 1973/4 and 1979/80. In the first crisis the price of oil quadrupled, and this was followed by a period of low world economic growth and a slight decline in the real price of oil. The second crisis involved a further doubling in the oil price, and was a major factor in causing the world economic recession in the early 1980s. The UK economy was hit by the world recession, and this alone would have caused a reduction in energy demand. However, in addition, the government had maintained a policy that oil produced by the UK should be sold at world market prices both for inland sales and for exports. The resulting increase in oil prices encouraged an increase also in the price of coal and, somewhat delayed, an increase in the price of gas. These higher energy prices, coupled with a government programme to encourage energy conservation, led to enhanced energy efficiencies and a reduction in energy compared to gross domestic product (GDP). The energy/GDP ratio, shown as a broken line in figure 1.1, had been declining in the UK since 1880, the peak of early industrialisation, but without the stimulus of higher prices and energy conservation this decline might have slowed down or reversed in the 1970s, as the rising use of energy for transport became an increasing component of energy consumption.

In later chapters we shall consider in more detail the structure of energy demand, showing how activities in different sectors give rise to different components of demand with different preferences for fuels or electricity. We shall also discuss energy supply and the factors that determine indigenous production potential and costs. One of the key issues with which we shall later be concerned is the balance between demand and supply and future levels of energy imports.

1.3   Energy questions and issues

We write in 1983 at a time when energy problems seem to have become submerged by economic problems in the UK and abroad, and attention has turned to questions of security and disarmament. But at any time the continuing conflicts in the Middle East could extend so as to disrupt the main artery of international trade in oil through the Straits of Hormuz. Even in a period of low demand for oil, such a disruption would require successful operation of the oil-sharing contingency plans of consumer countries in the IEA (International Energy Agency) in order to prevent another price explosion or actual scarcity of oil. If an interruption in world oil trade was prolonged it would be difficult for an orderly market to be maintained even if there was cooperation also from some members of OPEC (the Organisation of Petroleum Exporting Countries) and other oil producers.

A sudden change in world oil trade is a risk that will continue, and it will become a more serious threat to the UK as North Sea oil production declines and oil imports begin to impose a burden on the balance of payments. Quite apart from possible disruptions in world oil supplies there is an uncertain future for world energy. We shall see that world oil prices are likely to be higher in real terms when the UK once again requires oil imports. Thus the question of future import dependence is a major issue for energy policy. This dependence may not be confined to oil alone – there is likely to be an increasing need also for imports of natural gas and coal. We shall therefore also discuss world energy prospects so that the impact of alternative futures on the UK energy scene can be considered in relation to alternative options for indigenous energy production or increased imports.

Recent changes in the relation between UK energy demand and economic growth have led to a hope, and sometimes a belief, that future energy problems will disappear, or at least be reduced, by massive benefits from energy conservation. We shall analyse the characteristics of energy use in considerable detail in order to identify the levels of energy saving that can reasonably be expected. Our central view is based on continuing improvements in the technological and economic efficiency with which energy is used, but, with a plausible optimism about future economic growth, this still leaves a major task for the energy supply industries to meet both an increased demand and a pattern of fuel use that may be radically different from that of today. We shall discuss the difficulties that will be met by the supply industries in responding to these changes.

For some of the energy supply industries, major decisions are dependent on government policy and on the administration of that policy by the Department of Energy. We shall therefore examine the institutional arrangements which affect policies and their execution, and ask not only how they have fared in the past but also whether changes may be desirable in the future. One issue that arises directly from uncertainty and sudden changes in the energy scene is whether the procedures by which new energy developments take place are sufficiently flexible to avoid serious inefficiencies, or even energy scarcity, in the future. This issue raises questions that are technological as well as institutional: for example, could greater flexibility, or faster response through shorter construction times, become available for electricity supply through the option of smaller generating sets to meet part of future demand?

Decisions by the oil supply industry, although not tied institutionally to government administration, are strongly influenced by the fiscal regime in which they operate. With more costly oil developments on the UK sector of the Continental Shelf, the plans of oil companies are increasingly long term. These high costs will impose selection on the world oil industry, and, whether they increase or decrease, work on UK production will depend on world oil prospects and on the track-record of the UK in relation to taxation as well as on future intentions. These issues are not simply a matter for energy policy, they depend also on other objectives. The conflict of objectives presents one of the most difficult areas of energy policy to which we shall return in the final chapter of the book.

1.4   Analysis and modelling

The role of the energy analyst is to help to identify questions that need to be examined and other factors that are relevant to decisions on energy developments. Amongst the tools that are available to the analyst is an array of energy models that contribute to the understanding of energy supply and demand and may assist in pointing the way toward optimal decisions, or decisions whose merits remain robust in an uncertain future.

However, it is important to recognise that policy conclusions can rarely be derived from the mechanical operation of an energy model. At best the critical assumptions that provide the input to a model can be expressed in probabilistic form that might lead to a least-cost decision that remains valid for most input values. More generally, both the input and the structure of the model itself are too uncertain to provide more than a set of scenarios for the future that illustrate the kind of features that need to be considered. In later chapters we shall use quantitative modelling as a basis for discussion in this sense – it is not a mechanical device for reaching policy conclusions. Our aim is to identify and clarify issues which are (or should be) of concern in the short- to medium-term future, many of which will also have important implications for the long term.

Models of energy use fall into two types: those based on economics and those based on engineering (known colloquially as 'top-down' and 'bottom-up' models, respectively). Both types have strengths and weaknesses. Economic models, based as they are on interpretation of the past and its extrapolation into the future, may be myopic about the impact of technical change and innovation. Engineering models, on the other hand, may fail to take proper account of the consumers' economic response, assuming (at worst) that whatever is technically feasible must be both desirable and, in the long term, inevitable. In this study we shall make use of both types of model, though with a bias towards engineering-based 'bottom-up' models. The main reason for this bias is that many energy policy questions are couched in terms of technology. They involve decisions to construct or adopt new equipment, or they concern research and development, or measures to encourage the use of specific tehniques. Guidance on such questions arises more naturally from an engineering-style model.

Some energy models may also be classified as optimising models. In such cases, the aim is to choose values of control variables in such a way as to minimise an objective function (usually total costs). Optimising models, which generally make use of linear or non-linear programming techniques, may be used in individual sectors or for the energy system as a whole. This study makes some use of the optimisation approach, in particular in the modelling of the electricity supply industry. No attempt is made at an overall optimisation of energy policy, however. The technical requirements of the optimisation procedure usually enforce considerable simplification of the relationships concerned, which is likely to be unrealistic when applied to the complete system of energy supply and consumption. In addition, it is difficult to take uncertainty into account in a global optimisation approach, and the use of a single well-defined objective function over-simplifies the complexity of the real decision-making process.

The purpose of an energy model is to predict the consequences, in terms of the consumptions of different fuels (or the capacities of fuel-producing plant), of given values of other variables. The 'other variables' are, typically, the levels of economic activity and fuel prices. During the period of steady growth through the 1950s and 1960s, it was common practice to use a single, central, view of economic growth and fuel prices and to prepare a single forecast of (say) electricity demand from it. This could then readily be translated into a decision on the quantity of (in this case) electricity generating plant to be installed. Thus there was a simple linear connection between the initial assumptions and the final decision. Uncertainty, inasmuch as it was recognised at all, was taken into account by allowing a margin above the level of forecast demand.

In the much less certain world of the 1970s and 1980s, such a simple approach is no longer adequate. Instead, it is usual to recognise the uncertainties of the long term explicitly by examining a range of scenarios (e.g. Department of Energy, 1982). Decisions are then sought which are robust against a range of possible futures. A robust decision may be defined, for example, as a decision that: (i) remains nearly optimal for a variety of scenarios representing alternative futures, (ii) avoids excessive risk that could arise from a relatively unlikely event that could have serious consequences and (iii) leaves open some suitable options to change future energy plans so as to re-optimise later decisions if the future expectations are different from those that seem likely today.

A scenario approach for testing the robustness of decisions or plans is clearly preferable to the use of a single forecast, particularly in the longer term, but it does not remove by any means the problems of an uncertain world. First, the input assumptions which define the scenarios are necessarily judgement-based and may not encompass the actual course of events. This is particularly true when the scenarios cover many variables, as it is then not practicable to consider all combinations of values. Second, the presentation of a number of disparate scenarios, while usefully demonstrating the difficulty of the decision-making process, may not make that process any easier, unless a specific course of action emerges as being robust under most scenarios. If it is possible to assign probabilities (necessarily subjective) to the scenarios, then formal methods of decision theory may be applicable (e.g. Raiffa, 1970).

It is evident from the above discussion that there is a substantial subjective element in decision-making. This is seen in the choice and weighting of energy policy objectives (for example, the reduction of total energy costs may conflict with the need to maintain security by diversifying fuel supplies), the initial choice of scenarios and the assignment of probabilities to scenarios in order to evaluate specific courses of action. Formal decision analysis techniques do not replace this subjective element, but instead allow it to be recognised explicitly.

One consequence of the use of scenarios in energy planning may be to overwhelm the decision-maker with too much information. For this practical reason it is necessary to limit the number of scenarios, at the expense of some degree of coverage of possible futures. In this study, we use three economic scenarios for the UK, combined with a single future for world oil prices. Other, more specific, variants are considered in the context of particular policy issues.

Most scenarios used in the analysis of energy policy issues assume smooth changes in economic activity and fuel prices. This is unlikely to be the case in practice. Experience since 1973 would suggest that the future will be characterised by a strong business cycle (alternating booms and slumps in the world economy), with oil prices at times rising sharply and at other times static or falling. The response of individual countries, including the UK, to this unstable situation will differ from its response to any smooth scenario, in particular because the lack of stability may paralyse any long-term strategic thinking.

For a discussion of more general energy issues the reader is referred to *Energy Economics* (Eden et al., 1981).

1.5   Units and conventions

Energy analysis is complicated by the wide variety of units of measurement used. In appendix A, a list of definitions, conversion factors and approximate equivalents is given. In this book, we shall use multiples of the joule for describing energy in general. Where discussion is confined to a particular fuel, we shall often use also the 'natural' unit of measurement for that fuel, e.g. tonnes of coal or kilowatt-hours of electricity.

Energy flows from the original fuel resource, through various conversion and transmission processes, until it is finally consumed. The quantity of energy may be measured at different stages in this process, and the different definitions are sufficiently important to be introduced here.

Primary energy is measured in terms of the heat content of the fuel in the case of coal, oil or natural gas, as it comes from the ground. In the case of hydro or nuclear power, primary energy is usually defined as the energy in fossil fuel that would generate the same amount of electricity. Primary energy is almost always the largest of the three measures.

Delivered energy is the quantity of energy delivered to the final consumer. It is always less than primary energy, first because of conversion losses (nearly 70 per cent of the primary energy used to produce electricity is lost, for example) and, second, due to transmission losses.

Useful energy is the amount of energy actually put to a useful purpose in final consumption. For a domestic boiler, for example, the heat which goes into the water in the radiators is useful energy, whereas that which escapes up the flue is not. With a few special exceptions, useful energy is always less than delivered energy.

An example will illustrate the three measures. Suppose a householder receives 100 units of heating oil and 50 units of electricity. His energy use, in *delivered energy* terms, is then 150 units. Suppose, now, that his boiler has an efficiency of 65 per cent (that is, 35 per cent of its output is lost in flue gases and other losses), and that we regard his electrical appliances as 100 per cent efficient. His *useful* energy consumption is then

$$100 \times 0.65 + 50 = 115 \text{ units.}$$

Now suppose further that the overall efficiency of electricity generation (taking into account both conversion and transmission losses) is 28 per cent, and that the corresponding figure for domestic heating oil is 93 per cent, the losses in this case arising mainly in the oil refinery. Then in *primary energy* terms, the householder's energy consumption is

$$\frac{100}{0.93} + \frac{50}{0.28} = 286 \text{ units.}$$

Note the large difference of 171 units between primary and useful energy. This is made up of 128 units lost in electricity generation and transmission, 8 units lost in oil refining and 35 units lost in the householder's boiler.

1.6   Outline of the book

The book is structured in three parts. Chapters 1 to 5 provide the introduction, and place UK energy in a global and historical context. In chapter 2 we consider the world energy environment in which the UK is placed, and outline prospects for world energy and world fuel prices. In chapter 3 we review the history of energy policy in the UK and describe the institutional framework within which energy policy operates. Chapter 4 discusses the prospects for the UK economy, and defines the three economic scenarios which provide the starting-point for later analysis. Chapter 5 answers the question 'Where are we now?' displaying the current pattern of fuel use in the UK.

The second part of the book, chapters 6 to 12, contains the detailed analysis and discussion. Chapters 6, 7, 8 and 9 deal respectively with households, industry, transport and services. The electricity supply industry and the role of nuclear energy are discussed in chapter 10. Chapters 11 and 12 consider the supply picture for oil and gas and for coal.

Chapters 13, 14 and 15 form the third part of the book. Chapter 13 reviews policies on energy conservation. In chapter 14, the results of the analysis described in the second part of the book are brought together to indicate possible energy prospects for the UK. Chapter 15 examines energy policy objectives, and considers how they may be related to the problems and issues that are identified by the studies in the book.

2

World energy background

2.1   World energy and the UK

The world energy scene has an inescapable impact on the UK economy, both directly through the cost and availability of fuels and indirectly through its influence on world economic activity. During the 1950s and 1960s the ready availability of internationally traded oil at low cost led the UK, like other countries, to substitute oil for coal as the main fuel to meet increasing energy demand. In the same period cheap oil was one of the factors that aided world economic growth and increased world trade giving conditions favourable to economic growth in the UK.

In contrast the doubling and redoubling of OPEC oil prices in October 1973 and January 1974 not only produced a radical change in the fuel market but also contributed to the world economic recession in 1974–5 and adversely affected the UK economy. The second oil price rise in 1979–80 had even more striking effects on both the world fuel market and the world economy, with the economic recession reacting back on the fuel market in general and on world oil prices in particular. The second increase in oil prices came at a time when the UK was approaching self-sufficiency in oil production, but this seemingly favourable position so strengthened the pound sterling in relation to other currencies that the UK was unable to maintain its markets for manufactured exports in the face of competition from other countries during the subsequent world economic recession. This led to a decline in UK manufacturing industry, particularly in energy-intensive industries such as iron and steel and paper manufacturing, and accelerated the process of structural change in the UK economy as a whole.

In this chapter we comment on some aspects of the historical role of oil, showing how its key role in world energy has been associated in recent years with the development of OPEC. We then discuss the outlook for oil, its role as market leader in the fuel market and the circumstances for change. This brings us to a discussion of other fuels, their resources and potential for production, and the problems of bringing them to the market. Next we give results from an illustrative 'central' projection of world energy demand, which show also the

12

important role played by energy conservation. Finally, we summarise the main conclusions from a study of the world energy outlook which we have reported in more detail elsewhere (Eden, 1983).

2.2 Oil in the world economy

In the period 1950–73 the world experienced a period of unprecedented economic growth, with real annual growth averaging 5.2 per cent. Average growth in total energy demand was the same, but for oil demand it was 7.6 per cent – the total use of oil increased more than fivefold in the period. The centrally planned economies (USSR and China regions) grew rapidly from a low base due to the ravages of war. Whilst this factor was important also in Europe and Japan, the continued high growth in the market economies as a whole (denoted WOCA, world outside communist areas, i.e. excluding USSR and China regions) was substantially aided by other features of the period.

In the immediate post-war period the United States used its large current account surplus to provide both aid and investment to help towards recovery in those countries whose economies had been seriously damaged by the war. Economic growth was helped also by the extension of free trade, the stable monetary regime with nearly constant exchange rates following the Bretton Woods agreement and the institutional flexibility (including changed labour practices) that was possible following the traumatic destruction of the war. The availability of cheap oil in ever-increasing quantities was an important factor in permitting continued high growth. The real price of oil fell by nearly one-half between 1950 and 1970 and many industrialised countries were able to finance massive and increasing imports of oil with relatively modest increases in their exports of manufactured goods. The replacement of coal by oil as the dominant fuel led to improved energy efficiencies in most sectors of their economies, with the notable exception of road transport, though oil prices were too low to encourage serious attempts at energy conservation in most areas of consumption.

By the early 1970s there were already signs of economic problems. High growth had led to higher costs for raw materials including oil, and some key countries were running budget deficits to maintain growth. The US, with its central role in the stability of exchange rates and international trade, was additionally affected by the impact on its economy of the Vietnam war. Inflation was already becoming serious before the oil price rise in 1973.

The production of oil in the US reached its peak in 1970 and began to decline, whilst consumption continued to increase at 5 per cent per annum. This caused a rapid rise in oil imports to the US, from 2 MBD (million barrels per day) in 1967 to 6 MBD in 1973 (36 per cent of total oil consumption). Warnings of the increasing economic and political exposure of the US through these growing oil imports (Akins, 1973) caused concern, though this was partly countered by the classical economic experience of the instability of cartels, which suggested that Middle East oil, priced at nearly $2 per barrel in 1972, was too far above its cost of production (around 10 cents a barrel) for the price to be maintained, let alone increased (Adelman, 1972).

However, on a global scale the major oil companies were increasingly becoming aware that average annual oil discoveries would not for long keep pace with continuing exponential growth in world oil demand, even if this were to be much lower than the average annual growth of 7 per cent that had held for most of the twentieth century until 1973 (Drake, 1974). Thus, some observers were pointing to the inevitability of an oil crisis within a few years, simply because proved reserves would be inadequate to maintain increased production.

In October 1973 the Arab members of OPEC imposed an oil embargo on those countries they believed were providing Israel with assistance in the war between Israel and her neighbours. No doubt the publicity given to the importance of oil in the US and elsewhere was observed in the oil-producing countries themselves. However, neither they nor the oil-importing countries can have been prepared for the resulting panic in the (very small) spot market for oil where the price of oil rose to more than $20 per barrel in a few weeks, compared with $2.70 before the Israel–Arab war. Meantime OPEC unilaterally increased the official price, first to $3.65 and then by steps to reach $9.30 by March 1974, over four times its level a year earlier.

It should be recalled that the original catalyst for the formation of OPEC in 1960 had been the decline in the real price of oil during the 1950s culminating in a unilateral reduction by Esso in the price they would pay for Middle East oil – a reduction that was followed (reluctantly by some) by other oil companies. At that time (1960), Middle East production was some 5 MBD shared fairly equally between Iran, Iraq, Kuwait and Saudi Arabia. Elsewhere Venezuela, which played a key role in the formation of OPEC, was producing nearly 3 MBD, and total OPEC production was 8.5 MBD. During the 1960s and early 1970s, as oil production in OPEC increased (reaching over 25 MBD in 1973), the organisation gradually gained a larger role in the setting of oil prices, until by 1973 it was conducting negotiations (on behalf of all its members) with representatives of the major oil companies. By coincidence in October 1973, when the Israel–Arab war began, a meeting between representatives of OPEC and the oil companies was in progress. The negotiations were broken off and OPEC immediately raised the 'posted' or 'official' price for Saudi Arabian light crude (to which other oil prices are related) from $2.70 a barrel to $3.65. Since then all changes in the official price have been determined by OPEC, though these changes were strongly influenced by the spot market, or by contracts independently negotiated in the free market.

Following the fourfold oil price increase of 1973–4, because of lower growth in demand and worldwide inflation, the real price began to decline. In relation to the cost per unit of OPEC imports, by 1978 there had been a substantial oil price decrease – perhaps by more than a half – but in relation to inflation in OECD (the Organisation for Economic Cooperation and Development, covering almost all industrial countries) as a whole the decrease was more like 20 per cent though there were considerable variations between countries because of changes in exchange rates with respect to the dollar. This weakness in the oil price was due partly to lower economic growth, notably in the recession of 1975, partly to substitution for oil by other fuels (mainly in electricity generation and in steel-making), and partly to active measures for energy conservation. These effects reduced the growth in world oil demand to 2 per cent per annum over the period 1973–8, compared with its earlier value of 7 per cent.

In the second half of 1978 the revolution in Iran began to disrupt its oil exports which had previously been running at about 6 MBD. By the end of December they were suspended altogether and the spot price of oil soared. OPEC brought forward its planned increases in the official price (originally designed mainly to combat inflation) and set a price of $14.56 a barrel in March 1979. However, on the spot market oil was changing hands at more than $20 a barrel, so individual members of OPEC began to add a variety of premiums to the official price and to charge what the market would bear. In the next eighteen months OPEC sought to stabilise the market by successively raising the official price, reaching $32 a barrel by June 1980. The onset of the Iraq–Iran war in 1980 did nothing to help confidence or stability in the oil market.

The timing of the oil price increase in 1979–80 could hardly have been worse in relation to its impact on world economic growth and eventually its impact on OPEC members themselves. The industrialised countries in OECD had been in recession in 1974 and 1975, and had recovered to have economic growth of around 4 per cent in the next four years, though with continued difficulties due to inflation; but growth in 1979–80 fell to only about 1 per cent. The sudden removal from OECD countries of 2 per cent of their total GDP to pay the additional costs of oil imports led to defensive economic measures that reinforced the recession, with only 1 per cent growth in total GDP in 1980–1 and a decrease in 1981–2. Meanwhile, the oil-importing developing countries suffered not only from the increased costs for their oil imports, but also from the lost demand and weaker prices for their own exports, and from a formidable debt burden due to over-rapid expansion during the 1970s.

The effect of lower world economic growth on the demand for OPEC oil was magnified by other factors, some directly attributable to the higher oil prices.

The recession during 1979–83 was associated with a serious reduction in industrial activity in many countries, and within industry there was structural change away from energy-intensive industries, such as iron and steel. Meanwhile, measures for energy conservation and for substitution away from oil that had been set in progress following the 1973/4 price rise were accelerated. Finally, oil production increased in non-OPEC countries, so that, as residual supplier, the OPEC group bore more than its share of the impact of reduced world oil demand – enhanced by destocking (partly seasonal), since oil companies in general had overestimated the expected demand for oil. In March 1983 demand for OPEC oil fell to 14 MBD, compared to its peak of 31 MBD in 1979, and the official price was reduced from $34 to $29 a barrel. At the same time, quotas for production were introduced, designed to limit annual OPEC production to 17.5 MBD, with Saudi Arabia adjusting its production to reflect swings in demand. It is notable that the UK chose to make a corresponding adjustment to the price of North Sea oil that was carefully calculated to maintain sales without further destabilising the OPEC price.

The oil saga in 1973–83 showed that the oil market was not sufficiently flexible to respond to short-term perceptions of scarcity. The IEA (International Energy Agency) was set up by major consuming countries in 1974 in response to the first oil price rise. It was seen as a framework for allocating oil supplies and reducing demand in an emergency (such as the Arab oil embargo in 1973–4), and as a forum for information exchange and planning for the reduction of dependence on oil as an energy source. The emergency procedures were not brought into operation in 1979–80, and the IEA was singularly unsuccessful in moderating the second oil price rise. Its failure was due, at least partly, to the fact that its emergency procedures were based on the idea of a quantity shortfall (of 7 per cent) in oil supplies, rather than on market perception of scarcity; the latter may be almost unrelated to an actual shortfall of supply below the underlying real demand (i.e. excluding abnormal effects due to stock changes).

In the future, as in the past, we expect oil to meet a large part of the swings in world energy demand, and sudden changes in the price of oil, due to short-term expectations of scarcity or glut, will continue to affect economic growth. In the next section we place oil in its historical context of overall energy demand.

2.3   Energy demand and economic growth

During the period 1950–73, economic growth and the growth in world energy demand were almost the same, both averaging 5.2 per cent per annum. However, there were differences between regions. Both the centrally planned economies (CPE) and the group of developing countries (DEVC) had demands for total commercial energy (i.e. excluding woodfuel etc.) that increased faster

Table 2.1. *Energy intensities^a of world groups (1980 = 100)*

	1950	1960	1970	1980
OECD	127	113	117	100
Developing countries (DEVC)^b	61	84	97	100
Centrally planned economies (CPE)^c	122	135	108	100

Notes: ^{a} Energy intensity equals total commercial energy demand divided by total GDP.
^{b} Excluding China and centrally planned Asia.
^{c} USSR, East Europe, China and centrally planned Asia.
Source: OPEC, 1982.

than their economic activity, measured by total GDP. However, the more developed industrial countries, represented by the OECD total, had energy growth averaging 4.3 per cent per annum compared with economic growth of 4.8 per cent per annum, though the consequent decrease in energy intensity (defined as energy demand/GDP) did not take place uniformly through the period, as can be seen in table 2.1.

The increase in energy intensity for the group of developing countries shown in this table was substantially influenced by substitution from woodfuel (not included in total 'commercial' energy) to fossil fuel. By 1980, however, if woodfuel is represented by the amount of energy that would be contained in petroleum to meet the same requirements (its 'petroleum replacement value' or PRV) its use in the developing countries amounted to only about 6 per cent of the total energy consumed. This particular effect will therefore be less significant in the future than in the past.

The energy intensities and energy use per capita for the three main world groups are compared in table 2.2. Average energy intensities in the OECD and the DEVC are similar, though for North America the intensity is 40 per cent higher at 0.70 TOE (tonne of oil equivalent) per $1000, and for the rest of OECD it is lower, at 0.35 TOE per $1000. Similarly, in North America energy use per capita is much higher than the OECD average, namely more than 8 TOE compared with less than 3.5 TOE for the rest of OECD.

The importance of OPEC in world energy trade is shown by the consumption and production figures in table 2.3. The imports of energy to the OECD as a whole in 1980 amounted to 1.20 GTOE (billion tonnes of oil equivalent) and met nearly one-third of total consumption. Most of this total came from OPEC, though smaller amounts came from other developing countries and from the USSR, and most of it was in the form of crude oil.

Table 2.2. *Energy intensities in 1980, and per capita energy consumption in world groups*

Year 1980, units GJ[a]	Energy intensity TOE/$1000	Per capita use TOE
OECD	0.50	4.90
DEVC[b,c]	0.45	0.45
CPE[d]	1.00	1.55

Notes: [a] TOE = tonne of oil equivalent = 42 GJ.
[b] Excluding non-commercial energy.
[c] Excluding China and centrally planned Asia.
[d] USSR, Eastern Europe, China and centrally planned Asia.

Table 2.3. *Energy consumption and production (1980) in world groups*

Year 1980, units GTOE[a]	Consumption	Production[b]	Net-imports
OECD	3.82	2.62	1.20
Developing countries:			
OPEC	0.20	1.45	−1.25
Non-OPEC	0.79	0.65	0.14
CPE	2.13	2.22	−0.09

Notes: [a] 1 GTOE = 1000 MTOE = 42 EJ (lower calorific value).
[b] Including statistical adjustments.

Table 2.4. *Fuel shares of energy demand in 1980*

	Percentage share of consumption in 1980				
	Coal	Oil	Gas	Hydro-electric	Nuclear[a]
OECD	21	49	19	7	4
DEVC	16	62	11	10	1
CPE	48	29	19	3	1

Notes: Woodfuel is not included.
[a] Hydro-electric and nuclear primary energy at a nominal 35 per cent efficiency.

The oil dependence of the main groups in 1980 ranged from less than 30 per cent of the total commercial energy used for the centrally planned economies to more than 60 per cent for the developing market economies (table 2.4). These figures are mirrored by those for coal consumption – nearly 50 per cent of the total in the CPE group, but less than 20 per cent in the developing countries, where only India is a major coal user. The key question which we address in the remainder of this chapter is the manner in which world energy consumption will adjust to a future where the total production of oil is unlikely to increase much above its level in 1980.

2.4 Energy production potential

The worldwide balance between the various factors of production and demand for fuels eventually determines their prices. But, conversely, the price of each fuel and expectations about future prices will influence both factors of production and factors of demand. In this section, for each fuel we identify ranges of potential energy production that are compatible with a general picture of future energy demand associated with a medium level for future economic growth averaging between 2.5 and 3.0 per cent per annum. The consistency of our picture requires increases in the real price of oil, possibly not beginning until around 1990, reaching a value in the range \$40–\$60 per barrel (in 1980 dollars) by the year 2000. This would induce continued substitution of other fuels for oil and further energy conservation as outlined in the next section.

The factors that influence fuel production include:

- The availability of fuel resources that can be commercially recovered using existing technologies. Such resources identified at a particular time are called 'proved reserves'.
- The rate of discovery, namely gross additions to proved reserves. These include extensions to existing fields due to more information, new recovery technologies or higher prices, and discoveries of new fields.
- Lead-times for bringing reserves into production and the costs of bringing them to the market.
- Indigenous energy demand in the country where fuel reserves are located.
- Demand for energy exports from countries with energy resources.
- National policies on energy production and exports.

Table 2.5. *Oil production*

	Oil production GTOE per annum[a]		
	1980	2000	2020
Conventional oil:			
OECD	0.71	0.55-0.65	0.30-0.45
OPEC	1.37	1.30-1.55	0.90-1.30
Non-OPEC DEVC	0.28	0.50-0.70	0.50-0.70
Heavy oil total[b]	-	0.05-0.10	0.20-0.35
WOCA total oil	2.36	2.4-3.0	2.0-2.7

Notes: [a] GTOE per annum = 20 MBDOE.
          [b] Heavy oil, shale oil, tar sands, but excluding synthetic oil made from coal.
               Includes all regions.

Oil production

Current proved reserves and estimated gross additions to reserves can be used to indicate future production potential, which is then modified in the light of current oil production and expected national policies to give initial values for future production. From these one can derive cumulative oil production and the annual additions to proved reserves that are required for consistency, leading to the total oil that would have to be discovered in each world region by some future year. The results are required to satisfy constraints imposed by future annual additions to proved reserves, which must be in line with historical discovery rates and current geological knowledge and with future technology.

Our results for WOCA are given in table 2.5, and some of the parameters used for consistency checks are shown for a central view in table 2.6. Table 2.5 shows that oil production in WOCA is expected to lie in the range 2.0 to 3.0 GTOE per annum, or 40 to 60 MBDOE (million barrels per day oil equivalent). This may be compared with the actual range of 40 to 52 MBDOE during the period 1970–83. In addition, perhaps for a decade or more, the USSR plans to maintain oil exports to WOCA at about 1 MBDOE. China may also provide some quantities for export, but is likely to need future discoveries mainly for its own use in the longer term.

Table 2.6 shows that our assumptions and projections for future oil production would lead to a reduction in the overall reserves to production ratio (R/P) for WOCA from thirty-five years in 1980 to nineteen years in 2030. This would require average annual 'discoveries', or gross additions to proved reserves, to

Table 2.6. *Conventional oil reserves/production and implied discovery rates (central view)*

Conventional oil in:	Reserves/Production		Average annual discoveries[a] 1980-2030 GTOE	Percentage share of total oil discovered in WOCA by 2030
	1980 (years)	2030 (years)		
OECD	12	11	0.41	23
OPEC	45	31	0.66	58
Non-OPEC				
DEVC	44	11	0.50	19
WOCA	35	19	1.57	100

Note: [a] 'Discoveries means gross additions to proved reserves (see p. 19).

average about 1.57 GTOE or 11.5 billion barrels. This is less than the historical average over the past forty years which is dominated by the giant and super-giant oil fields found in the Middle East. Future new discoveries of such large fields are thought to be very unlikely, and most of the projected gross additions would need to come from extensions and improved recovery from existing fields.

In addition to conventional oil that will become available, the assumption of higher oil prices in the future allows our projections to include an increasing amount of oil produced from heavy oil deposits (particularly in Venezuela and in North America), and from tar sands and shale oil. The additional oil resources from deposits of heavy oil etc., recoverable at $30–$60 per barrel (1980 dollars), are comparable with the so-called 'ultimate' resources of conventional oil, which are estimated to be in the range 250 to 300 GTOE. However, their development will be slow compared with the historical growth of low-cost conventional oil production because of the enormous capital investment required, amounting to more than $50 000 million to produce 1 MBDOE.

Natural gas

It is generally accepted that the 'ultimate' resources of natural gas are likely to be comparable with those for conventional oil. However, the major part of future gas discoveries, as with existing reserves, are likely to be located inconveniently in relation to major markets, notably in Siberia and in the Middle East. Expansion of natural gas production is likely to be constrained not only by the investment cost of long-distance pipelines or LNG (liquefied natural

Table 2.7.   *Energy production potential in WOCA*

Units GTOE	1980	2000	2020
Coal	0.96	1.5-2.0	2.0-3.1
Oil	2.36	2.4-3.0	2.0-2.7
Gas	0.88	1.0-1.4	0.8-1.5
Wood etc.[a]	0.07	0.1	0.1-0.2
Hydro-electric	0.34	0.6-0.8	0.7-1.0
Nuclear	0.15	0.4-0.7	0.9-1.5
Total	4.76	6.0-8.0	6.5-10.0

Note: [a] Wood measured in terms of its petroleum replacement value (PRV) (about one-third of its thermal value).

gas) facilities, but also by political and security factors, such as East–West relations (for Siberian gas), or the stability of countries through which pipelines might need to pass (for Middle East gas). Thus, our projections for possible ranges of future gas production shown in table 2.7 take these factors into account, in addition to the constraints arising from reserves to production (R/P) ratios, discovery rates and estimated resources.

It is known that the USSR has very large proved reserves of natural gas and much larger probable resources which will be important for continued growth in their own energy needs. However, exports of Russian gas are likely to be limited more by transportation and security issues than by resource limitations. From the viewpoint of energy balances in WOCA it is therefore more informative to estimate these exports directly rather than as a difference between production and internal demand. We expect gas exports from the USSR to Western Europe to be in the range 40 to 80 MTOE (million tonnes of oil equivalent) by 2000, and 50 to 100 MTOE by 2020. Allowing for these imports it would be possible for natural gas demand in WOCA to increase by as much as 50 per cent above its 1980 values by 2000 and to maintain these higher levels for several decades (see table 2.7).

Coal production

Coal production is driven by demand and it is unlikely that there will be any general resource limits that would force the price substantially upwards until after the turn of the century – perhaps well after. However, as demand increases, the lower-cost producers will begin to take rent and move their prices up towards the marginal price for coal in international trade. This process may be accelerated by policies on resource depletion in Australia and South Africa that limit production and exports. Similar policies, coupled with environmental considerations, are expected, in due course, to limit production in some states in the US. Production in Western Europe is unlikely to expand very much because of the limited availability of low-cost reserves. In developing countries, coal exploration is likely to increase substantially and it is expected that considerable new resources of coal will be discovered, though not necessarily of high quality. Their role in international trade will depend on their quality as well as magnitude, and on costs of transportation to an ocean terminal as well as costs of production. Potential coal production in WOCA is summarised in table 2.7. Both the USSR and China have very large proved coal reserves and probable resources, but their location in both cases is not very convenient either for their own major markets or for exports. Thus coal imports into WOCA are likely to remain relatively small.

Woodfuel, biomass and solar

In view of their importance for developing countries, woodfuel and other biomass energy sources have been included in the illustrative projections given in this chapter. They are shown on a petroleum replacement basis, namely as the quantity of kerosene that would fulfil the same tasks – mainly for cooking. Solar energy is included on the same basis. Possible ranges for future supply are illustrated in table 2.7. These do not represent limits, or constraints, since these renewable sources are largely determined by demand (except in areas where there is serious scarcity of woodfuel), but they illustrate ranges in which future supply can be expected to lie.

Hydro-electric and nuclear power production

Hydro-electric and nuclear potential are also summarised in table 2.7, which shows the equivalent energy inputs that would be required to produce the same electricity output at a nominal 35 per cent efficiency. The boundaries of the ranges shown for nuclear energy, in particular, do not represent limits. Widespread social opposition, or lower growth in electricity demand, could lead to lower values. Conversely, if the need was there and nuclear power was more readily accepted, significantly higher production would be technically feasible.

2.5   Energy demand and conservation

We give results for an illustrative projection for energy demand in WOCA in tables 2.8 and 2.9. This corresponds to a 'central trend', and gives values for demand inside the ranges for potential supply of each fuel that are shown in

Table 2.8. *Energy demand and conservation in WOCA (central trend)*

	1972	1980	2000	2020
Population (billion)	2.5	2.9	4.2	5.8
Oil price 1980 $/barrel	2	34	40-60	50-90
Index numbers:				
GDP	78	100	169	270
Energy demand	84	100	135	174
Energy/GDP	108	100	80	65
Energy demand (GTOE)	4.0	4.8	6.5	8.4

Table 2.9. *Percentage fuel shares in total energy demand in WOCA (central trend)*

	1972	1980	2000	2020
Coal	19	20	24	29
Oil[a]	54	51	40	29
Gas	18	17	16	13
Woodfuel and solar[b]	2	2	2	2
Hydro-electric[c]	7	7	10	10
Nuclear[c]	1	3	9	16
Total	100	100	100	100

Notes: [a] Excluding synthetic oil from coal.
[b] At petroleum replacement values.
[c] Primary energy input at 35 per cent nominal conversion efficiency.

table 2.7. However, in order to reach this result it was necessary to assume the further substantial increases in oil prices given in table 2.8, namely, reaching between 20 per cent and 75 per cent above the 1980 value by 2000. Without such an increase there would be insufficient energy conservation and substitution away from oil. The energy intensity (energy/GDP), given for WOCA in table 2.8, shows a continuing reduction, which we associate with increasing overall energy costs and prices, improvements in technology and structural change.

2.6   Main conclusions

The two preceding sections provide an outline of methods and results taken from a more detailed study of the world (WOCA) energy outlook which we have reported elsewhere (Eden, 1983). The main conclusions of this study are noted below.

The supply and price of oil will continue to dominate the world energy scene through most of the period to 2020. As market leader, the price of oil will determine the ceiling for prices of other fuels, so determining the extent and rates of oil substitution and investment in other energy sources and conservation. Internationally traded oil will continue as the main balancing fuel to meet fluctuations in energy demand, and sudden changes in the price of oil due to scarcity or glut will in the future, as in the past, adversely affect economic growth.

World demand for oil is likely to remain below potential supply for several years unless there is a large and unexpected disruption of supplies from the Middle East. However, with a modest recovery in economic growth the margin of oil supply over demand will be small by 1990, and with continued growth the (real) price of oil will begin to rise. If average annual economic growth is within 1 per cent of the central trend shown in table 2.8, the price of oil is likely to be in the range $40 to $60 per barrel by 2000 (in dollars at 1980 values), but the timing of price movements – up or down – will remain uncertain due to future fluctuations in economic growth.

The key question for world energy in the longer term is whether there will be sufficient investment in new energy resources, including both energy conservation and new high-cost oil resources, so that there can be a reasonably smooth transition away from oil. The enormous investment requirements for many new energy sources, coupled with uncertainty about future energy prices and taxes on producers, are likely to inspire caution and may lead to such low growth in energy production potential that future energy crises are unavoidable.

We do not expect future economic growth to follow a smooth trend – there will be fluctuations whose magnitude, timing and duration will be uncertain. However, the long-term average trend is an important factor for energy planning and provides a basis from which to assess the impact and risks that may arise from fluctuations about this average. Our central trend projection for economic growth in WOCA averages 2.7 per cent per annum from 1980–2000. The growth rate for OECD is 0.5 per cent lower, and for the group of developing countries it is about 1.0 per cent higher.

Energy conservation may be summarised by the percentage decrease in the ratio of energy demand to GDP. In the OECD this ratio was almost the same in 1972 as in 1958, but by 1982 it had fallen nearly 20 per cent. Interactive contributions to this decline arise from price effects, technical change and structural change. For the OECD our central trend projection shows a fall in energy/GDP of 32 per cent by 2000 (compared with 1972) and nearly 50 per cent by 2020. For the group of developing countries we would have expected an increase in the ratio of energy demand to total GDP if energy prices have remained at their pre-1973 values. With the changed energy situation, following an increase of 7 per cent in 1972–80 we project a fall in energy/GDP of 4 per cent by 2000 and nearly 20 per cent by 2020 (compared with 1972).

Our central trend projection shows an increase of 35 per cent in world (WOCA) energy demand between 1980 and 2000, from 4.8 GTOE to 6.5 GTOE. Low and high projections suggest a range of possible energy demand in the year 2000 between 5.9 and 7.4 GTOE. By the year 2020, demand in the central trend will have reached 8.4 GTOE, or 74 per cent above its value in 1980. The major part of the future increase in world (WOCA) energy demand arises from the needs of developing countries, whose total demand doubles between 1980 and 2000, and reaches more than three times its 1980 value by 2020. Thus the percentage share of WOCA energy demand arising from developing countries increases from 21 per cent in 1980 to 31 per cent in 2000, and reaches 40 per cent by 2020.

We expect the demand for electricity in the OECD to increase in line with GDP until the year 2000 and a little slower thereafter. Thus, for the central trend, electricity demand increases by 60 per cent between 1980 and 2000, and by 2020 it reaches more than twice its 1980 level. In the developing countries there has been very rapid growth in electricity demand (nearly 9 per cent per annum between 1972 and 1980). For the central trend, we project much slower growth but still averaging more than 5 per cent per annum to 2000, then 3.5 per cent per annum from 2000 to 2020. This gives an almost threefold increase by 2000 and more than fivefold by 2020.

The projected levels of growth in energy demand in developing countries can be met only if demand growth in the OECD is moderated compared with the past, and if there is continuing substitution away from oil in all regions. The central trend projection shows oil's share of primary energy demand in WOCA declining from 51 per cent in 1980 to 40 per cent in 2000, and to 29 per cent in 2020 (or 32 per cent if synthetic oil from coal is included).

The production of oil in WOCA is likely to be limited by resource conservation policies, particularly in Middle East OPEC countries. Potential production in 2000, allowing for policy limits, is placed at 50 to 54 MBD (2500 to 2700 MTOE) if the price of oil was to remain near to $30 per barrel. But it could be in the range 50–60 MBD if the price began to rise by 1990 to reach $50 or more per barrel near the year 2000.

Some increase is expected in the supply of natural gas to WOCA, including imports from the USSR, and hydro production will increase both in the OECD and in developing countries. However, the main part of the incremental demand can be provided only through major increases in the production of coal and nuclear power. For the central trend, additional production from these two sources meets over 60 per cent of the incremental energy demand arising between 1980 and 2000, and nearly 90 per cent of the increase between 2000 and 2020. Meanwhile, woodfuel, biomass and solar energy remain relatively small contributors – less than 3 per cent when measured on a petroleum replacement basis.

Oil trade within WOCA will continue to be dominated by exports from OPEC, in the region of 24 MBD (1200 MTOE) in 2000 but somewhat less in 2020 for the central trend. Oil imports into WOCA from the USSR may be partly replaced by natural gas and coal, and there could be some imports of oil from China for a period, later to be supplemented or replaced by coal. Trade in natural gas within WOCA is likely to increase, but the most substantial increase in energy trade will come from coal. North America, Australia and South Africa will be large coal exporters, whilst Western Europe and Japan will remain large importers.

Our central trend projection provides relatively little increase in average income per capita in the group of developing countries. It seems likely that higher economic growth will be feasible only if the OECD also had higher growth so as to boost international trade. The high trend projection requires 15 per cent more energy in 2000 than the central trend, or nearly 1000 MTOE. This could, in principle, be met through equal contributions from oil, coal and conservation, with a smaller contribution from gas. However, to maintain high growth there will need to be a high degree of international cooperation and confidence to avoid energy scarcities and associated sharp movements in the price of oil that will otherwise have adverse effects on world economic growth.

3

The making of energy policy

3.1   Introduction

Energy policy has become one of the most complex and all-pervasive areas of decision-making. It involves macroeconomic and industrial affairs, international relations, environmental considerations and important areas of science and technology. It interacts with all of these in both directions. As a result it is not easy to sum up the content of energy policy in a compact and convenient definition although public debate and discussion have often required that the attempt should be made. The result has seldom been very helpful.

Policy may be considered *ex ante* or *ex post*. In the former case, it is usually thought of as a set of intentions or objectives to be pursued either as initiatives arising within the energy sector, or perhaps more often as responses to external events. In the latter case, *ex post*, it can be seen as the way in which those objectives have been implemented and as the totality of the decisions which have been made along the way by all those interests which have been involved. It is one important element in the making of energy policy to seek to anticipate as far as may be possible what those necessary decisions are likely to be.

For many years a form of words was adopted in government documents which described the objective of energy policy as being to ensure the provision of adequate and secure energy supplies at the lowest cost in real resources. To this there might be added the proviso that the supplies should be continuing and that regard should be paid to future as well as present costs. Although this remains quite a useful definition it inevitably raises further questions. What for example is meant by 'adequate' and 'secure', and how should 'costs' be determined and who should bear them? It also leaves out of account the issues which arise from interactions within the energy sector itself and those between the energy sector and the rest of the economy. Moreover, it does not include reference to the means by which the objectives might be pursued and thus obscures many of the sharp dilemmas and potential conflicts of interest whose resolution provides the hard realities of political and economic choice.

An even less satisfactory definition of UK energy policy that was coined recently, has been the suggestion that it rested on the 'Coconuke' strategy of

28

coal, conservation and nuclear power. This may describe some of the ingredients of such a policy but even in the few years since it was adopted it would be difficult to explain much of what has happened in those terms. Even if the list of ingredients was complete (and it makes no reference to gaseous, liquid or renewable forms of energy), most recipes require at least some indication of quantities and cooking times if the dish is to be edible. How much coal, conservation and nuclear power? How should they be mixed? When are they to be deployed, and at what cost?

Altogether energy policy is made up of all those decisions affecting the supply of and demand for fuels in particular uses. The decisions are made by the government, by fuel producers and by consumers acting within an environment of great uncertainty and change. There are certain policy issues which are internal to the energy system itself: choices about the production and consumption of different primary fuels which are dominated by resource availability and comparative costs. They involve considerations such as the balance and timing of investments and the determination of prices. The investment decisions are often very large and technologically complex and the issues surrounding the determination of absolute and relative prices can have very wide implications for the economy at large. Moreover, decisions concerning one fuel or one use will be likely to impinge on others, and the processes of adjustment may be difficult. The search for optimal solutions within the energy sector is therefore the first level of decision-making.

Such decisions can seldom be taken in isolation because the issues arise in a wider context of other national and international considerations, both economic and political. Some internally generated energy policies have an external impact so important as to determine whether and how far the energy objectives can be pursued. The relationship between nuclear power and the environment is one of many examples. At the same time energy policy decisions may sometimes be determined by wholly non-energy considerations, such as the imperatives of national security, public expenditure or the balance of payments. In such cases energy policy is responsive rather than active.

Because of the long time horizons which are involved in making changes in the energy system, most of the decisions made involve, inevitably, a view about the future and therefore contain an element of uncertainty. How this forward view is formed and how the problem of uncertainty is accommodated are therefore essential ingredients in the policy-making process.

3.2   Background

Since the end of the second world war in 1945, the UK has passed through four major phases which have had an important effect on the course of national energy policy. First, there was the period of immediate post-war shortages and economic recovery which lasted until the early 1950s. It was dominated by coal shortages and the establishment of the major public corporations responsible for coal, gas and electricity. Second, there was a period of some fifteen years in which the economy grew fairly steadily and in which ideas of indicative planning by consensus were developed. In the energy field the coal industry was in decline, there was a great expansion of oil consumption and by the end of the period the development of the North Sea resources of oil and gas had begun. The third phase emerged in the 1970s and was characterised by rapidly rising oil and other energy prices, there was a growing awareness of the international dimension to energy policy, and it was also a period of much slower economic growth. Coal once again came to be seen as central to UK energy policy along with other indigenous energy resources and there was a new emphasis on efficiency in energy use and on conservation. The fourth phase has so far seen deepening recession and energy surpluses alongside a retreat from planning and consensus politics and the re-emergence of debate about the role of market forces and the frontier between the public and private sectors in the fuel industries. How long this present phase will continue is uncertain, but already the outlines of a new one can be discerned: it is the post-North Sea and possibly the post-oil period which lies well within the time-scale of current policy decisions.

Each one of these broad phases of national life over the past forty years has also experienced recurrent short-term problems and crises in economics, politics, technology and industrial relations which have determined the course of UK energy policy and have ensured that its path has never been smooth.

3.3   Policy institutions

Much of the substance of energy policy is concerned with fuels, technology and economics but the institutions and procedures which contain them are often equally important. Policy issues arise, are formulated, debated and eventually implemented within specific forms of government organisation, industrial structures in the fuel industries, and in a variety of other official and non-official agencies representing consumer and other interests.

The prime responsibility for UK energy policy rests with the Secretary of State for Energy and his department although other ministries also have a major influence, most notably the Treasury through its responsibility for public expenditure and investment and overall economic management. The Foreign and Commonwealth Office, too, has for many years been concerned with the international aspects especially those concerned with the political implications of the operations of the oil companies in various parts of the world. The departments dealing with industry, employment and the environment are also liable to be closely involved. In addition to the major departments of state there has grown up over the years a network of subsidiary agencies to support, investigate or monitor particular aspects of the energy scene, and while they do not have executive responsibility for policy decisions they nevertheless have often had considerable influence in defining and determining them.

The Department of Energy has a long history dating back to the time when 'energy policy' was concerned with little more than health and safety in the mines. Indeed its changing role has been reflected in its changing title over the years: from Mines to Power, to Fuel and Power, to absorption within the super-ministries of Technology and Trade and Industry of the 1960s and finally after the first major oil crisis of 1973 to its emergence as the Department of Energy responsible for the administration of the whole energy sector with all the day to day decision-making which that involves.

If the structure of central government is important in the making of energy policy so too is the structure of the energy sector itself. On the supply side it has been dominated by a small number of large, powerful public or multinational corporations while on the demand side the consumers of energy are large in number and diversity. This is the major reason why, until very recently, energy policy has been chiefly concerned with problems of supply. One of the first post-war attempts to examine the UK energy scene as a whole was made by the Ridley Committee, set up in 1951 in the period of acute fuel shortages. Apart from its short-term recommendations dealing with the problems of fuel supply it made proposals for the development of wider and more formal consultation between the government and other interests involved. This effort to broaden the basis of energy discussion and consensus was one which continued intermittently for the next thirty years.

At first the major participants apart from the government were the fuel supply industries. The Ridley Committee (Ridley, 1952) had recommended that there should be greater coordination between them on such issues as planning, pricing and the role of nuclear power, and a coordinating committee was set up at the end of 1952 involving the minister and the chairmen of the nationalised industries. There had, of course, always been bilateral contacts but the new ingredient was the effort to achieve wider participation in establishing a common approach to national fuel policy. The committee achieved very little and effectively died after two or three meetings although it formally survived into the early 1960s.

In 1965 an Energy Advisory Council was set up with a wider membership, reflecting the tripartite spirit of the times and the attempts at national planning through the National Economic Development Council and the National Plan. The Energy Advisory Council played a part in the discussions leading up to the important Fuel Policy White Papers (Cmnd 2798 and Cmnd 3438, Ministry of Power, 1965 and 1967) but its role was presentational rather than substantive and it too finally withered away. In the 1970s similar fates overcame the National Energy Conference and the Energy Commission which after flurries of public interest and some useful documentation also lapsed into inactivity under the weight of changes in political attitudes, specific short-term problems and general indifference.

There are many reasons behind these failures to establish a broader basis for the discussion of overall energy policy issues. Some of them lie in the structural arrangements within the energy sector itself. Others derive from the fact that most energy problems arise in a highly specific form – an oil shortage, a coal strike, pricing policies or major investment decisions – in which the exposure of such issues to the scrutiny and observations of third parties is not seen by the direct participants as particularly helpful. Moreover, the problem of finding a continuing agenda of substantial policy issues for wide debate leading to practical results has proved difficult, while general reviews on non-urgent, non-sensitive issues lead to boredom and a loss of political momentum.

Much the most effective contribution to the energy debate outside the government and the industries has been through more specific agencies such as Royal Commissions (e.g. on Environmental Pollution), Advisory Councils (e.g. on Conservation or Research and Development), the parliamentary Select Committees (e.g. on Energy or the Nationalised Industries), Public Inquiries (e.g. on the Belvoir coalfield or the Sizewell nuclear power station), the Monopolies Commission (e.g. on the coal industry), consumer groups and independent academic or lobbying organisations.

3.4   The role of government departments

The principal mechanism through which public policy in the form of control, guidance and direction is exercised in the industrial sector of the economy is by way of the so-called sponsoring departments of the government. It is their task to represent the interests of the government to individual industries and to ensure that government policies and requirements are carried out. At the same time they provide the channel for communicating the interests of the industries to the government. The greater part of manufacturing industry is the responsibility of the presently labelled Department of Industry, the Department of the Environment deals among other things with transport and the construction industry, and the Department of Energy looks after the fuel industries: coal, gas, oil, electricity and the nuclear industry.

The strength and effectiveness of the relationship between the sponsoring department and its clients is strongly influenced by the structure of the industries and by the positive commitment of the government towards them. In the case of the energy industries, the coal, gas, electricity and nuclear industries are almost entirely under public ownership and are therefore expected to pursue national as well as commercial objectives. The oil industry, too, has for many years had an element of state involvement although until the development of the North Sea the government's relationship with it was much more 'arm's length' in character, and with foreign rather than energy policy considerations playing the greater part.

In carrying out its sponsoring role the Department of Energy is organised vertically in a number of rather self-contained industrial divisions each dealing with one specific fuel industry in the case of coal, gas, electricity or atomic energy, or with some aspects of petroleum. These are supplemented by a number of 'horizontal' divisions dealing across the board with general energy policy questions, or providing common technical and advisory services. The intimacy and effectiveness of the two-way relationship between the industry and its sponsoring division can be a crucial element in the formulation and implementation of energy policy. So too is the relative balance of influence between the vertical 'fuel' divisions and the horizontal 'energy' divisions.

3.5   Public ownership

The issue of ownership is relevant to energy policy in so far as it may determine or influence the objectives and performance of the fuel industries and their interactions with one another in supplying the total energy market. For more than a generation it seemed as though the issue of ownership in the fuel industries had been resolved. The structural problems of the coal industry had pointed towards the possibility of a public ownership solution since the end of the first world war although it was not formally implemented until the end of the second world war. Gas and electricity were seen as public utilities where the need for integrated supply networks and common standards also made public ownership seem appropriate and relatively uncontroversial. The military and security aspects of atomic energy gave it a special status, too. Petroleum, with its diversity of products, its high risks and its multinational organisation and operations, was in a different category. The strategic and foreign policy implications of international exploration and production gave the companies a special protected status in relation to their national governments. Not until the development of home production from the North Sea in the 1970s did the issue of public ownership and participation become an active ingredient of policy and it was reinforced nationally and internationally by the crises of 1973 and 1979.

By the end of the 1970s, therefore, almost the whole of the energy supply sector had been brought into public ownership or close public control. Since 1980 the issue of ownership has re-emerged. Although in part this has been due to political rather than energy or industrial considerations, it has been reinforced by concern about the structural problems of nationalisation arising out of the decline of parts of the coal industry and by the expansion arising out of the peripheral activities by gas and electricity.

The formal relationships between the government and the nationalised industries are set out in the various Nationalisation Acts dating from the mid-1940s. The appointment of chairmen and board members is the ultimate source of the minister's authority, but in operational terms it is his power to approve the industry's capital investment programme and in general to ensure that the industries are efficiently run which provides the real point of leverage and power. In principle, the day to day operations of the industry are not the concern of the government but, given control over major investments, general concern about the levels of wages and prices, interest rates and borrowing, it is clear that the boundary between general policy guidance and day to day operations is not always easy to define. In practice the involvement of the sponsoring department in these operations is often very close. It involves frequent personal contact between ministers and senior government officials on the one hand and chairmen, board members and managers on the other on matters of industrial tactics as well as strategy. There are, moreover, almost continuous exchanges of operational information and advice at technical and administrative levels.

The dual role of acting as the two-way interpreter of the interests of the government and the industry is both subtle and complex. Members of the industry in varying degrees enjoy having a political role in the corridors of Whitehall, while civil servants likewise enjoy the taste of entrepreneurial life and may become heavily committed champions of their protégés. As the Select Committee on Nationalised Industries pointed out in 1978, 'the informal and practical arrangements which have grown up over the years . . . are even more important than the formal power set out in the statutes'.

Whatever initial problems might have been resolved by public ownership of the major fuel industries in the late 1940s, it quickly became clear that many of the underlying industrial problems of efficiency and labour relations remained and that in addition a new set of issues had emerged. These were concerned with the practical problems of achieving a balance between commercial and operational objectives on the one hand and, on the other hand, of meeting the political, economic and social purposes which lay behind the Nationalisation Acts. During the 1950s a number of inquiries took place into the industries' performance and several common problems began to emerge: the need for

adequate scrutiny by Parliament, monitoring, financial control and accountability.

In 1961 there appeared the first of what was to be an important series of White
Papers on the Financial and Economic Objectives of Nationalised Industries
(Cmnd 1337, Treasury, 1961), which sought to establish a common framework
for the industries by the setting of financial targets and requiring a target rate of
return to be achieved on capital or turnover. This, it was argued, would simulate
the disciplines of the market economy and ensure that the industries pursued
appropriate production, pricing and marketing policies.

By 1967 it had become clear that these guidelines were inadequate. In
monopoly trading conditions a satisfactory final out-turn could be achieved
simply by raising prices, while within the wide range of activities covered by
most of the industries it was possible to conceal or absorb inefficiencies by
cross-subsidisation of different activities. At the same time, and in the planning
climate of the time, it was considered necessary for the often very large
investment decisions to be taken on the basis of common criteria in order to
ensure the best use of national resources. A new White Paper (Cmnd 3437,
Treasury, 1967) addressed itself to these problems by supplementing the pursuit
of appropriate financial objectives with more rigorous rules about pricing policy
and investment criteria. Prices were to be related to long-term marginal costs
and capital expenditure was to be appraised by the use of a standard test
discount rate.

Although both concepts are straightforward in principle they involved many
difficult and contentious problems of measurement and accounting in the fuel
industries. Could the same rules be applied to a homogeneous product like
electricity as to a revitalised and expanding natural gas industry with problems
of depletable resources to consider? And what of coal which faced long-term
decline as well as short-term problems of high-cost pits operating alongside
low-cost collieries and cheap open-cast output? As to investment criteria, what
was to be the basis of the standard discount rate? Should it be applied to new
investments only or to all investments? How should the problems of inflation
and accounting conventions be handled? These and similar arguments continued
through the early 1970s among both academics and accountants, but also in the
hard context of actual investment and energy strategy considerations. Two areas
where the problem of interest rates was crucial were the evaluation of future
costs and benefits in the choice between coal- and nuclear-fired power stations,
and the optimum rate of depletion of North Sea oil and gas.

In 1978 the Treasury produced a further refinement of the investment
guidelines (Cmnd 7131, Treasury, 1978) and the framework within which
performance could be monitored, although in practice their application has
remained fairly loose and pragmatic. Thus, although a basic framework of

economic regulation for the nationalised industries had been set in principle from the late 1960s, it has never been possible to establish either the self-policing mechanism which had been hoped for, or a set of operating criteria which could withstand the imperatives of the short-term crisis.

The political problems of control and accountability have proved no more susceptible to rules and guidelines. The Nationalisation Acts themselves give little guidance and have had to be interpreted over the years in rapidly changing industrial situations and by politicians, officials and managers with very different objectives and styles of operation. Ministerial powers of appointment, dismissal and general direction to the industries' boards provides them with considerable powers for overall policy control but they seldom intervene in day to day policy formulation and implementation. Specific powers of direction have been rarely and reluctantly used. In the energy sector too the problems are compounded by the fact that the fuel industries are often in competition with one another and therefore do not necessarily share common objectives in national or even 'energy' terms. This diversity and independence is also reflected in the organisational structure of the Department of Energy.

Another consideration is that energy policy is now not only concerned with the terms and conditions of fuel supply, which have dominated it in the past, but also with issues of fuel consumption and use. These have traditionally been matters which were left to the free choice among consumers of the fuels they used with a realistic cost-related pricing system providing the basis of that choice. With the exception of taxes on transport fuel and such occasional devices as the tax on fuel oil and assistance in boiler conversion from oil to coal, the government has generally been content to leave the demand side of the energy equation to itself. But this is now changing within the framework of the conservation programme and through the development of information, advisory and management services. Alongside these the growth of consumerism and environmental concern have added to a widening of the area of public and parliamentary scrutiny and accountability.

3.6   Planning the use of resources

The early 1960s began to mark important changes in the approach to policy-making. After an initial reaction against the wartime and post-war systems of planning and controls the Conservative administrations of the late 1950s were moving towards adopting ideas of economic management and intervention in an attempt to improve the economic performance of the UK. The success of indicative planning in France and elsewhere heightened concern about the need for faster growth and a more effective allocation and use of national resources. The 1961 Treasury White Paper cited above (Cmnd 1337) had been an early expression of the new attitude to resource allocation between and within the nationalised industries. In 1962 the National Economic Development Council and its subsidiary bodies were set up to establish a tripartite consensus between the government, trade unions and management about the conditions and means of achieving faster growth.

In 1964 the incoming Labour government picked up these strands and sought to formalise them within an overall National Plan. The Plan itself contained little that was new so far as the energy industries were concerned, although the 4 per cent annual growth rate which it postulated would have involved a considerable expansion of energy supply, most of it coming from oil because the decline of the coal industry was expected to continue.

There were other parallel developments in train in the energy sector. A separate review of the prospects for coal and fuel policy generally was taking place and the Energy Advisory Council (mentioned in 3.3 above) was set up in 1965 as an attempt to reach a broad basis of agreement. The result of this review led to two White Papers on Fuel Policy (Cmnd 2798 and Cmnd 3438, Ministry of Power, 1965 and 1967). The first was principally concerned with the problems of coal, while the second looked additionally at the possible implications of what were expected to be growing supplies of nuclear power and the potential availability of gas from the North Sea. Exploratory drilling had begun in the North Sea in 1964 and the first significant finds of natural gas were made less than a year later. Having made an early start on the development of nuclear power for electricity generation, Britain was well on the way to becoming a four-fuel economy with all the extra dimensions of energy policy which that was to entail.

Unfortunately, attempts to improve the country's economic performance by a form of national planning and consensus fell well short of the hopes which had been raised. Nevertheless, within the energy sector at least, a framework of planning has survived, although it has owed more to the pressure of events than to ideology. Through the 1970s the rate of economic growth slackened and the hitherto steady rise in energy consumption began to level off. While the total energy market was slack it was having to adjust to the momentum of a rapid penetration by natural gas (whose market share rose from 2 per cent to 20 per cent between 1969 and 1979) and to the effect of rapid changes in absolute and relative fuel prices. The structural adjustments required within a static or contracting market were much greater and the management and government responses much more difficult than in a climate of steady expansion. At the same time too the international responses to the energy crisis were imposing new requirements on the energy sector. It was against this background that planning in the energy sector began to take a new form.

Alongside the attempts at national resource planning there had developed within industry a variety of procedures and management practices which are generally described as corporate planning, ranging from broad and loosely quantified statements of objectives, resources and constraints affecting the enterprise to rigorous and well-researched analyses of future prospects and targets within a range of alternative scenarios and external conditions. In the nationalised industries the corporate plan provides a framework within which it can meet its statutory obligations to present its forward investment programmes for government approval as well as serving its own internal management purposes. In 1974 the Department of Energy set up a Corporate Planning Division which aimed to strengthen and coordinate the links between the government and the industries in this field and at about the same time it established a high-level energy strategy group to review the broad issues of energy planning and to seek a common approach to the assessment of future prospects within the energy sector and beyond.

The need for this coordination arose from the fact that left to themselves the individual industries were liable to produce inconsistent or incompatible views about their future prospects and competitive performance and hence about the investment and other resources required to achieve and maintain it. In addition if their individual perceptions of the general macroeconomic climate and external factors such as movements in prices and interest rates were different then forward market assessments could be irreconcilable.

It was no accident that as the vogue for planning developed so too did the analytical techniques required to support it. Data and information systems were expanded and forecasting, appraisal and optimising methodologies were developed. Within the government there was a long history of statistical recording and analysis dating from the earliest days of its concerns with health and safety in the mines. By the early 1970s the Department of Energy had developed a range of forecasting and optimising models covering the whole of the energy sector and which had grown out of the need to meet some of the analytical problems which had emerged from the 1965 and 1967 Fuel Policy White Papers and national macroeconomic planning. These models provided a quantitative basis for examining many aspects of energy policy during the 1970s and made it possible for the department to engage in informed discussions with the planners in the fuel industries who were in many respects more familiar with the technical and analytical approach to corporate planning issues. The aim of the government was not to elaborate an 'energy plan' itself, but more modestly to encourage the individual fuel industries to carry out their own planning with due regard to the objectives and intentions of the others and on the basis of a common appreciation of the wider sectoral and national considerations involved.

The oil companies were of course in a different situation from the nationalised fuel industries, although there were growing links between them and the government in respect of their UK and offshore activities and in their international operations which might affect UK interests. These links became much closer in the 1970s as international cooperation among oil-consuming countries developed especially within the IEA (see below) and as North Sea production grew. International cooperation aimed at common supply and demand management policies for the participating countries and sought to establish standardised information and reporting procedures between them. North Sea developments led to new oil policies through joint government–industry participation arrangements, the setting up of the British National Oil Corporation (BNOC), new forms of taxation, new industrial policies related to offshore equipment and supplies, the licensing of exploration, decisions about depletion policy and discussion about the use of the oil revenues. All of this involved a closer collaboration with the oil companies than ever before and consequently, although less formally than in the case of the nationalised industries, a greater sharing of experience and expertise in the development of a common approach to strategic energy problems.

3.7   The international dimension

The 1973 oil crisis had the effect of internationalising energy policy. The main formal expression of this was the establishment of new areas of cooperation among the oil-consuming countries, in particular through the IEA. At the same time it encouraged individual countries to pay more attention to the global issues of energy policy – world resources, trade and the role of the developing countries – in their analysis of domestic policies. The special expertise of the oil companies in this field, developed over many years, once more helped to move them closer to the centre of governments' energy policies and analysis.

The principal purpose of the IEA, which was set up in 1974 with the participation of twenty-one member countries of the OECD, was to establish an international programme of cooperation in all forms of energy supply and use, but especially to deal with the risks of disruption of oil supplies. Four specialist standing groups were established dealing with emergency questions, the state of the oil market, long-term cooperation and relations with producer countries and other consumers. The groups dealing with the oil market and emergency questions were the most active and important and they built up a strong network of information systems among the member countries so that in the event of significant disruptions occurring the members could prepare and activate the necessary measures to curtail demand and share the available supplies. It has yet to be seen how effective these might be in a situation where individual national interests might be affected by collective action.

3.8   Fuel policies in practice

In the light of all the domestic and international developments discussed in the preceding sections, the general picture of the UK energy sector by the end of the 1970s was one in which a great deal of common ground and agreed practices in the formulation of energy policy had been established. It is tempting to see this progress towards a more orderly and structured approach to policy-making as offering the prospect of greater stability, certainty and assurance in the future. But if the means of dealing with problems has been formalised and improved there still remain as many areas of specific difficulty, contention and uncertainty as ever: pricing policy, power station fuelling, structural problems in the coal industry, taxation, environmental problems, nuclear power and so on. These remain the hard currency of day to day decisions in the energy field as much as they have done in the past and unless the future were to show a quite remarkable change it is likely that they will continue to be so.

It has become common to regard the energy sector as one in which for technical and structural reasons rapid changes in policy are difficult if not impossible. And yet in retrospect it is remarkable how often and how rapidly objectives and priorities have shifted and how policies have altered.

The changes in official attitudes to the coal industry are a clear example. Views about the appropriate size of the industry have ranged from aiming at an annual output of over 250 million tonnes a year in the late 1940s down to as low as 80 million tonnes or less by the end of the 1960s. Four or five years later production objectives were back to 150–200 million tonnes. Through the period there were times when oil consumption was encouraged in preference to coal only to be followed within months by pressures and incentives to burn coal. By the beginning of the 1980s even the 115–20 million tonnes being produced could not be sold and it was being argued in some quarters that even if coal as a fuel should be required in increasing quantities it did not necessarily have to come from the home industry but could be readily imported from abroad. With the exception of occasional worries about industrial relations problems the main influence on coal policy has been external to the industry itself and has coincided with an anxious or relaxed attitude to the country's balance of payments.

The evolution of the gas industry has undergone equally dramatic changes of fortune, but for different reasons. The major technological changes from being a coal-based manufacturing industry to a distributor of natural gas have transformed it from a Victorian relic into a sophisticated and successful distribution and marketing agency displacing other fuels in domestic and many industrial uses. Its well-developed transmission and distribution network could provide the basis for the long-term future of coal-based synthetic gas and hence become crucial in the possible long-term expansion of the coal industry. In its battle for improved market shares and its impact on the other fuels gas policy has been dominated by general pricing considerations while the industry's technological momentum has also led it into wider areas of activity in exploration and development of hydrocarbon resources which have raised contentious political issues about the industry's proper role in the economy. It was the pace of development of the gas industry and the matching of increasing supplies in the 1970s to the growth of demand which stimulated concern with problems of depletion policy and the balancing of future needs and resources. From the start these were matters which involved the government in new areas of regulation and decision-making which not only required political judgements in unfamiliar fields but also the creation of a new apparatus of analysis, data and information systems.

Oil has traditionally provided the main international strand in UK energy policy. Oil matters were dominated by foreign policy and the balance of payments until with the arrival of North Sea oil the government found itself directly engaged in the oil business with the content of oil policy becoming entrepreneurial as well as political and diplomatic. In one sense North Sea oil did not present any fundamentally new issues of 'energy' policy in the limited sense of concern with the choice and use of fuels. By far its greatest effect was to enlarge the macroeconomic component in energy policy: the balance of payments effect, the strength of sterling and the timing and disposal of the massive new revenues which would be generated. It remains to be seen what new policy issues will emerge as North Sea production and revenues begin to decline in the late 1980s and 1990s if the rest of the economy, weakened by the prolonged recession, cannot generate alternative government income and foreign exchange.

Internal and external factors have also buffeted the electricity industry over the years. There have been shifting preferences between oil and coal for power station fuelling and for new generating capacity. There have been changing views about pricing policy, the prospects for economic growth and public expenditure targets.

Nowhere has the ambivalence in policy been greater than in relation to nuclear power where the UK industry has swung between considerable success and high expectations on the one hand and great disappointments on the other. Up to the early 1950s there was considerable caution in assessing the future prospects for nuclear power. The Ridley Report (Ridley, 1952) said it would be 'many years' or 'a generation' before nuclear power could make a significant contribution to electricity supplies and the First Nuclear Programme (Ministry of Fuel and Power, 1955) was appropriately modest. Only two years later in the wake of the Suez oil crisis the programme was trebled in size. Within a further two years the easing of the crisis and the pressures of public expenditure, as well as technical and administrative problems, led to the programme being once more scaled down. Despite this, by the mid-1960s Britain was generating more nuclear power than the rest of the world and the policy debate shifted from 'How much nuclear power?' to the still unresolved problems of reactor choice with its concentration on technology and safety and waste disposal.

A growing concern with environmental questions stemming from doubts about the possibility, even the desirability, of faster economic growth has broadened the technical problems of reactor safety into a much wider political and philosophical arena. It is a matter which has become a crucial part of energy policy and it has been accompanied by a range of new statutory requirements and planning procedures which have to be negotiated when energy choices are being made. These apply not only to the immediate effects of energy installations and activities such as the opening of new coalfields or the siting of nuclear power stations, but also have international implications, as in the issues of 'acid rain' or nuclear waste disposal. Issues such as these are not only concerned with aesthetics and amenity factors but they can bear heavily on the costs of producing and using energy, and as in the case of protracted planning procedures they can impose lengthy and expensive delays on the implementation of policy decisions once taken.

3.9   Conclusions

It was said earlier that energy policy is made up of decisions affecting the supply of and demand for fuels in all their uses. It is clear that, in the light of all the issues, institutions and historical developments which have influenced that policy over the years, the policy-making process is a highly complex one. Moreover, the objectives and priorities have changed, sometimes very rapidly, as time has passed and it must be one of the lessons for the future that this situation is more likely to persist than to disappear. In the course of reaching decisions even on apparently narrow and specific issues many wider considerations have to be taken into account. One recurring lesson has been that an energy policy decision is at least as likely to be responsive to some external development at home or abroad as to arise from conditions or objectives within the energy sector itself. Also energy policy decisions seldom arise as a clear choice between one solution or another but rather as how much of one element as compared with how much of another. Timing is also crucial: when will a particular result be required and at what rate is it possible or desirable to achieve it? Above all, perhaps, what are the costs and benefits involved in accounting terms, in real resources, and to society?

There has been no shortage of energy policies in the UK but there have been few clear and consistent threads. This is perhaps inevitable as the country has developed since the 1940s from being a single-fuel economy based on coal (and that in severe shortage) to becoming an energy-rich four-fuel economy with the additional options of a fifth in the form of conservation and the potential of a sixth in the shape of renewable energy sources. Perhaps the luxury of abundant choice has contributed to the indecision. The easy availability of oil from the 1950s solved the problems of the coal shortages. Natural gas and North Sea oil in the 1960s and 1970s provided further relief to the energy system. Even the oil crises from 1973, by contributing to the industrial countries' recession, reduced the pressure of demand and weakened the sense of urgency in the approach to the future of coal, nuclear power, conservation and renewable energy. The slower economic growth reduced the pressure on resources and hence on the need to sharpen and refine the policy objectives. Pragmatism and flexibility have been the terms most commonly used to define UK policy but they could well prove insufficient for a future marked by declining supplies of gas and oil, an uncertain nuclear industry and a diminished coal industry.

4

Prospects for the UK economy

4.1   Recent history

The period since the last war, until the early 1970s, had been characterised in the UK by steady economic growth. Figure 4.1 shows the value of GDP between 1953 and 1980 (these and other historical data are from Central Statistical Office, 1983). The near doubling in real terms of GDP over this period clearly indicates a substantial increase in prosperity. However, the growth of GDP has been unstable since 1973 and has recently been negative.

The post-war period has seen significant changes in the structure of economic activity. Figure 4.2 shows the ratio to GDP of three other economic indicators: total industrial production (TIP), consumers' expenditure and services' output (in each case the ratio is scaled to a 1970 value of 100).

We see from figure 4.2 that consumers' expenditure, though showing some irregularities, generally follows GDP. The relationship between industry and

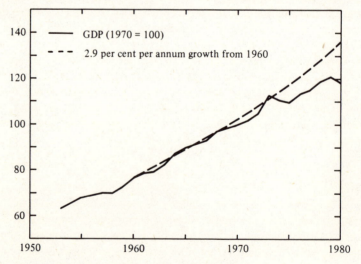

4.1 Gross domestic product for the UK, 1953–80

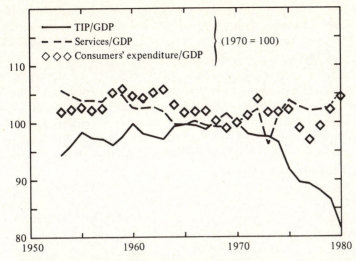

4.2 The changing structure of the UK economy, 1953–80

services, however, shows a reversal of trend around 1969. Prior to this date, industrial production rose relative to GDP (the ratio being markedly influenced by the business cycle), and there was a corresponding fall in the ratio of services to GDP. After 1969, there was a rapid and continuous fall in industrial output relative to GDP, matched by a more gradual rise in services. It is significant that this turning-point occurred before the rise in oil prices of 1973. This and subsequent energy crises may have accelerated industrial decline (though this is by no means self-evident), but the basic cause of the phenomenon must be sought elsewhere.

The causes of de-industrialisation in the UK and other developed countries are complex, and their analysis is beyond the scope of this book. The interested reader is referred to Barker and Brailovsky (1981), Kilpatrick and Lawson (1980), Blackaby (1979) and Kaldor (1966). For our present discussion, it is sufficient to note that such changes in economic structure have important implications for the demand for energy in the UK.

4.2 Possible futures

There is clearly great uncertainty about the future structure and performance of the UK economy. At one extreme, industrial decline might continue to be rapid, and overall economic growth low, with the UK becoming a relatively poor, service-dominated economy. At the other extreme, de-industrialisation may be a temporary adjustment process, which will bottom out, or possibly be reversed, in the future. The latter view, combined with healthy economic growth, would imply a return to the experience of the 1950s and 1960s. Other possibilities include the development of a service-dominated economy combined with moderate or high economic growth.

In a study of energy policy issues, it is not very helpful to consider scenarios in which economic conditions are so adverse that energy issues would be outweighed by more extreme and urgent social problems. At the same time, it is widely believed that, for the industrialised countries in general, the levels of economic growth experienced in the 1950s and 1960s are unlikely to be exceeded in the long term. These two views provide the basis from which the scenarios used in this study are constructed.

The scenarios (also referred to as the high, central and low cases) make informal use of the results of a range of models (e.g. National Institute of Economic and Social Research, 1981), but no attempt is made to fit the energy analysis into a detailed macroeconomic model. The main economic variables included in the scenarios are GDP, TIP, consumers' expenditure, services output and agricultural output. Agriculture, though of minor importance in the UK from an energy viewpoint, is dealt with separately because of its very specific energy needs. Industrial production is further subdivided into the output of sixteen specific sectors, including the construction industry but excluding the energy industries. 'Services' comprise communications (but not transport), distributive trades, banking and other business services, ownership of dwellings, professional and scientific services, public administration and defence, and other miscellaneous services.

The overview of the world energy scene given in chapter 2 included a 'central view' of future oil prices, and although this is not intended as a forecast, it is a useful starting-point for the examination of energy policy issues. Most of the analysis in this study is based on this projection of world oil prices, though variants on it are considered when appropriate.

The relationship between fuel prices and economic growth involves policy issues (such as fuel taxation and the use of petroleum revenues) as well as basic economic mechanisms. Since the UK is very dependent on external trade, UK economic growth tends to follow world growth. For the world as a whole, high growth must either be associated with high energy demand (requiring the use of high-cost fuel resources) or with high energy conservation. In both cases it is likely that high growth will be associated with high prices. Conversely, a combination of low fuel prices and a stagnant economy is plausible. The combination of low fuel prices with high world growth, or of high fuel prices with low world growth, appears less stable. The period since 1973 has been characterised by sudden transitions between the two stable states.

For the UK (as indeed for any oil-producing country with a significant manufacturing sector) the interaction between oil prices and economic growth is particularly complex. On the positive side, as long as world oil prices exceed oil production costs, production creates revenues which may be used elsewhere in the economy. Conversely, the initial investment required to develop energy resources may be made at the expense of investment elsewhere, particularly in manufacturing industry, and the export of oil may lead to a strengthening of the currency which hinders other exports and encourages imports of manufactured goods. For a fuller discussion of these and similar issues, see Barker and Brailovsky (1981), Noreng (1980), Hamilton (1978) and MacKay and Mackay (1975).

The analysis presented in this study generally uses 1980 as a base year, though, in the construction of scenarios, data for 1981 and the early part of 1982 have also been used. The time-scale extends to 2020, though uncertainties (always substantial) increase markedly beyond the end of the century. This time-scale reflects the long investment lead-times associated with developments in energy supply. For example, the planning and construction of a nuclear power station may take ten years, and the station could then provide power for a further thirty years.

In order to compare scenarios or other features, it is desirable for numerical assumptions and results to be quoted with some precision. The reader should not be misled, however, into thinking that the degree of precision implies any commensurate accuracy of the projections. On the contrary, numerical results are no more accurate than is implied by the general statements in the text. We stress that the detailed scenarios are intended to provide plausible backgrounds against which energy policy issues may be discussed. They are in no sense intended as either forecasts or targets.

4.3 Central economic scenario

The average rate of growth of the UK economy between 1953 and 1973 was just under 3 per cent per annum, and since the latter date it has been very small. We have noted earlier that for energy planning it is appropriate to study futures which are fairly optimistic in economic terms, while remaining aware of the special implications for energy policy of more adverse futures. For the central scenario, therefore, we postulate a fairly rapid recovery from the recession of the early 1980s, followed by a resumption of steady economic growth. Specifically, we assume that GDP recovers to its 1979 level by 1984 or 1985, and grows thereafter at an average rate of nearly 2 per cent per annum to the year 2010, after which there is a slight reduction.

Due to the depth of the current recession in industrial output, the latter is assumed to recover more quckly than GDP in the period to 1990. Thereafter,

Table 4.1. *Economic indicators for the central scenario*

Indices (1975 = 100)
(Average annual percentage growth rates in brackets)

Year	GDP	Industrial output[a]	Agricultural output	Other services output	Consumers' expenditure
1980	107.3	95.4	128.5	110.0	110.5
1985	113.9 (1.20)	102.2 (1.39)	127.5[b] (−0.16)	114.1 (0.73)	113.8 (0.59)
1990	124.9 (1.86)	112.1 (1.87)	137.4 (1.51)	125.0 (1.84)	124.4 (1.80)
2000	152.2 (2.00)	134.8 (1.86)	156.2 (1.29)	154.0 (2.11)	151.6 (2.00)
2010	185.5 (2.00)	161.4 (1.82)	174.3 (1.10)	189.6 (2.10)	184.4 (2.00)
2020	223.9 (1.90)	191.5 (1.72)	194.4 (1.10)	231.1 (2.00)	223.0 (1.90)

Notes: [a] Including construction.
[b] The fall between 1980 and 1985 is the result of the very high level of output (assessed at constant prices) in 1980.

industrial production grows more slowly than GDP, indicating a gradual move towards a service-orientated economy. The speed of this transition is taken to be much slower than that experienced between 1969 and 1984 (see figure 4.2). Output in the services sectors rises slowly at first, but later more quickly than GDP. Agricultural output has not in the past shown any clear link with GDP, but has risen (with fluctuations due to the weather) as technical changes have improved productivity. This trend is assumed to continue. Finally, consumers' expenditure is taken to recover more slowly than GDP, but later moves in line with it. The economic indicators and growth rates are summarised in table 4.1.

Note that smooth growth is assumed for this, and for the high and low, cases. In reality, of course, economic growth is likely to follow the usual cyclic pattern (the business cycle) with a period of about five years. On this may be imposed shocks (due perhaps to sudden rises in the oil price as occurred in 1973 and 1979) which could have important economic effects. The timing of such events is unpredictable but special consideration will be given later in the book to the energy policy implications of the business cycle and sudden changes in the world energy scene.

The structure of industry has important implications for energy use, due to the wide variations in energy intensity between sectors (see chapter 7). In all the scenarios, we assume a continuation of the trends in industrial structure that have been evident in recent decades. The shares in industrial output rise for electrical, mechanical and instrument engineering, chemicals, china, paper and

Table 4.2. *Output of industrial sectors, central scenario (1975 = 100)*

Sector	1980	1985	1990	2000	2010	2020
Iron and steel	67.1	75.0	84.0	96.0	109.2	124.3
Non-ferrous metals	97.2	103.0	115.4	143.0	170.0	198.6
Mechanical and instrument engineering	88.1	99.0	111.2	139.2	172.6	208.2
Electrical engineering	113.1	117.7	130.9	163.7	204.6	255.8
Shipbuilding etc.	67.8	72.1	76.7	85.8	94.6	104.0
Vehicles	92.0	94.9	99.5	112.0	126.6	142.3
Other metal goods	83.4	98.5	111.5	140.8	170.9	203.2
Food, drink and tobacco	106.6	114.2	126.3	151.5	180.7	211.1
Chemicals and allied trades[a]	109.7	119.3	133.5	165.3	204.1	251.0
Textiles, leather and clothing	84.3	86.3	90.0	101.4	112.6	121.9
Paper, printing and stationery	105.1	109.8	122.7	152.5	189.4	235.0
Bricks, etc.[b]	86.8	96.3	107.1	123.9	143.2	163.9
China, earthenware and glass	98.6	109.0	122.7	151.5	183.5	221.1
Cement	85.5	91.0	98.3	113.5	130.6	149.4
Construction	95.9	102.1	109.0	125.9	145.3	167.3
Other industries[c]	98.6	104.2	117.0	147.7	186.0	229.0

Notes: [a] Excluding coal and petroleum products.
[b] Including tiles, fireclay and other building materials.
[c] Comprising timber, furniture and other manufacturing industries not specified elsewhere.

other industries. The shares enjoyed by shipbuilding, vehicles, textiles, cement and construction fall steadily, while the metals industries, other metal goods, food and bricks maintain fairly stable shares.

The picture of industrial structure presented is one of slow change, with few major surprises. Other, more extreme, changes are certainly possible, and could have important consequences for total energy use and fuel shares.

Table 4.2 shows the output levels implied by these sectoral shares and the TIP assumed for the central scenario. Growth occurs in all sectors, though at widely differing rates. Only two sectors fail to regain their 1975 output levels by 2000 (steel and shipbuilding), while eight sectors have done so by 1985.

4.4   High economic scenario

For the high economic scenario, we assume that the economy recovers during the 1980s as in the central scenario, but that steady growth is then experienced at an annual rate of about 2.5 per cent. This represents an economic performance

Table 4.3. *Economic indicators for the high scenario*

Indices (1975 = 100)
(Average annual percentage growth rates in brackets)

Year	GDP	Industrial output[a]	Agricultural output	Other services output	Consumers' expenditure
1980	107.3	95.4	128.5	110.0	110.5
1985	113.9 (1.20)	102.2 (1.39)	127.5[b] (−0.16)	114.1 (0.73)	113.8 (0.59)
1990	128.0 (2.36)	116.9 (2.72)	138.0 (1.60)	126.4 (2.07)	128.6 (2.48)
2000	164.0 (2.51)	150.5 (2.56)	157.5 (1.33)	161.4 (2.47)	164.6 (2.50)
2010	209.9 (2.50)	193.8 (2.56)	177.5 (1.20)	206.0 (2.47)	210.7 (2.50)
2020	266.1 (2.40)	246.6 (2.44)	200.0 (1.20)	260.3 (2.37)	267.1 (2.40)

Notes: [a] Including construction.
[b] The fall between 1980 and 1985 is the result of the very high level of output (assessed at constant prices) in 1980.

slightly worse than the best long-term post-war growth rate, and would generally be regarded as an optimistic view of the future of the UK. The main economic indicators are shown in table 4.3, which may be compared with the central scenario values in table 4.1.

In contrast to the central scenario, industrial output leads economic growth, so that the process of de-industrialisation is halted. However, the recovery of the ratio of TIP to GDP is only sufficient to bring this ratio close to its 1979 value by 2020; in effect the economic structure becomes stable, with the balance between industry and services tilted towards the latter in comparison with the situation prior to 1970. In general, we would expect the industry/GDP ratio to be higher in times of high growth, because of the component of industrial output which comprises investment goods and is therefore directly growth-dependent. The same relationship has been demonstrated in the recent past by the industrial decline which has accompanied the slowing-down of the economy as a whole (figure 4.2). The services sector is, as always, complementary to industry, while consumers' expenditure moves with GDP. Agricultural output is only slightly higher than in the central case, reflecting the weak link between agricultural output and GDP.

The shares in industrial output are assumed to be the same as in the central scenario. In reality, a higher growth rate would probably imply higher shares for those sectors which are important in the production of investment goods, and conversely for consumer goods. However, quantification of these effects without the use of a detailed structural model of the economy is difficult, and for the appraisal of energy policy issues the simple approach used here is preferred. By 2000, only shipbuilding remains below its 1975 output level. The high growth sectors may be placed in perspective by comparing past and assumed future growth rates. For chemicals, for example, the assumptions of output imply an average annual growth rate between 1980 and 2020 of 2.74 per cent, which is much lower than the 6.29 per cent experienced between 1953 and 1973.

4.5   Low economic scenario

Recent economic performance raises the possibility of a very adverse economic future for the UK. For example, the CEGB (Central Electricity Generating Board) (1982) considers a range of economic scenarios, in the lowest of which the average annual rate of growth between 1980 and 2000 is minus 0.5 per cent. Similarly, the Department of Energy (1982) quotes a range of economic growth rates starting from 0.5 per cent per annum for the same period. However, such low rates of growth would be likely, over such a long period, to be associated with major structural change and possibly acute social tensions, not least as a result of unemployment. Though from an economic planning viewpoint such scenarios certainly need to be considered, their relevance to energy planning is doubtful unless the evidence for such a pessimistic view becomes much stronger.

For this study, our low economic scenario is based on an average GDP growth rate between 1980 and 2000 of 1.0 per cent per annum, arising from a slow recovery followed by growth at around 1.25 per cent. De-industrialisation occurs rather faster than in the central scenario, with a complementary rise in services, and with consumer's expenditure generally following GDP. The detailed economic assumptions are shown in table 4.4.

Once again, the shares in industrial output in each subsector are assumed to match those for the central scenario. With such a low rate of industrial growth, this scenario presents a bleak picture. By 2020, four sectors have failed to attain their 1975 output levels, and in only three sectors does growth between 1975 and 2020 exceed 1 per cent per annum.

4.6   Comparison between scenarios

Figure 4.3 shows the historical course of GDP from 1950 to 1980, with the projections for the three scenarios from 1985 to 2020. The average annual growth rates for the three scenarios between 1980 and 2020 are 2.3, 1.9 and 1.1 per cent, which are low in comparison with the 1950s and 1960s. In the authors' view, a long-term growth rate below our central case is more likely than one above the central case. Simple analysis of the trends in the labour force and

Table 4.4.   *Economic indicators for the low scenario*

Indices (1975 = 100)
(Average annual percentage growth rates in brackets)

Year	GDP	Industrial output[a]	Agricultural output	Other services output	Consumers' expenditure
1980	107.3	95.4	128.5	110.0	110.5
1985	109.0 (0.31)	97.2 (0.37)	127.5[b] (−0.16)	111.3 (0.24)	113.8 (0.59)
1990	114.8 (1.04)	101.6 (0.89)	136.7 (1.40)	117.8 (1.14)	119.1 (0.91)
2000	130.0 (1.25)	111.4 (0.93)	154.0 (1.20)	135.7 (1.42)	134.7 (1.24)
2010	147.2 (1.25)	122.0 (0.91)	170.1 (1.00)	156.3 (1.42)	152.5 (1.25)
2020	165.0 (1.15)	132.1 (0.80)	187.9 (1.00)‐	178.2 (1.32)	171.0 (1.15)

Notes: [a] Including construction.
[b] The fall between 1980 and 1985 is the result of the very high level of output (assessed at constant prices) in 1980.

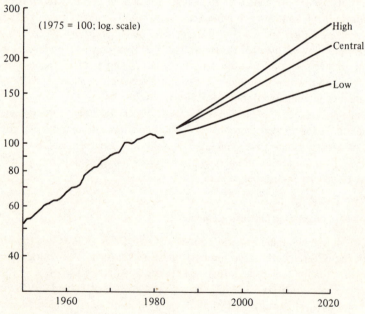

4.3 Past and future UK gross domestic product

in labour productivity, however, indicate that unemployment is likely to remain serious for the UK for at least the next decade. The range of industrial output spanned by the scenarios is greater than the range of GDP, and conversely for services; this is a result of the tendency for de-industrialisation to proceed more rapidly under low growth.

5

Fuel use in the UK

5.1   Energy and economic activity

The purpose of this chapter is to present an overview of the present patterns of fuel use in the UK. First, however, we shall look at the relationship between total energy use and economic growth.

Energy use is a natural result of economic activity. Individuals whose wealth is increased through economic growth use some of that wealth to keep warm, to replace their own labour by machinery of one sort or another, and to travel. Over a very long period, the process of economic development is usually associated with increasing energy intensity up to some maximum value, and then a gradual fall. This is demonstrated for the UK by figure 5.1 (Humphrey and Stanislaw, 1979) which shows the primary energy/GDP ratio between 1700 and 1975. The figure shows that the UK has been in a period of declining energy intensity since 1880.

The variation of the same ratio in the more recent past is shown in figure 5.2 (Department of Energy, 1983a and earlier editions). Apart from occasional anomalies, there is a steady downward trend in energy intensity.

This downward trend is the result of many different mechanisms, among which we may note:

(a) Technical changes (for example in manufacturing processes) which lead to increases in efficiency.

(b) Changes in the mix of industrial products away from high-energy products such as steel.

(c) Changes in the overall structure of the economy, in particular the growing role of service activities.

(d) Changes in fuel mix: some of these, such as the replacement of coal by oil or gas, often improve energy efficiency; while others, notably the growth of electricity's share in final consumption, worsen primary energy efficiency.

(e) Activities aimed specifically at energy conservation, in response to publicity or increased energy prices.

54

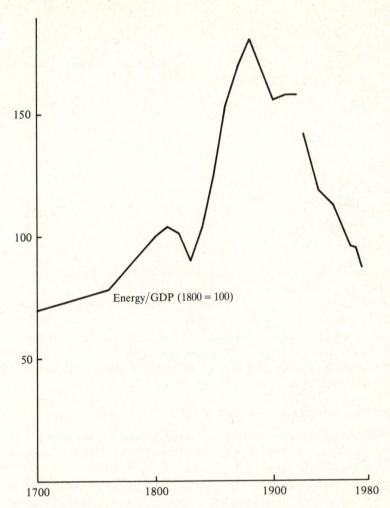

5.1 UK energy intensity (primary energy/GDP), 1700–1975. Figures up to 1920 include Eire

The diversity of these mechanisms of change illustrates the difficulty of interpreting simple parameters such as the energy/GDP ratio, and should also provide a warning against the use of forecasts based on the extrapolation of such ratios. In order to understand the process of change more fully, we need to look at energy use in much more detail.

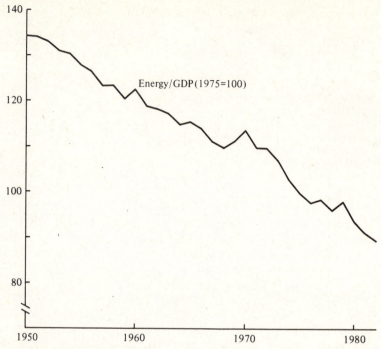

5.2 UK energy intensity (primary energy/GDP), 1950–82. Primary fuel use is temperature-corrected

5.2   Analysis by sectors and fuels

Table 5.1 shows the way in which final energy consumption was divided between fuels and sectors in 1980 (Department of Energy, 1983a). We observe that, even seven years after the oil crisis, oil was still the most important fuel in final consumption with a share of 43.9 per cent (its share in 1973 was 48.7 per cent). Over half of this oil was used in transport, and more than one-quarter in industry. Gas was the second most important fuel in final consumption in 1980 at just under 30 per cent. Of this, one-half went to households, and most of the remainder to industry. Coal and other solid fuels were split about equally between households and industry, with a small amount being used in commercial and public buildings (the services sector). Electricity's share in final consumption was similar to that of solid fuels, and households, industry and services were all important consumers.

The distinction between primary and delivered energy (introduced in chapter 1) is important in understanding these figures. Electricity is generated at an efficiency of around 30 per cent. Small losses are also involved in the production

Table 5.1.   *UK fuel use in 1980 (final consumers; PJ; percentages of total in brackets)*

	Solid fuel	Oil products	Gases	Electricity	Total
Iron and steel	132	70	67	33	302 (5.1)
Other industry	220	646	600	254	1720 (28.8)
Transport	2	1476	0	11	1489 (25.0)
Households	350	115	890	310	1665 (27.9)
Agriculture	1	47	0	14	62 (1.0)
Other services	62	263	217	185	727 (12.2)
Total	767 (12.9)	2617 (43.9)	1774 (29.7)	807 (13.5)	5965 (100.0)

Note: Gas use in other industry includes about 183 PJ used as a chemical feedstock which is shown separately in table 5.6 below. Other differences between tables 5.1 and 5.6 are due to rounding errors.

of other fuels. If deliveries into final consumption were expressed in terms of the equivalent quantity of primary energy, the share of electricity would rise to around 33 per cent.

The split of energy into sectors shows that 'other industries' and households are the major consuming sectors, with transport a close third. The services sector, though it contributes more to GDP than does industry, accounts for only one-eighth of delivered energy use. Agriculture is a very minor sector in energy terms, but is of interest because of its very high dependence on oil.

It is instructive to compare the pattern of fuel use shown in table 5.1 with that twenty years earlier, shown in table 5.2. The sectoral structure is not markedly different; transport has increased in importance since 1960, while iron and steel has fallen substantially. Fuel use in 1960 was, however, dominated by solid fuels, with oil products a very poor second. Gas in 1960 was, of course, almost all manufactured from coal and was therefore expensive; its low share is not surprising. The very substantial increase in electricity's share between 1960 and 1980 should be noted. This mainly results from technical change, specifically the increased use of domestic appliances and the use of electrical machinery in industry.

5.3   Analysis by end-use

Energy is not an end in itself. Consumers purchase fuels in order to obtain a range of benefits, including comfort, light, transport, the transformation of

Table 5.2.   *UK fuel use in 1960 (final consumers; PJ; percentages of total in brackets)*

	Solid fuel	Oil products	Gases	Electricity	Total
Iron and steel	522	133	70	23	748 (14.0)
Other industry	945	343	79	137	1504 (28.2)
Transport	297	624	0	8	929 (17.4)
Households	1193	71	137	121	1522 (28.6)
Agriculture	13	43	0	8	64 (1.2)
Other services	316	139	50	59	564 (10.6)
Total	3286	1353	336	356	5331
	(61.6)	(25.4)	(6.3)	(6.7)	(100.0)

materials involved in industrial production or domestic cooking and so on. Since different fuels are differently suited to these various uses, we need to be aware of the different applications in order to assess the prospects for energy conservation and inter-fuel substitution.

Bush and Matthews (1979) present an excellent summary of the structure of fuel use in 1976, from which the details presented in this section are taken. The data are the result of a complex process of analysis, and the reader is directed to the reference cited above for details of the data sources and assumptions used.

A breakdown of final energy consumption by end-use and sector is given in table 5.3. Note that other industry, households and services are all dominated by the use of fuels for low-grade heat. As expected, transport and agriculture are dominated by motive power, while in iron and steel, high-grade heat is the most important end-use.

Overall, low-grade heat accounts for nearly one-half of total final consumption, and the most important sector is households. Here, and in services, space and water heating are the major applications, so that the key issue for energy conservation is the thermal performance of the building structures. In 'other industry', which accounts for about one-third of total low-grade heat use, only 35 per cent of fuel used for low-grade heat is for space and water heating, the remainder being for industrial process use. In the same sector, 82 per cent of the fuel used for low-grade heat is consumed in boilers.

Motive power is the second largest end-use category in table 5.3, accounting for 33 per cent of final consumption. About one-fifth of this (mainly in other industry and households) is stationary motive power, for which electricity is the

Table 5.3. *Final energy consumption in the UK, by end-use and sector, 1976 (PJ; percentage of total in brackets)*

	Low-grade heat[a]	High-grade heat[a]	Motive power	Lighting etc.
Iron and steel	93	516	35	4
Other industry[b]	975	365	247	25
Transport	0	0	1500	0
Households	1279	127	105[c]	24
Agriculture	24	0	49[d]	0
Other services	505	50	37	70
Total	2876	1058	1973	123
	(47.7)	(17.6)	(32.7)	(2.0)

Notes: [a] Low-grade heat is usually defined as heat at an end-use temperature below 200 °C. High-grade heat is heat at 200 °C or over, and includes cooking and electrochemical applications.
[b] Other industry excludes petrochemicals. Quantities of energy are measured downstream of combined heat and power (CHP) systems where applicable.
[c] All domestic electrical appliances other than lighting and cooking are included under motive power.
[d] Lighting in agriculture is included in motive power.

major fuel. The remainder – almost entirely in transport – is mobile motive power, which is almost wholly dependent on oil products.

High-grade heat, including domestic cooking, accounted in 1976 for about 18 per cent of final consumption. The most important sectors are iron and steel and other industry. Lighting and other electricity-specific applications apart from motive power are a small proportion of the total, though they are of considerable importance in the services sector.

The relationships between the end-use categories and the use of specific fuels are summarised in table 5.4 . Low-grade heat is dominated by oil and gas, with solid fuel in third place. It is worth noting that, whereas oil use for low-grade heat is concentrated in other industry and services, both gas and solid fuel use are dominated by the household sector. At first sight, solid fuels appear to lead in the production of high-grade heat. However, this element of solid-fuel use is almost wholly due to the iron and steel sector (418 PJ) and, when this sector is excluded, the major fuel for high-grade heat applications is seen to be gas, with substantial contributions from both oil and electricity. For each of these fuels, other industry is the most important sector, with households also of considerable importance for gas (94 PJ). Motive power is, of course, dominated by oil (the

Table 5.4.   *Final energy consumption in the UK, by end-use and fuel, 1976 (PJ)*

	Low-grade heat[a]	High-grade heat[a]	Motive power	Lighting etc.
Solid fuels	607	499	3	3
Oil products	929	161	1594	2
Gases	929	277	1	0
Heat (from CHP)	210	0	0	0
Electricity	200	121	374	118

Note: [a] Low-grade heat is usually defined as heat at an end-use temperature below 200 °C. High-grade heat is heat at 200 °C or over, and includes cooking and electrochemical applications.

Table 5.5.   *Economic structure and energy intensity, 1960 and 1980*

	Manufacturing and construction		Other services (excluding transport)	
	1960	1980	1960	1980
Contribution to GDP (%)	42.7	29.8	43.1	55.1
Percentage of delivered energy	42.3	33.9	10.6	12.2
Energy intensity (MJ/1980 £ contributed to GDP)	43.7	33.1	10.8	6.4

transport sector), with electricity, in which the largest element is stationary motive power in industry, coming a rather poor second. Lighting and other specialised non-heating applications are, of course, dominated by electricity.

5.4   Structure and energy intensity

It was noted in section 5.1 that the historical decline in overall energy intensity was in part the result of structural change in the economy as a whole and within industry. Table 5.5 shows the relative sizes of the industry and service sectors, and their respective energy intensities, in 1960 and 1980 (these and other statistics in this section are taken from Central Statistical Office, 1983; Department of Energy, 1983a and earlier editions). It may be seen that the services sector, which (in terms of its contribution to GDP) is four to five times less energy intensive than industry, has been growing in importance. Energy efficiency has improved substantially in both sectors over this twenty-year period.

Within industry itself, both changes in energy intensity over time and the differences between sectors are important. The iron and steel industry is about six times as energy intensive as industry as a whole, and building materials (bricks, china and cement) and chemicals also show higher than average energy intensity. On the other hand, engineering, which represented 37 per cent of industrial output in 1980, has an energy intensity of about one-half the average. In most sectors there has been a marked fall in energy intensity over the last few decades, and there has been a tendency for energy efficiency to improve most in the more energy-intensive sectors. Furthermore, structural change (particularly the decline of iron and steel) has led to overall energy savings. This is a topic to which we shall return in chapter 7.

5.5   Energy balance table

In chapter 1, the concepts of primary, delivered and useful energy were introduced. Most of the discussion in the present chapter has been in terms of delivered energy. Energy delivered to final consumers is a mixture of primary fuels (coal, natural gas) and secondary fuels such as oil products and electricity. The industries which produce these fuels are themselves, of course, major consumers of primary fuels. In the process of secondary fuel production some energy will inevitably be used up, and for both primary and secondary fuels some losses may occur in distribution.

These processes, all of which occur 'upstream' of the final consumer, need to be understood if the overall pattern of UK fuel use, and in particular the level and composition of any fuel imports, is to be examined. An energy balance table, which provides a convenient way of displaying the complete pattern of fuel use in a specific year, is given for the UK in 1980 in table 5.6.

Though the table appears at first sight to be very complex, its basic structure is straightforward. We start at the top with a fairly detailed breakdown of final consumption by fuel and sector, including non-energy uses of fuel (i.e. uses as lubricants, solvents, chemical feedstocks etc.). We then follow the implications of these demands through the conversion sectors – mainly electricity generation and oil refining – taking into account distribution and conversion losses. For example, in 1980 the total fuel input to the electricity supply industry was 2812 PJ (2526 + 3 + 283), and electricity output was 907 PJ (net of the industry's own use but before subtraction of distribution losses), giving an overall thermal efficiency of 32.2 per cent. We may then bring these primary energy needs and any outstanding secondary fuel demands together to find the total energy

Table 5.6. *UK energy balance table, 1980(PJ)*

		Primary fuels					
	Total energy	Total primary	Coal	Crude oil	Natural gas	Nuclear energy	Hydro-electric energy
Households	1665	1160	275	0	885	0	0
Iron and steel	302	52	5	0	47	0	0
Other industry	1537	615	208	0	407	0	0
Transport	1489	2	2	0	0	0	0
Services	789	264	48	0	216	0	0
Final energy demand	5783	2094	538	0	1555	0	0
Non-energy uses	496	182	0	0	182	0	0
Distribution losses	118	37	0	0	37	0	0
Electricity supply industry	1905	2526	2139	0	15	323	50
Oil refineries	333	3902	0	3902	0	0	0
Solid-fuel manufacture	112	446	446	0	1	0	0
Gas manufacture	16	14	0	0	14	0	0
Energy conversion sectors	2366	6889	2584	3902	29	323	50
Coal industry	42	21	18	0	3	0	0
Oil industry	0	0	0	0	0	0	0
Natural gas industry	48	48	0	0	48	0	0
Primary energy sectors	90	69	18	0	51	0	0
Total energy required	8852	9271	3140	3902	1856	323	50
Production	8738	8681	3288	3583	1437	323	50
Net imports	539	802	101	282	419	0	0
Bunkers	−107	0	0	0	0	0	0
Stock decrease	−288	−296	−242	−53	0	0	0
Statistical difference	−30	84	−6	91	0	0	0
Total energy available	8852	9271	3140	3902	1856	323	50

Note: Summations may not be exact owing to rounding errors.

Secondary fuels

Total secondary	Manuf'd solid fuel	Oil products				Other oil prods.	Manufactured gases			Electricity
		Total oil prods.	Fuel oil	Gas oil/ diesel	Gasoline		Total manuf'd gas	SNG	Other manuf'd gas	
505	74	115	3	26	0	87	5	3	2	310
250	128	69	55	12	0	1	20	0	20	33
922	13	646	386	194	0	65	9	2	8	254
1487	0	1476	5	351	899	220	0	0	0	11
525	14	310	100	209	0	1	2	1	1	199
3689	230	2616	549	793	899	374	36	6	30	807
313	0	313	0	0	0	313	1	1	0	0
81	2	0	0	0	0	0	4	0	4	75
−621	3	283	275	8	0	0	0	0	0	−907
−3569	0	−3572	−1015	−1007	−780	−769	0	0	0	3
−335	−305	0	0	0	0	0	−30	0	−30	1
2	0	11	0	0	0	11	−11	−7	−4	1
−4523	−302	−3277	−740	−999	−780	−758	−41	−7	−34	−903
20	0	0	0	0	0	0	0	0	0	20
0	0	0	0	0	0	0	0	0	0	0
0	0	0	0	0	0	0	0	0	0	0
20	0	0	0	0	0	0	0	0	0	20
−419	−70	−349	−191	−206	119	−71	0	0	0	0
58	0	58	0	0	0	58	0	0	0	0
−263	−30	−233	−100	−151	86	−68	0	0	0	0
−107	0	−107	−73	−35	0	0	0	0	0	0
8	−41	49	50	1	−2	0	0	0	0	0
−114	1	−115	−68	−22	35	−61	0	0	0	0
−419	−70	−349	−191	−206	119	−71	0	0	0	0

required, classified by fuel. This must match (apart from statistical differences and stock adjustments) the fuel available from indigenous production and net imports, less fuel use for marine bunkers, i.e. for international shipping. The table shows that UK fuel imports amounted in 1980 to 539 PJ, some 6 per cent of total requirements. Natural gas was the main import (419 PJ); crude oil imports were largely offset by a net export of oil products, while there was a small net import of coal. Note also the increase in coal and other solid fuel stocks due to the recession.

The energy balance table also shows the losses incurred in moving from primary fuels to final consumption. Of the 8852 PJ total energy requirements, 2573 PJ (29 per cent) is lost in extraction, conversion and distribution. Most of this loss, 1905 PJ, arises from electricity generation, with oil refining (333 PJ) the second largest factor.

Finally, we may note the shape of the primary fuel mix. Nuclear energy and hydro-electric power account respectively for 3.7 and 0.6 per cent of total energy requirements – a very small proportion – though nuclear energy provides nearly 12 per cent of the energy input for electricity generation. Though coal and other solid fuels account for only 13 per cent of final demand, they represent some 35 per cent of primary energy, reflecting the importance of coal in electricity generation. Oil and gas respectively account for 40 and 21 per cent of primary fuel use, compared with 47 and 28 per cent of final energy demand plus non-energy uses.

6

Energy use in households

6.1   Introduction

History

In 1980, the household sector used 28 per cent of all energy delivered into final consumption, a figure which has been rising slightly since 1973 (Department of Energy, 1983a). Figure 6.1 shows that the total amount of energy used has risen somewhat over the recent period, though over the longer term it has remained fairly stable. Due to the increase in the number of households, energy use per household shows, if anything, a gradual fall, but energy conservation following the 1973 oil crisis seems as yet to have had little impact on total energy use in this sector.

The same period has seen a major shift away from solid fuel and towards gas. This has been accompanied by steady growth in electricity's share of the market, and by the penetration of central heating. Oil has always been a minor fuel in this sector.

Methodology

There are two principal approaches to modelling domestic energy use. In the 'top-down' approach, energy use and fuel shares are related to income, fuel prices and other relevant parameters by means of econometric models. The 'bottom-up' approach makes use of more detailed knowledge of the stocks and technical characteristics of fuel-using appliances and the buildings themselves to construct an overall picture of fuel use. Both approaches have strengths and weaknesses. In this study, we use the 'bottom-up' approach, but including economic relationships where these are clearly relevant. This approach seems particularly appropriate for the household sector, where decisions are rarely made on strictly economic grounds, and where the slow replacement rate of the housing stock makes econometric modelling difficult.

One result of the approach used in this study is that there is no explicit link

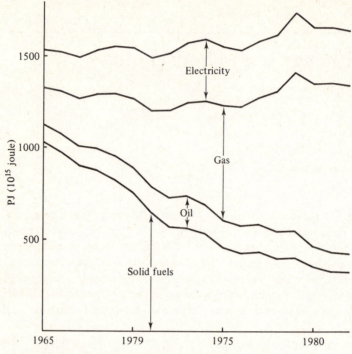

6.1 Fuel use in the household sector, 1965–82

between income and household energy use. Though such a link probably exists, it is complex, and would be expected to operate in a number of ways, including:

(a) increased income leading to an increase in both building and demoli- tion rates, improving the average standard of buildings,

(b) increased income leading to increased propensity to invest in insula- tion, or conversely to a decreased awareness of energy costs as the latter form a smaller component of total expenditure,

(c) increased income leading to higher levels of comfort, or larger houses, and so increasing energy use.

These effects occur over widely-differing time-scales, and depend on fashions and expectations as well as, for example, on government policy on the building regulations. It is far from easy to quantify these mechanisms on the basis of past experience, and it seems preferable to leave the energy–income relationship as a matter for discussion rather than to incorporate it formally into the model.

Figure 6.2 shows in simplified form the logical relationships used in this study to model household energy use. The starting-point is a model of the housing

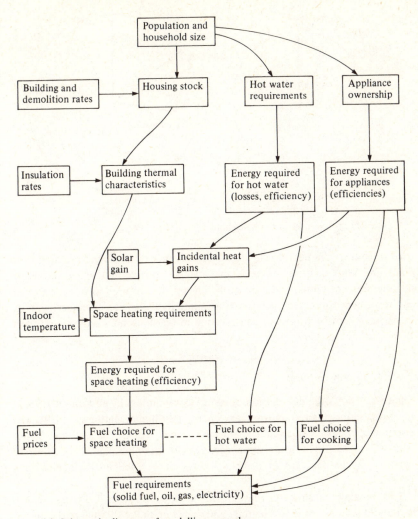

6.2 Schematic diagram of modelling procedure

stock, disaggregated by age and type. From this model, the thermal characteristics of each type of dwelling, under a range of insulation assumptions, are calculated. Linked models deal with the ownership and use of cookers and other appliances, and with the supply of hot water. These uses of energy, together with solar gain and heat from the occupants themselves, make a contribution to the space heating of the dwelling. The remaining requirement for space heating is met by the central (or other) heating system itself. Appliance efficiencies are

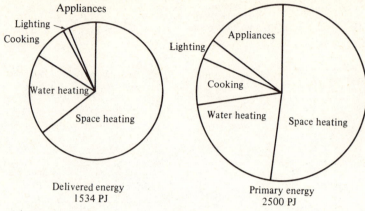

6.3 Energy end-uses in the household sector, 1976

used to convert the need for heat into the quantity of fuel input required. For many individual end-uses, there is only a single possible fuel; space and water heating are exceptions, and here economic criteria are used as a guide to fuel choice in new equipment, alongside a simple model of stock replacement. A useful review of fuel use and conservation in the household sector is given in Watt Committee, 1979.

Energy end-uses

Figure 6.3 shows the distribution of energy consumption by end-use in 1976, in terms of both delivered and primary energy (Bush and Matthews, 1979). The dominance of space and water heating is evident. Cooking is less than 10 per cent of the total. Lighting and appliances account for only 8 per cent of delivered energy, but 19 per cent of primary energy due to the losses in electricity generation.

This breakdown suggests that the main scope for energy savings in the household sector is in space heating, and therefore in the thermal performance of the building itself; later analysis will confirm this observation.

6.2   The housing stock

Households

The most convenient unit for analysing energy use in the domestic sector is the household. The number of households depends on the population (taken from Office of Population Censuses and Surveys, 1981) and the number of persons

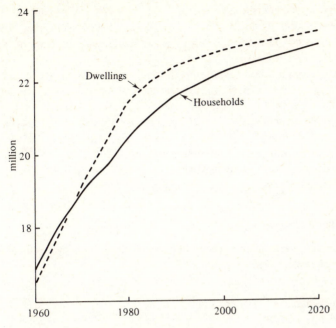

6.4 Projections of households and dwellings

per household. The latter figure has been declining steadily through the post-war period, and it is assumed that this decline will continue, though at a slower rate. Figure 6.4 shows the projections of both households and dwellings (see below) for the period to 2020.

Dwellings

It is important to distinguish the number of dwellings from the number of households. Except in times of housing shortage, there is usually a small excess of dwellings over households, as figure 6.4 shows, representing houses awaiting demolition or occupation. For the purpose of energy analysis, we need to know not only the number of dwellings, but also their age distribution and type. This requires an examination of the process of stock replacement.

Building and demolition rates are very sensitive to fluctuations in the economy as a whole. Demolition rates have changed erratically in recent years, and are a poor guide to the long term. Building starts have fallen sharply since 1970, and it is assumed that the high levels of the 1960s will not be attained in the lower-growth environment anticipated for the long-term future. This implies some ageing of the housing stock as a whole, with an emphasis on refurbishment rather than replacement. From an energy point of view, the slower turnover will impede conservation, in particular because of the number of solid-walled houses which will remain in use, and this represents an important interaction between housing and energy policies.

The age structure of the housing stock is important, in particular, because of the difference in thermal performance and ease of insulation between solid-walled and cavity-walled houses. We assume (following Romig and Leach, 1977) that all houses built prior to 1935 are solid-walled, and all built thereafter are cavity-walled, though in fact the transition was more gradual. We also assume that 85 per cent of all demolitions are of pre-1935 houses, and that 95 per cent of all unoccupied dwellings are pre-1935 properties awaiting demolition, while the remaining 5 per cent are new buildings.

Dwelling types

Building thermal performance is very dependent on the type of dwelling. We distinguish five categories:

> Detached
> Semi-detached (including end-terraced)
> Middle terrace
> Top-floor flat
> Other flat

Romig and Leach (1977) indicate that the proportions of different dwelling types in the total stock have changed significantly over the past sixty years, notably in the increase of semi-detached rather than terraced houses. However, recent figures in the General Household Surveys (Office of Population Censuses and Surveys, 1979 and earlier editions) suggest that this change has ceased. We assume, with Leach (1979), that the proportions of different dwelling types found in recent years will be maintained. Following Romig and Leach (1977), we assume that one-quarter of 'terraced' houses are end-terrace and are therefore treated as semi-detached for energy analysis purposes. Using age breakdown data from the General Household Surveys, we can construct the housing stock structure shown in table 6.1.

Building dimensions

Average floor areas in new dwellings have shown a marked decline in recent years (Romig and Leach, 1977; Department of the Environment, 1981 and earlier editions) and we assume that this decline will continue at a slower rate, flattening out around the end of the century. Heat loss from buildings depends

Table 6.1. *Structure of the housing stock*

Year of measurement	Year of construction	Occupied dwellings (m)				Unoccupied dwellings (m)
		Detached	Semi-detached	Terraced	Flat	
1980	Before 1935	1.31	2.92	3.34	1.75	
	1935-74	1.87	3.52	2.31	2.30	
	1975-79	0.26	0.16	0.27	0.45	
	Total	3.44	6.60	5.92	4.50	0.93
1985	Before 1935	1.28	2.91	3.32	1.72	
	1935-79	2.13	3.68	2.58	2.74	
	1980-84	0.12	0.14	0.27	0.20	
	Total	3.53	6.73	6.17	4.66	0.91
1990	Before 1935	1.27	2.90	3.30	1.72	
	1935-84	2.24	3.82	2.85	2.93	
	1985-89	0.14	0.24	0.13	0.12	
	Total	3.65	6.95	6.28	4.77	0.78
2000	Before 1935	1.15	2.78	3.13	1.64	
	1935-89	2.37	4.03	2.96	3.04	
	1990-99	0.26	0.28	0.37	0.26	
	Total	3.78	7.09	6.45	4.94	0.68
2020	Before 1935	0.98	2.58	2.87	1.43	
	1935-99	2.59	4.27	3.29	3.26	
	2000-19	0.32	0.54	0.54	0.36	
	Total	3.89	7.39	6.70	5.05	0.35

on the areas of exposed walls, roof, windows and ground floor, and typical ratios of these areas to the floor area are taken from Building Research Establishment, 1976. These data are summarised in table 6.2.

6.3   Insulation and heat loss

Thermal properties of building elements

All the heat input to a house, whether from the space heating system, the hot water system, electrical appliances or other sources, will find its way eventually to the environment. The effect of insulating the house is to slow down this movement of heat so that, for a given internal temperature, a smaller heat input is required.

The rate at which heat moves through any solid element of a building is controlled by the thermal transmittance, or U-value, of the material. Thermal transmittance is the reciprocal of thermal resistance; where the building element

Table 6.2. *Building dimensions*

	Detached	Semi-detached	Terraced	Flat (apartment)		
Floor area (m²):						
1980	105	87	81	61		
1985	105	87	80	61		
1990	104	86	80	61		
2000	103	86	79	60		
2020	101	84	78	59		
Areas (ratio to total floor area):				*Ground floor*	*Intermediate*	*Top floor*
Wall	1.25	1.00	0.75	0.75	0.75	0.75
Roof	0.50	0.50	0.50	0.00	0.00	1.00
Ground floor	0.50	0.50	0.50	1.00	0.00	0.00
Window	0.18	0.18	0.18	0.18	0.18	0.18

comprises a series of layers across which the heat must pass (e.g. for cavity wall, plaster + block + cavity + brick) then the total thermal resistance is the sum of the resistances of each part, including the resistances represented by the surfaces themselves. The latter can be important, particularly for thin structures such as windows. For further details of the physical processes involved, see O'Callaghan, 1978 and Fisk, 1981.

The rate of heat flow through any building element is proportional to the U-value, the area of the element and the difference between the inside and outside temperatures; and the total rate of heat loss *through the building fabric* is:

$$Q_f = \Sigma_j \ A_j U_j (T_i - T_o)$$

where the summation is over building elements of area A_j and U-value U_j, with inside and outside temperatures T_i and T_o. To this must be added loss through *ventilation*, the rate of which is given by

$$Q_v = V \times 330N(T_i - T_o)$$

where V is the internal volume of the dwelling, corrected for dead spaces, N is the number of air changes per hour, and 330 is the energy (in watt-hours) needed to raise the temperature of $1 \, m^3$ of air through $1°C$. The quantities Q_f and Q_v are measured in watts.

Table 6.3 gives some examples of U-values for different building elements; these are by no means complete, and the reader is referred to more detailed sources for further information (CIBS, 1980, Open University, 1978).

Table 6.3. *U-values for typical building elements*

Element	U-value (W/m² °C)	Notes
Solid wall	2.1	220 mm brickwork, 13 mm dense plaster
Cavity wall	1.3	105 mm brick, cavity, 100 mm medium concrete block, 13 mm lightweight plaster
Insulated cavity wall	0.55	As above, plus 50 mm urea-formaldehyde foam
Single-glazed window	5.0	Wood frame occupying 20 per cent of total area, normal exposure
Double-glazed window	3.7	Aluminium frame with thermal break, occupying 20 per cent of total area, normal exposure
Roof, no insulation	2.2	Pitched, tiled roof over plaster-board ceiling
Insulated roof	0.34	As above, with 100 mm glass fibre quilt
Floor (detached house)	0.59	Indicative values only; actual value depends on size and shape of floor,
Floor (semi-detached)	0.53	number of exposed edges, and on whether floor is of solid concrete
Floor (terrace or ground-floor flat)	0.44	or suspended timber construction; see CIBS, 1980

Note: The above values are examples of situations which are often found in practice. In some cases, different values are used in the analysis, e.g. typical loft insulation thickness is taken to be 80 mm.

Inside and outside temperatures

Table 6.4 shows the average external temperatures on a monthly basis; in this study we make no explicit allowance for variations between different parts of the UK.

Internal temperatures depend on family income, the ownership of central heating and insulation, and the proportion of the day that the dwelling is in use. There has been a slow increase in average temperature over time. The present study is based on a future in which fuel prices rise steadily, so that, although extreme measures are not required, there is a continuing awareness of the cost of fuels and of the need for conservation. We assume that inside temperatures will rise only slightly over the period to 2020. It is expected, however, that there

Table 6.4. *External temperatures for the UK (°C)*

January	3.7	July	16.7
February	4.0	August	16.5
March	6.1	September	14.3
April	9.0	October	11.5
May	12.0	November	7.4
June	15.1	December	5.0

Note: These are averages over an eighteen-hour day to take account of the intermittent nature of the heating load.

Table 6.5. *Inside temperature assumptions (°C)*

	Central heating, poor insulation	Central heating, good insulation	No central heating, poor insulation	No central heating, good insulation
1980	17.0	18.0	14.0	15.0
1985	17.1	18.1	14.2	15.2
1990	17.3	18.3	14.5	15.5
2000	17.5	18.5	14.5	15.5
2020	18.0	19.0	15.0	16.0

Note: 'Good insulation' in this context means at least cavity-wall insulation plus loft insulation.

will be a significant increase in comfort, resulting from an improvement in temperature control. Table 6.5 shows the inside temperatures assumed.

Insulation levels

There are major uncertainties both in the ownership of home insulation and in the factors which influence householders to invest in such measures. Very few householders carry out economic assessments of insulation measures; the decision to invest seems to be influenced mainly by the prevailing climate of opinion, by publicity and advertising and by the perceived impact of the measure on the market value of the house. It is also important to recognise that some measures may bring other benefits than fuel saving; double glazing, in particular, may reduce noise, increase comfort by modifying the temperature distribution in the room and solve problems caused by deterioration in existing windows.

Estimates of the current level of cavity wall insulation vary widely; for this study we use a mid-range figure of about nine hundred thousand homes in 1980 (based on ACEC, 1982). For a future in which there is a continuing awareness of energy costs, we assume a continuation of the present installation rate (about 100 000 retrofits per year) to 2020. In addition, all new houses are assumed to be built with cavity insulation as a result of recent changes in the building regulations. The proportion of cavity-walled dwellings which are insulated rises from 8 per cent in 1980 to 24 per cent in 1990, 38 per cent in 2000 and nearly 60 per cent by 2020. It should be noted that decisive government action in this field could lead to much faster penetration of the market, particularly since a coordinated campaign in a particular area allows costs to be reduced.

Concern has recently been expressed about health risks due to the leakage into the living space of formaldehyde vapour from urea-formaldehyde foam used for cavity insulation. However, this appears to result from inadequate pre-installation checks by the installer rather than from an intrinsic problem of the technology, and adequately enforced codes of practice should eliminate the problem. In any case, this does not apply to new houses, nor to existing properties except for a fairly short period after installation, nor to other methods of cavity insulation.

The proportion of suitable roofs with some sort of loft insulation was around 66 per cent in 1980 (ACEC, 1982). This is one of the most straightforward and cost-effective insulation options and is likely to penetrate rapidly. We assume about 85 per cent penetration by 2000 and 90 per cent by 2020. Insulation thickness is difficult to predict; we assume an average of 80 mm throughout, though 'best practice' will be 100 mm or more.

As noted above, double glazing is not generally cost-effective when regarded solely as an energy conservation measure. The present level is around 16 per cent, and we assume that this rises to 26 per cent by the end of the period.

No explicit assumption is made about draughtproofing, but the assumption of one air change per hour for ventilation heat loss calculations implies wide use of this measure.

Internal or external insulation of solid walls is possible (e.g. Southern, 1981), but is generally very expensive and often disruptive to the occupants. These options are assumed to have a negligible impact in this study (one circumstance which would justify a more optimistic view would be the installation of these measures as part of a large scale programme to refurbish older property).

The use of controls to allow a reduction in average room temperature without loss of comfort has already been noted. Though improvements in control are likely to be substantial (due both to better systems and penetration into the market of existing techniques), there seems little scope in this sector for the sophisticated building control systems being developed for the services sector.

Table 6.6. *Heat loss from average semi-detached, 1980 (GJ/annum)*

	Insulation level				
	None	Loft	Loft, d. glazing	Loft, cavity fill	Loft, d. glazing, cavity fill
Solid walls, central heating	81.1	70.4	64.4	N/R[a]	N/R
Solid walls, no central heating	52.3	45.4	41.5	N/R	N/R
Cavity walls, central heating	55.9	45.3	39.3	41.5	34.5
Cavity walls, no central heating	36.0	29.2	25.3	27.1	22.6

Note: [a] Not relevant.

Clearly, many combinations of insulation measures are possible. We make some simplifying assumptions (e.g. that any householder owning double glazing or cavity-wall insulation will also, if relevant, have installed loft insulation) to identify eight categories:

> Solid walls, no insulation
> Solid walls, loft insulation
> Solid walls, loft insulation, double glazing
> Cavity walls, no insulation
> Cavity walls, loft insulation
> Cavity walls, loft insulation, double glazing
> Cavity walls, loft insulation, cavity insulation
> Cavity walls, loft insulation, double glazing, cavity insulation

Heat loss

The assumptions outlined above enable us to estimate the rate of heat loss, on a month by month basis, with different insulation options. Table 6.6 gives some examples of annual heat losses for semi-detached houses, using building dimensions for 1980. These take into account the increase in room temperature resulting from the ownership of central heating or insulation. Note that ownership of central heating increases annual heat loss (because of higher internal temperatures) by over 50 per cent. For solid-walled houses, the maximum saving is 21 per cent, of which nearly two-thirds is due to loft insulation. For cavity-walled houses, heat loss before insulation is less than 70 per cent of that for solid-walled houses, and savings of up to 38 per cent are possible, about half being from loft insulation. This means that a fully insulated

Table 6.7.   *Ownership levels of energy-using appliances (Number per 100 households)*

Appliance	1980	2000	2020
Cooker:			
electric	44	54	58
gas	55	48	45
other (e.g. solid-fuel range)	2	0	0
Washing-machine	75	83	84
Tumble-drier	18	49	50
Refrigerator	72	51	45
Fridge/freezer	32	50	55
Freezer	22	45	45
Electric kettle	78	87	88
Colour television	67	94	100
Monochrome television	48	25	10
Dishwasher	4	27	36

Note: Other appliances included in the analysis were spin drier, drying-cabinet, iron, vacuum cleaner, hi-fi unit, toaster, heated towel rail and electric blanket.

cavity-walled house has just over half the heat loss of a solid-walled house which is fully insulated except for wall insulation.

6.4   Energy-using appliances

In this section we consider the ownership and use of appliances, other than central heating systems, which consume fuel. As well as being an important component of fuel demand, these may also make a partial contribution to space heating requirements. Most use electrical energy, though cookers may use gas or other solid fuels. Hot water supply is very often integrated with a central heating system, and will be considered later.

Cookers

Various annual energy consumption figures are published for a typical gas or electric cooker. In this study we assume 80 therms (8.4 GJ) for a gas cooker and 1,230 kWh (4.4 GJ) for an electric cooker. At past and current prices, gas is very much the cheaper option, but in spite of this electricity has gained steadily relative to gas. Since the price advantage of gas is likely to fall in the future, we assume the preference for electric cookers to be permanent. Ownership levels are included in table 6.7 above. A significant improvement in the efficiency of

Table 6.8. *Consumption of energy-using appliances (kWh per appliance per year)*

Appliance	1980	2000	2020
Cooker:			
electric	1230	800	800
gas	2360	2085	1950
other (e.g. solid-fuel range)	5560	5560	5560
Washing-machine	200	200	200
Tumble-drier	425	375	350
Refrigerator	325	300	300
Fridge/freezer	600	575	550
Freezer	1000	850	800
Electric kettle	250	200	175
Colour television	500	300	250
Monochrome television	250	160	160
Dishwasher	850	850	825

Note: Other appliances included in the analysis were spin drier, drying-cabinet, iron, vacuum cleaner, hi-fi unit, toaster, heated towel rail and electric blanket.
1 kWh = 3.6 MJ = 0.034 therms.

electric cookers is expected, because of better insulation, changes in cooking habits and the increased use of microwave ovens. A rather smaller improvement is expected for gas cookers, as shown in table 6.8.

Other appliances

Analysis has been carried out for seventeen types of electrical appliance (lighting is considered separately). In each case ownership has been estimated on the basis of a logistic penetration curve with a judgement-based saturation level, fitted to historical data, and likely improvements in efficiency have been assessed. Special consideration has been given to appliances which are in some measure substitutes for one another, such as refrigerators and fridge/freezers. The resulting ownership and consumption figures are shown in tables 6.7 and 6.8. The assumed efficiency improvements are certainly more modest than what could be achieved in principle (see, for example, Nørgard, 1979). However, for most appliances, energy saving is not a major design criterion, and there is as yet little evidence that energy efficiency is a major consumer priority.

Lighting

Energy use per household for lighting rose sharply through the period 1955 to 1973, and then levelled off. There is substantial scope for saving, both through the use of fluorescent tubes and by the avoidance of wastage. However, the strong upward trend in the past suggests that the benefits of improved efficiency may be largely offset by higher levels of illumination. We assume a very gradual rise in electricity consumption per household for lighting, from its 1980 value of 332 kWh per annum to 338 kWh in 2000 and 344 kWh in 2020.

6.5 Space and water heating

Hot water

The fuel required to provide hot water depends on many factors, including the water temperature required (currently 55–60° C but probably slightly lower in the future), the requirement per person, the household size, losses (e.g. from tanks and pipework) and the efficiency of the water heating appliance. We assume that the use of hot water will rise from its 1980 value of 35 litres per person per day to 50 litres by 2020. The effect of this rise on energy consumption is offset by the reduction in household size, the lowering of water temperature and the reduction in tank and pipework losses resulting from better insulation (these losses account for 30–50 per cent of energy use for hot water at present). The net effect is that the total useful energy (i.e. heating appliance output) for hot water rises from 270 PJ in 1980 to 300 PJ in 2000, remaining almost stable thereafter. The corresponding fuel input depends on the type of appliance and, since this service is often combined with space heating, appliance efficiency will be considered in the latter context.

Where hot water is not produced using a central heating system, it may be based on an independent electric immersion heater or an independent gas heater, with or without storage facilities in each case. More rarely, oil or solid-fuel fired systems may be used. In many cases, an electric immersion heater is fitted to systems which are normally heated from the central heating system, and this may be preferred in summer when the efficiency of the central boiler is at its lowest (see discussion below). We assume that this practice will grow as the price advantage over electricity is reduced. A more detailed survey of domestic hot water production is found in ACEC, 1981b.

Incidental heat gains

The requirement for space heating is reduced by incidental heat gains from a number of sources, including solar gain, other energy uses, and the occupants themselves.

Figure 6.5 shows the monthly pattern of incidental heat gains for a 1980 cavity-walled semi-detached house, and the pattern of heat loss with and without basic insulation. Gains from occupants and other energy appliances

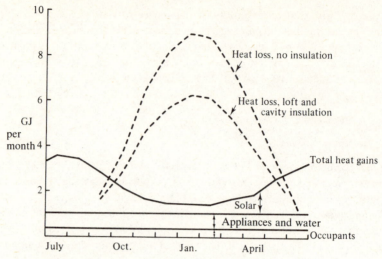

6.5 Heat gains and losses for a typical semi-detached house (1980 cavity-walled semi-detached house with central heating)

(including hot water) vary only slightly over the year. Gains from appliances are less than total appliance energy use as much of the heat is released in the kitchen and will contribute only partially to the house as a whole. The percentage allowed ranges from 10 per cent for freezers (which are often sited in a garage) to 80 per cent for lighting and television. Solar gain is, of course, out of phase with heat losses, but is substantial in spring and autumn. The demand on the space heating system is represented by the area above the total heat gains curve and below the heat loss curve. It will be seen that the insulation measures reduce total heat loss by about 30 per cent but, because of the incidental heat gains, space heating demand is reduced by nearly 40 per cent and the heating season shortened by about a month.

The gain from solar energy may be increased by the design and orientation of the building; this is known as passive solar heating and will be discussed in section 6.7 with other technological developments.

The structure of incidental heat gains varies little between different types of dwelling. Changes over time are also small; improvements in appliance efficiency are largely offset by increasing ownership levels.

Space and water heating systems

Table 6.9 shows the assumptions used for the current and future efficiencies of a range of heating systems. A distinction is made between winter and summer

Table 6.9. *Central heating system efficiencies*

Fuel and date of installation	Winter efficiency %	Summer efficiency %
Solid fuel, open fire + boiler:		
Before 1972	55	N/A[a]
From 1972	65	N/A
Solid fuel, closed system:		
Before 1975	65	55
1975-84	70	65
1985-99	75	70
2000-20	80	75
Gas, with radiators:		
Before 1972	60	50
1972-79	70	60
1980-89	73	65
1990-99	85	75
2000-20	88	80
Gas, ducted air:		
Before 1972	65	N/A
1972-84	72	60
1985-99	80	70
2000-20	88	78
Electric	95	N/A
Oil:		
Before 1972	65	55
From 1972	75	65

Note: [a] Not applicable.

efficiencies; the latter, which correspond to a water heating rather than a space heating load, are lower as a result of low load factors (Whittle and Warren, 1978). A substantial increase in efficiency is expected over the period, especially for gas boilers where it is expected that the introduction of condensing boilers (see section 6.8) will have a marked effect. Note that the figures in the table refer to boilers installed at a given date; at any particular time the average efficiency of the boiler stock will be lower due to the mix of old and new boilers.

Electric heating systems are here assumed to have an efficiency of 95 per cent. Though their physical efficiency at the first stage is 100 per cent, storage heaters release some heat when it is not required so that their effective efficiency is lower. The efficiency of solid-fuel heating systems of the closed type (i.e. free-standing boilers or enclosed room heaters) is likely to rise due to improved

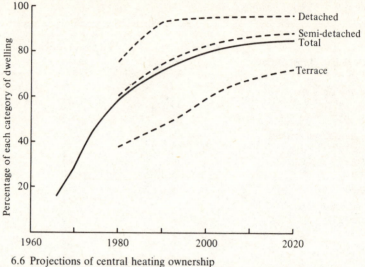

6.6 Projections of central heating ownership

combustion and more effective control. Little improvement is foreseen for oil, which is a minor fuel in the household sector.

Other technological developments, including solar energy, CHP (combined heat and power) and heat pumps, are discussed in section 6.8 below.

Direct-acting heaters are used in many homes instead of, or as well as, a central heating system. Gas fires are the most common, followed by electric fires, and solid fuel, with oil fulfilling a minor role. Total ownership of such systems is expected to fall, especially that of oil and solid-fuel systems. Gas is expected to strengthen its position until around 2000, thereafter losing some-what to electricity. Improvements in appliance efficiency are expected, though only to 70–75 per cent (from the 1980 range of 55–65 per cent) for gas heaters. Where direct heaters are used to supplement a central heating system, we assume that they meet 5 per cent of the heat demand.

In this study we assume a continuation of the historic trend in central heating ownership, which rises to 85 per cent by 2020. Figure 6.6 shows the ownership levels used, broken down by type of dwelling (flats follow the 'total' curve). In small and/or well-insulated dwellings, the incentive to install a centralised system is less than in larger dwellings, and this is reflected by the different rates of penetration shown in the figure.

Fuel choice

Apart from cooking (where, as we have seen, fuel choice appears to be based on non-economic criteria), it is only in the installation of space and water heating

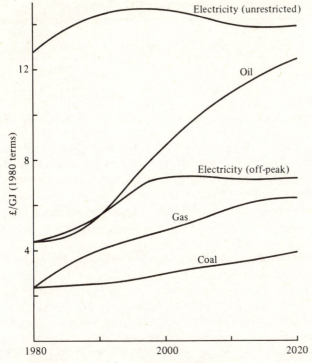

6.7 Projected fuel prices in the domestic sector

systems that the user can exercise any choice over the type of fuel used. In this area, too, it is likely that economic criteria (which are rarely explicitly evaluated) act alongside fashion, convenience, familiarity and other non-quantifiable criteria to influence fuel choice.

For this study, we assume that the decision is made in two stages. First, the householder decides between electricity and fossil fuels. This is modelled using a constant elasticity of substitution model based on fuel prices corrected for appliance efficiencies, and with an allowance for unquantifiable preference factors. A similar model is used for the second choice, between coal and gas (oil is assumed to remain a minor fuel). The models have been calibrated using historical data and match past behaviour satisfactorily.

Figure 6.7 shows the assumed prices of fuels in the household sector, and their implications for new acquisitions of heating systems are shown in table 6.10. The steep rise in oil prices makes this fuel insignificant in new plant acquisitions. The rise in coal prices is modest (see chapter 12), with the result that coal's share in new acquisitions rises significantly until around the end of the century, when it is

Table 6.10.   *Fuel shares in new space heating investment (%)*

	1980	2000	2020
Solid fuels	2	29	23
Gas	78	39	24
Electricity	20	32	53

limited by competition from off-peak electricity. Gas prices rise steeply at first, mainly for reasons of policy, but their later rise is more gradual. The ratio of gas to coal price is lower than would be expected from the cost of manufacturing gas from coal, but this is due to the high ratio of domestic coal price to average coal cost, reflecting both coal quality and distribution costs. The popularity of gas in new plant acquisitions falls as a result of the combined pressure from electricity and coal.

The low price of coal combines with the increased role of nuclear energy from around 2000 to create fairly stable electricity prices. The price of electricity on an off-peak tariff is loosely related to the marginal cost of generation in nuclear stations, but is also influenced by policy considerations. We assume an initial rise broadly similar to that for gas, flattening later as the nuclear component of the system becomes more important. By the end of the period, off-peak electricity and gas prices are close to each other in both delivered energy and useful energy terms, and this is reflected in the growing role of electricity in new plant acquisitions. It must be stressed that the scope for expansion of the off-peak market is very dependent on the scale of future developments in nuclear energy in the UK.

This approach to the modelling of fuel choice is, of course, a simplification of the real situation, and we highlight this in two important respects. First, the criteria for fuel choice will vary with the size and type of dwelling: for example, coal may be a good choice in houses with a high fuel requirement, but is much less suitable for very small or well-insulated houses because of technical and cost problems with very small coal-fired systems. Second (and particularly in new dwellings), the decision on fuel choice interacts with the decision on the level of insulation: in a highly insulated dwelling with a small net requirement for space heating, the high running cost of electricity-based systems in the early part of the period may be offset by their low capital cost; whereas in poorly insulated dwellings, particularly those with solid walls, low running cost will be of paramount importance. Future fuel mix will therefore be related in practice to the changing structure of the housing stock and to the rate of adoption of conservation measures.

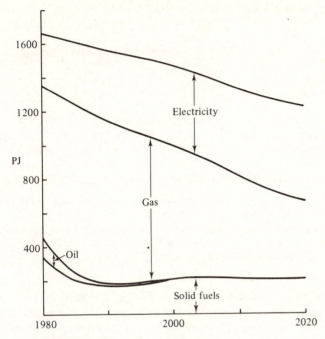

6.8 Projected fuel use in households

6.6   Total energy use

The implications of the above discussion for total fuel use are shown in figure 6.8. In total, energy use declines by 27 per cent over the period (corresponding to a 35 per cent fall in energy use per household). Oil virtually disappears from the market, though it must be recognised that inertia (which is not adequately modelled in this simple approach), together with structural effects such as incomplete access to natural gas, may slow down this change. Initially, the increase in the efficiency of solid-fuel use (due mainly to the scrapping of open fires) leads to lower solid-fuel use, but this trend is later reversed as a result of the price advantage of coal over gas in new installations. Solid fuel's share in 2020 is 17 per cent (20 per cent if non-heat uses of electricity are excluded). Gas use grows up to the late 1980s, and then declines as a combined result of conservation and competition from electricity; its share in 2020 is 38 per cent (45 per cent of fuel used for heat), compared with 53 per cent in 1980, and more than 60 per cent during the late 1980s. Gas heat pumps make a small but growing contribution from around 2000.

Electricity enjoys a growing market, its share rising to 45 per cent by 2020. If

Table 6.11.   *Payback periods for domestic energy conservation*

Measure	Range of payback period (years)
Draught stripping	1 - 6
Hot water cylinder insulation	0 - 5[a]
Loft insulation	1 - 5
Cavity-wall fill	4 - 10
Double glazing (heated living-room)	6 - 25
Double glazing (whole house)	9 - 85
Adequate control system	2 - 5

Note: [a] More generally (e.g. ACEC, 1981b) the payback period for cylinder insulation is found to be a few months.

Source: Taken from Select Committee on Energy, 1982, using data from the British Gas Corporation, the Association for the Conservation of Energy, the Department of Energy and the Glass and Glazing Federation.

we consider only the use of fuels for heating and cooking, however, we find that electricity's share rises from 11 per cent in 1980 to 21 and 35 per cent in 2000 and 2020 respectively, so that even at the end of the period gas is the most important heat fuel. Electric heat pumps become a significant element from around 1990 (see section 6.8 below).

The use of electricity for lighting and appliances (but excluding cooking) grows from 152 PJ in 1980 to 198 PJ in 2000, after which it remains stable. This represents an average annual rate of growth over the whole period, on a per household basis, of 0.4 per cent as increasing appliance ownership just outstrips efficiency improvements.

6.7   Energy conservation economics

Many assessments have been made of the economics of domestic energy conservation. Clearly these depend not only on the cost of purchasing and installing the conservation measure itself, but also on the type and cost (now and in the future) of the fuel saved, the internal temperature of the house (which may itself be affected by the insulation measure) and the behaviour of the occupants.

The most common measure of economic viability in this context is the simple payback period, the ratio of capital cost to annual savings at today's fuel prices. Select Committee on Energy (1982) draws on a number of sources to give the results shown in table 6.11. Clearly, draught stripping, hot water cylinder

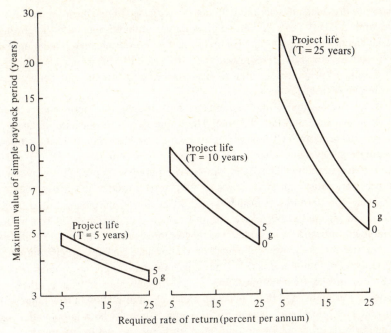

6.9 Payback periods and rates of return for investment appraisal (g is the expected annual percentage rise in real fuel costs)

insulation and loft insulation are very worthwhile, with control system improve-ments and cavity-wall insulation also economically justified. Double glazing, regarded solely as an energy conservation measure, is more doubtful, though it may well be justified if installed on a DIY (do-it-yourself) basis.

The simple payback period is clearly a rather poor measure of cost-effectiveness, ignoring future fuel price rises, the life of the measure and the interest rate. Figure 6.9 allows these other factors to be taken into account. For example, if the measure is expected to last twenty-five years and the house-holder's required rate of return (which is often equated to the real interest rate) is 10 per cent, then on the basis of constant real fuel prices he should go ahead with projects whose simple payback period is ten years or less, extending this limit to fifteen years if he expects real fuel prices to rise at 5 per cent per annum. Many householders may expect to move house within a few years, and may not feel that the market value of their house will adequately reflect any investment which they have made in conservation. This will severely limit the measures which they will be prepared to undertake, as the results in the figure for T = 5 and T = 10 show.

Although inflation does not affect the overall economics of a particular measure provided all costs and benefits are expressed in real terms, it may affect the timing of cash flows. In particular, where a measure is funded by borrowing, repayments will fall with time (in real terms) as a result of general inflation, but may well exceed the fuel savings in the early years of a measure's life. This can represent a substantial barrier to investment, since all the net benefits are pushed into an uncertain future.

A detailed account of the cost-effectiveness of domestic energy conservation is given in Leach and Pellew, 1982. Their approach is to calculate the 'cost of conserving energy' (CCE), which is defined as the annuitised investment required to save one unit of fuel, using a 5 per cent rate of return and a twenty-five-year life. The CCE can be compared with present (or possible future) fuel costs. Indicative prices (in 1982 terms) used in this assessment are £2.20/m^2 for 100 mm loft insulation, £2.60/m^2 for 50 mm mineral fibre cavity insulation (around £1.50/m^2 for urea-formaldehyde foam) and £20–£60/m^2 for double glazing (the lower end of the range representing a simple DIY system). These are installed costs and make some allowance for bulk purchasing; wide variations are found in practice. They conclude that a vigorous programme for full loft and cavity-wall insulation in existing housing is well justified on economic grounds, and that the economic levels of insulation in new houses (at current fuel prices) are 200 mm for lofts and 50 mm for both floors and walls. Higher levels of insulation are indicated for homes heated by electricity.

Another approach to the economic analysis of energy conservation in new houses is to optimise the heat supply and building fabric as a whole. In this case, capital savings through the use of a smaller space heating system may be added to the fuel savings to set against the capital costs of insulation. Clearly, such an analysis will indicate a higher level of insulation than one based on fuel savings alone. The optimisation can also be extended to the choice of fuel: as noted earlier, high levels of insulation may favour electricity, which has higher running costs and lower capital costs than gas.

6.8   Technical developments

Energy conservation

It is clear that the present scope for energy saving in houses is very large, that much of it is highly cost-effective, and that the technology is readily available. Obstacles to the realisation of these savings are therefore primarily institutional and are further discussed in section 6.9 and chapter 13.

An important area where current technology is inadequate is the insulation of solid walls. Solid-walled houses today account for about 46 per cent of the building stock, and will still account for 34 per cent in 2020 on the assumptions used in this study. Attention needs to be given to ways of reducing the cost of both internal and external insulation (within which installation cost is a very important element), as well as to reducing the inconvenience to occupants.

Improvements in the efficiency of current types of fuel-using equipment are likely to take place over the next few decades due to the initiative of manufacturers, provided that there is a continuing awareness of the need to save energy.

Condensing boilers

Combustion of natural gas produces carbon dioxide and water. The water is normally lost from a central heating boiler as water vapour in the flue gases. A substantial quantity of heat can be recovered if this water vapour is condensed. This is the principle of the condensing boiler, which can raise efficiency from around 75 per cent to over 85 per cent. It is predicted (Green and Pattison, 1981) that condensing boilers will be available in the UK from around 1985, and will account for around 35 per cent of the sales of gas central heating systems by 1990. All new gas boilers are expected to be of the condensing type by the end of the century.

Electric heat pumps

A heat pump is a device which uses work, in the form of shaft power from an electric motor or oil- or gas-fired engine, to transfer heat from a cool source to a warmer output medium. A refrigerator (in which heat is transferred from the already cold food to the air in the kitchen) is a familiar example. The technique can readily be adapted to warm a house, usually using the outside air as a heat source (though the ground itself may also be used) and with warm air or hot water as an output medium. The amount of heat supplied to the house is up to two or three times the quantity of electricity used (this factor is known as the coefficient of performance, or COP), so that the device displays an efficiency in electricity use of 200–300 per cent.

The capital cost of a heat pump is, of course, much greater than an equivalent capacity of direct electric heating, and it is usually economic to combine a somewhat undersized heat pump with supplementary direct heating. This will, of course, significantly reduce the overall system efficiency.

Electric heat pumps are beginning to appear in the services sector, but are as yet negligible in the domestic sector. Their adoption is hindered by a range of technical and economic problems:

(a) Early models have shown problems of noise and reliability.
(b) In the damp climate of the UK, frosting of heat exchangers often occurs, requiring special provisions which reduce the COP and increase cost.

(c) The devices are generally bulkier than other central heating units, and therefore present siting difficulties.

(d) Units sized for a whole house represent a type and size of load for which current domestic power supply networks are not designed.

(e) Because (in general) a low outlet temperature implies a high COP, heat pumps are better suited to ducted air heating systems than to radiator systems. The latter, however, are the established tradition in UK central heating systems, and retrofitting of warm air systems is usually difficult.

(f) Capital costs are high relative to those of other systems.

(g) The strong cost advantage of natural gas over electricity in this sector (a ratio of 5:1 between the prices of the two fuels in 1980/1) more than cancels out the efficiency advantage of electric heat pumps.

For these reasons we do not expect early penetration of this technology into the market, except possibly in larger houses not connected to the gas distribution network, where the main competitor is oil. However, as noted in section 6.6 above, their contribution in the long term could be substantial if electricity prices are low.

For further discussion on heat pumps in general, see Heap, 1979.

Gas heat pumps

It is also possible to operate a heat pump on gas, either using a gas engine to provide shaft power for a normal vapour compression cycle heat pump, or using an absorption cycle. In the latter, the compression stage of the conventional system is replaced by the absorption of the refrigerant into a solvent, and the subsequent regeneration of the refrigerant at a higher pressure using direct heating by gas or any other fuel. In either system, waste heat from the fuel combustion may be added to that from the pump itself. It is hoped that with further development, domestic-sized units with COPs of around 1.5 and 1.2 for the compression and absorption systems respectively may be practicable. However, the technology is not yet mature and these systems share some of the obstacles noted above for electric heat pumps.

District heating and CHP

It is straightforward, in principle, to supply heat to a number of dwellings from a single boiler, thus creating a district heating system. If electricity is produced at the same time, the result is a combined heat and power (CHP) system. CHP systems are attractive for two reasons. First, they save energy when compared with the separate provision of the same amounts of heat and electricity. Second, they may replace premium fuels (e.g. natural gas) by the cheaper fuels such as coal which are more suited to centralised use. District heating by itself only offers the second of these attractions; while the central boiler may be more efficient than boilers in individual houses, this gain is offset by losses in heat distribution, and possibly by less efficient use of the system by householders. The latter has been a problem in some systems, where costs have been met through a fixed charge so that the user has had no incentive to save, or where poor system design has made control by the user impossible. Accurate, reliable and reasonably cheap heat metering is essential for the future development of these systems.

The cost of the heat distribution network is a major part of the cost of a district heating or CHP scheme. As a result, these schemes are usually only feasible in areas of high housing density, and then only if a large proportion of householders make use of the system. Implementation of CHP in an existing urban area also causes substantial disruption.

CHP and district heating have been the subject of a major government study (Combined Heat and Power Group, 1977 and 1979). This concluded that the restriction to high-density housing meant that at most some 30 per cent of UK dwellings could benefit. The economic case appeared marginal, though it was likely to improve as fuel prices increased. Substantial government intervention would be needed, in part because of the long time-scale required to build up the heat load (typically fifteen years). In line with these conclusions, we assume in this study that the contribution to domestic heating of CHP or heat-only district heating systems will be small, at least to the end of the century.

The interaction of district heating with other conservation options is of particular interest. It is very desirable that economic insulation measures should be carried out before the installation of district heating, and that the system be sized accordingly; later insulation of dwellings already connected to a district heating system is likely to damage the economics of the system to a marked degree. It is also possible that any economic benefits of district heating will be more difficult to achieve for well-insulated dwellings than for poorly insulated ones, even if the system is correctly sized for the insulated dwellings.

The same general conclusion applies to solar energy: installation of solar energy systems (particularly for space heating) reduces the load factor on a district heating system and so increases the unit cost of the heat supplied.

The rather gloomy prospects for CHP and district heating in the UK contrast with the emphasis placed on this technology in some other European countries, notably Denmark, Sweden, Finland and West Germany, as well as in many Eastern European countries. In some cases, extensive post-war reconstruction provided an opportunity for district heating; other contributory factors include the minor role of gas in the domestic sector compared with the UK, and different traditions in housing density.

Solar energy

Figure 6.3 above shows that over 80 per cent of energy delivered into the domestic sector is used for low-grade heat. This is therefore a natural sector for the direct use of solar energy. There are two approaches to the collection of solar energy in individual houses (or occasionally for groups of houses). Active systems, usually comprising solar panels fitted to the roof of an existing house, capture energy in a circulating fluid; they are usually used to provide part of the energy required for hot water. Passive solar energy is captured by modifying the house itself in order to increase solar gain; such an approach is best suited to reducing the fuel requirements for space heating. The modifications may include the orientation and location of the house itself, the concentration of glazed areas on the south side, the addition of conservatory areas, or the replacement of parts of the roof with glazing. Clearly, most of these are only applicable to new buildings. The distinction between active and passive systems is not a rigid one; a passive system may, for example, include a motorised fan which circulates warm air.

The effectiveness of solar energy systems is limited by the mismatch between heating demand, which peaks in the winter, and the availability of sunshine. The cloudy skies characteristic of the UK are also a problem. Nevertheless, active solar systems can provide a substantial proportion of summer hot water, and passive solar heating, when combined with a high level of insulation, can reduce the total fuel required for space heating to a very low level.

Solar water heating may be competitive at present with the use of electricity on an unrestricted tariff in some parts of the country (depending on the rate of return on investment required by the householder), but not with off-peak electricity or gas. Solar space heating through modified house design is difficult to assess economically because the incremental costs cannot be readily identified; modifications to existing houses appear less economic than loft or cavity-wall insulation, but may be attractive to some householders (see Turrent et al., 1980). It is likely that a consideration of the benefits of solar gain will increasingly influence architectural practice over the next few decades. For general reviews of solar energy, see Flood, 1983 and ETSU, 1976 and 1984.

6.9   Policy issues

It is clear that the main energy issue in the household sector is the encouragement of straightforward energy conservation measures. Adoption of such measures is hindered by lack of knowledge as well as by economic and institutional barriers. Possible actions to remove these obstacles are discussed below.

Education

Schools should ensure that young people are aware of energy issues and of the measures which are available to householders to reduce their fuel bills. The fuel supply industries have excellent opportunities to inform users of the value of energy conservation. Though attitudes to conservation in the fuel industries are inevitably ambivalent, both the gas and electricity industries are seeking to promote conservation measures, and it is to be hoped that this will increase. High Street showrooms, and regular metering and billing, provide convenient points of contact with the general public. Field trials are being carried out on fuel metering systems which provide continuous and readable information on both fuel use and expenditure.

The industry which provides conservation materials is fragmented and lacks direct contact with the public. However, retail outlets already promote loft insulation (and maintain competitive prices), and the success of the double-glazing industry also shows the potential of effective marketing. The recent establishment of the Association for the Conservation of Energy provides the industry with a single voice, and is to be welcomed.

Though the amount of energy consumed by most appliances is fairly small, clear energy labelling would help to create a general consciousness of the importance of energy efficiency.

Financial

Gas prices in the domestic sector fell in real terms between 1973 and 1980 by some 24 per cent. This did not encourage energy conservation. Prices have risen since then, both because of the use of higher-cost gas (see chapter 11) and as a deliberate part of government policy. This policy has been opposed by some on the grounds that it causes hardship to those least able to meet rising fuel bills. However, general arguments of economic efficiency would indicate that fuels should be priced at a level related to their long-run value (i.e. a high price for a scarce resource), and that social needs should be met directly. While the energy industries should be (and are) sensitive to hardship, it is not their role to be agents of social policy in general.

Electricity prices have risen in real terms since 1973, largely through the relaxation of the government price control which was in force at that time.

It is widely suggested that the government should provide more direct financial aid to encourage domestic energy conservation. Against this, it is argued that the government should not subsidise actions which are already in the consumers' interest. Clearly, education and publicity are priority needs which can be met fairly cheaply. There is, however, a case for further government financial involvement. Because basic conservation measures are highly cost-effective at the discount rate used in the public sector, a tax on domestic fuel, the proceeds of which were entirely used for grants towards domestic conservation, would leave the average householder better off, with no other effect on public sector finances. Practical measures could, however, have significant distributional effects:

(a) Funding through a tax on fuels would penalise those for whom conservation is not straightforward, principally those living in solid-walled houses.
(b) Funding through general taxation would discriminate in favour of those below the tax payment threshold.
(c) Direct grants would probably benefit those in cavity-walled houses more than those in solid-walled houses.
(d) Payment taking the form of tax relief for conservation would not benefit those below the tax threshold.

As for any financial assistance, the expectation of increased aid in the future may inhibit conservation activity now, and this argues for clear and decisive government action. The existing grant scheme for loft insulation, though clearly well intentioned, is on too limited a scale to have a substantial effect.

Institutional factors

In 1981, 56 per cent of dwellings in Great Britain were owned by their occupants, 31 per cent were rented from local authorities, and 13 per cent were privately rented. In owner-occupied property, conservation investment has little effect on the market value of the house (double glazing is probably an exception), with the result that conservation may not be worthwhile for a householder who expects to move within a few years. It is to be hoped that growing awareness of energy will change this situation. Building Societies may have a practical role to play, either by drawing to the attention of potential buyers any lack of basic insulation in the property, or by requiring purchasers to undertake basic conservation measures as a condition of receiving a mortgage. The structural problems (e.g. damp ingress) which are occasionally experienced subsequent to cavity insulation discourage this degree of commitment from Building Societies.

Some 70 per cent of rented properties are owned by local authorities and, of these, about three-quarters have cavity walls. Very few, however, have cavity insulation (Leach and Pellew, 1982). Local authorities find insulation difficult, both because the scope for obtaining a return on investment through higher rents may be limited, and because of general financial stringency. It is important that the financial relationship between central and local government should permit local authorities to make investments which attract a real return exceeding 5 per cent, and that the setting of rents should be flexible enough to allow this return to be realised in practice. For loft and cavity-wall insulation, this aim can readily be achieved together with a net benefit to the tenants. A coordinated scheme for (say) cavity insulation will also involve much lower costs per dwelling than piecemeal operation, and will overcome problems of publicity and information.

It is encouraging that the building regulations, rather than merely reflecting good practice in the industry, are now acquiring a normative role in such matters as energy conservation. It should be remembered that new houses are expected to be in use for sixty years or more, and therefore the recommended insulation standards (especially for walls, where later improvement is difficult) should be appropriate to the energy market in twenty to thirty years' time.

The building industry is fragmented, and is (often wisely) conservative in its methods. Organisations such as the National House Building Council, the Royal Institute of British Architects and the Chartered Institution of Building Services provide avenues for the dissemination of information on energy conservation. Cavity-wall insulation has received bad publicity both on health grounds and because of occasional problems with damp; provisions for the training and licensing of operators in this field need to be strengthened, and the contract between installer and householder should include insurance to cover the cost of overcoming any structural problems.

Fragmentation of the building and conservation industries has in the past been matched by a fragmentation of government responsibility for conservation. The recent establishment of an Energy Efficiency Office, to cover all aspects of government involvement in energy conservation, is welcome.

Other government policy

Energy conservation cannot be isolated from other areas of government policy. Economic growth may promote conservation (see section 6.1), and low inflation will encourage conservation by removing the short-term cash flow problems caused by high inflation, as well as by allowing fuel costs to be more clearly perceived.

Housing policy is clearly important for energy conservation. In this study we have assumed the continuation of low building and demolition rates. Faster replacement of the housing stock would allow the benefits of improved techniques to penetrate the market more quickly, particularly if it led to the earlier replacement of solid-walled houses. The government's influence on private house building is, of course, more limited than that on the public sector.

There are several arguments for the large-scale refurbishment of older property, particularly in currently unpopular city-centre areas, and this may become more necessary if low building rates lead to a general ageing of the building stock. Such schemes, which would clearly require government involvement, would provide a good opportunity for the external insulation of solid walls and, if economic, for combined heat and power schemes.

7

Energy use in industry

7.1   History

In 1960, UK industrial energy use was 42 per cent of all energy delivered to final consumers (this and other statistics are taken from Department of Energy, 1983a and Central Statistical Office, 1983, and earlier editions). This proportion remained fairly stable until 1973, after which it fell sharply to reach 34 per cent by 1980. This fall was partly due to substantial reductions in industrial energy intensity (see below), and partly due to the recession, which hit industry harder than other parts of the economy.

Oil's share in industrial fuel use rose from 21 per cent in 1960 to nearly 45 per cent in 1973, but then fell to 35 per cent by 1980. In that year, industry accounted for 27 per cent of all oil used in final consumption, or 62 per cent of oil used outside the transport sector. Thus the industry sector has a very important role to play in substitution away from oil.

Energy intensity

In contrast to most other sectors, UK industry has, over the post-war period, seen a steady decline in energy intensity. Figure 7.1 shows industrial output (excluding the energy industries themselves) and the energy/output ratio between 1953 and 1981. This shows the slowdown in industrial growth after 1973, the increased severity of the business cycle, and the sharp recession from 1979. Over the period as a whole, energy intensity fell at an average annual rate of 2.1 per cent. The post oil crisis period is of particular interest. Between 1973 and 1979, despite higher fuel prices, the average annual fall in energy intensity was only about 1 per cent. This is partly because, in a recession, the gradual improvement in efficiency resulting from the installation of new plant is suppressed, and partly, it would appear, because factories were under-utilised and energy overheads were larger in relation to output. In 1980, there was a sharp improvement in efficiency, only partly explained by the collapse of the iron and steel industry. Possibly this deeper recession led to the closure of

97

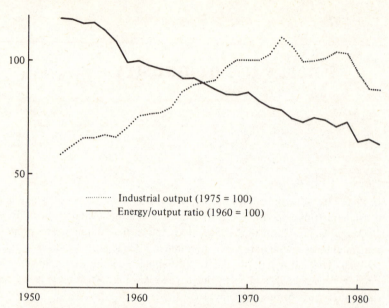

7.1 UK industrial output and energy intensity, 1953–82. Industry includes construction and non-energy mining and quarrying; energy excludes oil and gas used as feedstocks or for other non-energy purposes

inefficient factories and the concentration of production in more economic (and often more energy-efficient) establishments.

The above discussion illustrates the complex mechanisms underlying changes in energy intensity. Structural change within industry is another important factor. Table 7.1 shows the changing structure of industrial output and energy use disaggregated into eight sectors. In 1953 the two most energy-intensive sectors accounted for less than 10 per cent of output but 47 per cent of energy use. By 1980 these sectors had fallen to 5.8 per cent of output and only 27 per cent of energy. The table also shows the general tendency for energy intensity to fall more rapidly in the most energy-intensive sectors.

Structural change is also important at a more detailed level. Jenne and Cattell (1983) have compared the five-year periods before and after 1973, with the results shown in table 7.2. Based on a breakdown of industry (excluding 'other trades', which is mainly construction), into 104 categories (minimum list headings, MLH), this analysis shows that structural change accounted for about half the fall in energy intensity between 1973 and 1978, though it was much less important in the previous five-year period. In total, energy intensity appears to have fallen more quickly after 1973 than before, though this ceases to be the case if iron and steel is excluded (differences from figure 7.1 are due to the

Table 7.1. *Energy intensity and structural change: sector level*

Sector	Percentage of total output		Percentage of total energy		1980 energy intensity (relative to average)	Energy intensity ratio 1980/1953
	1953	1980	1953	1980		
Iron and steel	6.2	2.6	32.8	16.4	6.42	0.67
Bricks, pottery, glass, cement	3.2	3.2	14.1	10.8	3.35	0.42
Chemicals	4.0	8.6	10.8	13.8	1.60	0.32
Food, drink, tobacco	10.6	11.2	7.2	10.8	0.96	0.78
Paper, printing, stationery	6.0	7.7	5.0	6.3	0.82	0.54
Textiles, leather, clothing	11.8	7.5	10.9	5.4	0.72	0.43
Other trades (mainly construction)	22.9	21.6	6.9	15.1	0.70	1.26
Engineering and non-ferrous metals	35.4	37.6	12.2	21.4	0.57	0.91

Table 7.2. *Energy intensity and structural change: industry level*

	Percentage change in energy/output ratio	
	1968-73	1973-78
All industry[a]:		
Total change	−9.9	−12.5
Due to structural change	−1.5	− 6.8
Due to other factors	−8.4	− 5.7
Industry excluding iron and steel:		
Total change	−8.5	− 6.7
Due to structural change	+1.2	− 3.2
Due to other factors	−9.7	− 3.5

Note: [a] Excluding the energy industries and 'other trades'.

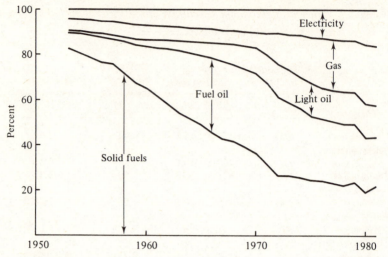

7.2 Fuel shares in UK industry, 1953–81. Feedstock uses of oil and gas are excluded

exclusion of other trades). It is of particular interest that the fall in energy intensity attributable to factors other than structural change has been slower since 1973 despite higher fuel prices. This casts serious doubt on a simple analysis of aggregate energy conservation as a response to fuel prices.

Fuel shares

The post-war period has seen major changes in industrial fuel shares, as shown in figure 7.2. Coal has been in steady decline, being ousted by oil through the late 1950s and 1960s, and gas in the 1970s. After 1973, gas also took over part of the market from oil. Electricity grew steadily in importance throughout the period.

Industrial fuel use may be divided conveniently into three categories: non-premium or bulk heat applications, which in most sectors are steam-based; premium heat; and specific uses of electricity. The post-war period has been, in many sectors, one of transition from non-premium to premium uses of fuel, as 'clean' fuels – distillate oil, natural gas and electricity – have prompted technological advances in direct fuel use. In most cases, this change has reinforced the trend towards higher energy efficiency by obviating the losses associated with steam distribution and use. If increased oil and gas prices prompt a reversal of the trend towards premium fuels, the improvement in energy efficiency may be curtailed.

The use of electricity as a heat fuel is of particular interest. Many techniques

Table 7.3. *Structure of UK industrial fuel use, 1976 (PJ; excluding iron and steel and petrochemicals)*

	Solid fuels	Oil products	Gases	Electricity	Heat	Total
Public supply	255	785	457	244	6	1747
Internal supply	-	-	-	38	204	242
Total supply	255	785	457	282	210	1989
Input to CHP	62	203	111	-	-	376
Use via steam/ water system	102	372	156	-	169	799
Direct heat	89	147	180	29	41	487
Electrochemical	-	-	-	38	-	38
Motive power:						
Stationary	-	22	1	181	-	204
Mobile	-	39	-	4	-	43
Other uses	3	1	8	30	-	42

Note: Summations may not be exact due to round-off in converting to PJ.

have been developed in recent years, including induction furnaces, infra-red, dielectric, mircrowave and radio frequency heating and heat pumps. Though electricity is intrinsically inefficient in primary energy terms, this may be more than offset by the precision and efficiency with which electricity can be used, and by its dependence on relatively low-cost primary fuels.

Specific uses of electricity (i.e. those for which there are no practical alternative fuels) include stationary motive power, lighting and electronic control. These uses have grown steadily in importance, unaffected by the energy crisis, as a by-product of technical changes in manufacturing processes. The robustness of this trend in the past suggests that it will continue in the future, but there is considerable scope nevertheless for technical conservation both in the use of electric motors and in lighting.

End-uses

Table 7.3 shows the structure of industrial fuel use in 1976 (excluding iron and steel and petrochemicals), classified by fuel and end-use (Bush and Matthews, 1979). We note several features of this breakdown:

(a) Nearly three-fifths of the fuel purchased from public supply is used for steam-raising, of which about one-third is used in CHP plant.

(b) Oil accounts for nearly 60 per cent of the fossil fuel used for steam-raising, with gas providing most of the remainder.
(c) Oil and gas are both very important in the direct heat market.
(d) Other uses of fuels are mainly electricity-specific.

7.2   Modelling industrial fuel use

Methods

In the household and transport sectors, we analyse fuel use in detail, on the basis of the stock of fuel-using equipment (houses, appliances, cars etc.) and its changing characteristics over time. This very detailed approach is not possible for industry because of the diversity of industrial fuels and processes. For this reason a simpler model is used, based on the simulation of the main mechanisms which lead to changes in the pattern of fuel use. This is outlined below.

Many detailed technical issues arise in the discussion of energy conservation and inter-fuel substitution in industry. With present knowledge, it is rarely possible to incorporate these into a formal modelling approach, but the results of more broadly-based modelling work provide a background against which they can be considered.

Simulation model

It is possible here to give only a very brief description of the simulation model, and for more detail the reader is referred to Bending (1982). The model simulates changes in fuel use from year to year resulting from four mechanisms: plant retirements, new plant installations, conversion of plant from one fuel to another and changes in end-use efficiency. The main exogenous variables are the output of the sector being studied and the prices of fuels, all varying with time. The model uses a number of parameters, many of which (such as the efficiency of combustion of a particular fuel) have a direct meaning in engineering terms, while others are drawn from economics. Some of these parameters have values specified by the user on the basis of engineering or economic judgement; the remainder are chosen by a model calibration process using historical fuel-use data.

The retirement of fuel-using equipment is assumed to depend only on its 'natural life', which varies from fuel to fuel but not with the year of installation of the plant. Fuel prices and sector growth are assumed to have a negligible effect.

The scale of new plant installation is determined in the model by the gap created by plant retirements on the one hand and sector growth on the other, after taking into account changes in end-use efficiency (see below). The efficiency of fuel-using equipment is assumed to increase with the year of installation, but to remain constant for a given piece of equipment during its life. Efficiency varies, of course, from fuel to fuel.

In most sectors, the choice of fuel for new plant proceeds in two stages. The split between premium fuels and non-premium fuels (defined in section 7.1 above) is related to marginal premium and non-premium fuel prices through a constant elasticity of substitution model. Fuel prices are lagged by one year, augmented by an excess cost term representing non-fuel costs (such as annuitised plant capital cost, maintenance and labour costs, fuel handling and storage and environmental protection), and take into account fuel combustion efficiency. The excess costs are inferred from historical patterns of fuel use in the course of the calibration process. The second stage of the fuel allocation process is a simple identification of the lowest price fuel (where fuel prices are defined as for the premium/non-premium split) in each of the premium and non-premium categories, the fuel allocation being modified to allow for some use of the apparently less attractive fuels. In sectors dominated by furnaces (iron and steel, bricks, china and cement) the classification into premium and non-premium fuels is not applicable, and the stage involving the premium/non-premium split is omitted.

Both the scale and direction of plant conversions (which can only occur within the premium or non-premium categories, not between categories) are assumed to be related to fuel prices. All conversions within a fuel category are assumed to be in favour of the lowest-price fuel (where some or all non-fuel costs are again included), and the proportion of plant converted in each year is an increasing function of the fuel price differential. In practice, conversion can be a fairly important mechanism in the non-premium category (where it represents the switching of boilers from one fuel to another), and in specialist areas such as cement kilns, but is rather less important for premium fuel uses.

End-use efficiency links the energy available after fuel combustion to the output of the sector. Changes in this factor represent physical changes in (for example) steam-use efficiency or advances in process technology. They may also represent structural change within a sector (see section 7.1 above). The model uses a simple logistic time trend, multiplied by a constant elasticity price term, using average fuel prices lagged by one year.

Specific uses of electricity are modelled separately from other fuels. They are assumed to be proportional to a linear combination of output and employment in the sector considered, and also to follow a logistic time trend. No explicit price mechanism has been included, since electricity costs are normally a minor factor in the design of production plant.

The model has been calibrated for ten sectors of industry, using data from 1953 to 1980.

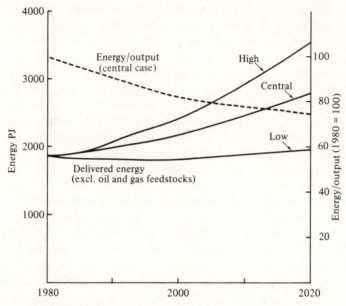

7.3 Projections of energy use and energy intensity in industry

7.3   Results of analysis

Total energy use

Figure 7.3 shows total delivered energy for the three economic growth cases introduced in chapter 4. The central case shows a 16 per cent rise between 1980 and 2000, and a 48 per cent rise over the whole period to 2020; the faster rise in the second half of the period is the result of a slowing down in the improvement in energy efficiency as conservation opportunities are used up. In the low case, growth in industrial output very nearly matches the improvement in energy efficiency, and energy use is almost stable. The broken curve shows the energy/output ratio for the central case (the differences between cases are small). The ratio falls at 1.0 and 0.5 per cent per annum respectively between 1980 and 2000 and between 2000 and 2020. This is slower than in the past (see figure 7.1) when aggregate energy conservation was aided by the move from coal to oil and gas and from steam-based systems to the direct use of premium fuels.

In the future, as in the past, the rate of change of energy intensity varies markedly between sectors. Cement, engineering, food and 'other trades' (which is mainly construction) show a very gradual improvement, while energy intensity falls more rapidly in chemicals, textiles and the china, pottery and glass sector. It was pointed out in section 7.1 that much of the historical improvement in energy

Table 7.4.   *Sector shares in total energy use, central case*

Sector	Percentage share in delivered energy		
	1980	2000	2020
Iron and steel	17.8	18.1	16.0
Engineering etc.	20.6	23.2	24.9
Food etc.	11.0	11.4	12.5
Chemicals etc.	13.4	11.3	11.2
Textiles etc.	5.2	4.1	3.1
Paper etc.	7.1	7.4	7.6
Bricks etc.	2.5	2.3	2.0
China etc.	3.4	3.0	2.4
Cement	4.9	5.6	5.3
Other trades	14.2	13.6	15.1

intensity has been due to structural change within and between individual sectors. Quantification of such changes in the future is not possible within the modelling framework used in this study, but it is likely to be pariculary important in the engineering and chemical sectors.

Changing industrial structure, together with different rates of change of energy intensity, leads to changes in the split of total energy use between sectors. Table 7.4 shows that these changes are projected as fairly small, though the increasing importance of engineering is reflected in its growing share of fuel use.

Fuel prices and expenditure

The fuel prices on which these projections are based are shown for the central case in figure 7.4. The main contrast is between the fairly steep rise of oil prices and the more modest growth for coal. Oil prices, as noted in chapter 11, are based on the expectation of a substantial rise in the world price, which is believed to be unavoidable in the long term if the world economy grows at a satisfactory rate. This is amplified for the UK in the early part of the period by the downward movement of the real dollar exchange rate. Coal prices, on the other hand, are based on the assessment of UK costs given in chapter 12. It is likely that world coal trade will become of major importance towards the end of the period, and there is a significant possibility of higher coal prices as a result. The price of gas is bounded by the cost of manufacturing substitute natural gas. As a result it remains below the price of fuel oil throughout the period, although initially it rises faster than the prices of other fuels. The electricity price is based

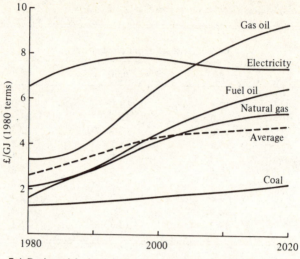

7.4 Projected fuel prices for industry (central case)

on a fairly strong nuclear programme (see chapter 10), and remains more stable than other prices. Note in particular that, taking into account the typical efficiencies of fuel-using appliances, electricity would achieve useful-energy price parity with natural gas towards the end of the period.

The figure also shows the fuel-share weighted average price for industry as a whole; this rises by 2.5 per cent per annum between 1980 and 2000, but by only 0.6 per cent per annum thereafter. Total expenditure on fuels as a proportion of industrial output rises by 33 per cent between 1980 and 2000 but is very nearly stable for the rest of the period.

Fuel shares

The changing pattern of fuel prices leads to the fuel shares shown in figure 7.5. Coal's share rises steadily, stabilising towards the end of the period at around 47 per cent. Oil use falls sharply until about 1995 due to competition from both coal and gas; the fall continues into the early years of the next century, at a slower rate. Gas continues to grow in importance, though more slowly than in the past, until the mid 1990s; thereafter competition from electricity and coal, in the premium and steam-raising markets respectively, reduces its share. Electricity continues the upward trend in market share which it has shown for most of the historical period, with major expansion into the premium heat market. Note the shift, over the period as a whole, from dominance by oil and gas to dominance

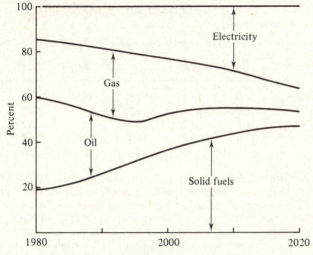

7.5 Projected fuel shares in industry (central case)

by coal and electricity. Though this represents a major change, it is less rapid than the move away from coal between the early 1950s and the present.

Sections 7.4 to 7.7 discuss the projections in more detail for each of the four fuels.

Energy end-uses

The modelling framework used in this study allows a simple breakdown to be made in terms of end-uses, though the classifications used are far from exact. Table 7.5 shows that the main change in shares over the period is due to the continuing growth of specific (i.e. non-heating) uses of electricity. The historical period has seen substantial growth in the premium heat category at the expense of bulk heat for steam-raising; the changed price outlook is expected to slow down this trend considerably. The fall in the share of bulk furnace heating (iron and steel and the building materials sectors) is largely due to changes in industrial structure.

7.4   Solid-fuel use

The main use of solid fuel in industry may be divided into two categories, furnaces and steam-raising. Furnace use of solid fuel (in the form of coke) is dominated by iron ore reduction in the iron and steel industry; an application which uses the chemical and physical properties of the coke as well as its heat

Table 7.5.   *Projections of industrial energy end-uses, central case (percentages of total delivered energy)*

End-use category	1980	1990	2000	2010	2020
Bulk heat, steam-raising	37.7	33.3	31.6	32.1	33.1
Bulk heat, furnaces	26.8	27.6	26.2	24.5	22.7
Other (premium) heat	24.3	25.2	25.9	25.7	25.5
Specific electricity	11.2	14.0	16.3	17.6	18.6

Note: For the purposes of this table, bulk heat (steam-raising) is defined as all non-premium fuel use in engineering, food, chemicals, textiles, paper and other trades, while other (premium) heat use is defined as all premium fuel use in the same sectors. Bulk heat (furnaces) is defined to include all fossil fuel use, together with the use of electricity for heating, in iron and steel, bricks, china and cement. All non-heating uses of electricity are classified as specific electricity, except that electrochemical uses are included as part of premium heat.

content and is open to fuel substitution to only a limited extent. Similarly, cement manufacture shows a clear preference for coal over other fuels since coal ash is a useful component of the end-product. The remaining significant furnace use of coal is in brick manufacture. Here switching between fuels occurs readily, and cleanliness and controllability create a technical preference for oil or gas. Nevertheless, under the price regime envisaged in this study, we foresee a substantial move to coal in this sector, with coal's share in total energy use rising from 20 per cent in 1980 to 90 per cent (its 1959 value) by 2000, remaining almost stable thereafter. A scheme to demonstrate the feasibility of coal use with modern brick-making technology is in progress as part of the government's Energy Conservation Demonstration Projects Scheme.

The projections for the central case imply a 60 per cent increase in total solid fuel in furnaces between 1980 and 2000, with just over a doubling for the period to 2020 as a whole. Figure 7.6 shows the projected use of solid fuels for both furnaces and steam-raising; the bar chart shows the dominance of iron and steel and cement in 2020 in the furnace use of solid fuels.

This also shows the rapid rise in the use of coal for steam-raising, which grows by a factor of more than six over the period as a whole, from 37 per cent of all solid-fuel use in 1980 to 54 and 64 per cent in 2000 and 2020 respectively. This market appears to be well spread between different sectors of industry.

Table 7.6 gives a more detailed picture of this change. Industrialists considering the installation of new boilers will only choose coal if its price advantage over other fuels is sufficient to offset the higher capital and non-fuel running costs

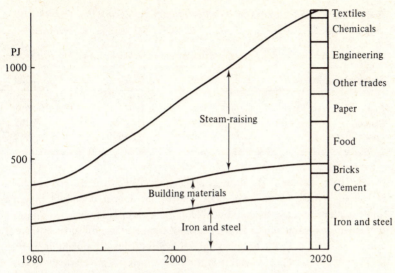

7.6 Industrial use of solid fuels, 1980–2020 (central case)

Table 7.6. *Switching to coal in steam-raising sectors (central case)*

| Sector | Threshold year[a] | Percentage share in non-premium fuel | | | | Non-premium/total (%) | |
		1980	1990	2000	2020	1980	2020
Engineering etc.	2003	31.7	24.9	50.6	75.3	38.7	26.6
Food etc.	1985	12.9	30.6	64.0	96.1	72.9	69.7
Chemicals etc.	1990	3.0	14.0	68.9	97.5	54.8	44.4
Textiles etc.	1989	22.6	47.4	76.6	98.4	59.6	47.9
Paper etc.	1981	27.5	58.0	86.9	99.8	77.4	71.9
Other trades	1996	18.3	20.5	41.8	86.4	40.9	39.5

Note: [a] i.e. year in which coal becomes the dominant non-premium fuel in new plant installations.

(see section 7.8 below). As the price gap widens, a time will be reached when coal becomes the 'best buy', and this is shown as the threshold year in the table. It varies between sectors, due to differences in prices and non-fuel costs, from 1981 in the paper sector to around the end of the century in 'other trades' and engineering; both sectors with generally small boilers and low load factors. Diversity within each sector, together with some conversions of existing boilers

Table 7.7.   *Solid-fuel use in industry for different economic growth cases*

Economic growth case	Total solid-fuel use (PJ)		
	1980	2000	2020
High	360	870	1621
Central	360	795	1305
Low	360	679	842

to coal (see section 7.8), allow coal's share to begin to rise earlier than the threshold year, and the projections imply an almost complete takeover of non-premium fuel use by coal by 2020 in most sectors. However, non-premium fuel use is generally a falling proportion of total fuel use for most of the period, and coal's share in total energy use in 2020 varies from 20 per cent in engineering to 72 per cent in paper. Gas has in the past enjoyed a price advantage through interruptible tariffs; we assume that these will be phased out.

Differences in solid-fuel use for the different economic growth scenarios are summarised in table 7.7. They are mainly the result of changed industrial output, with the shares of coal in total energy use varying little between scenarios. We assume a lower coal price for the low growth scenario (and conversely, see chapter 12), which tends to increase coal's share under lower growth. However, this is offset by the reduced opportunities for investment in new plant.

7.5   Oil use

The outlook for oil use in industry, under the fuel price assumptions used in this study, is one of major decline. Figure 7.7 shows the projection for the central case. Total oil use falls by 3.9 and 3.0 per cent per annum respectively between 1980 and 2000 and between 2000 and 2020; a total reduction by a factor of more than four. The fall is particularly rapid between the late 1980s and the late 1990s, when the natural period for retirement of plant installed in the oil-rich 1960s coincides with the steepest rate of increase of oil product prices (figure 7.4). The figure prompts several further observations:

(a) Fuel oil use (here taken to include all oil used in iron and steel, bricks, china and cement) falls particularly rapidly, to 38 and 13 per cent of its 1980 level in 2000 and 2020 respectively. It may be asked whether the UK (or European) refinery systems can accommodate such a rapid change in the shape of the oil product barrel, particularly in view of the

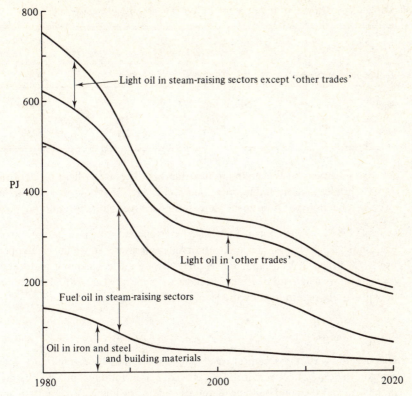

7.7 Industrial use of oil products, 1980–2020 (central case)

probable move out of fuel oil for electricity generation in countries where this is still a major use. If this shift cannot readily be met, or if the more advanced petroleum cracking facilities which it implies lead to significant cost increases, companies may prefer to clear the market by offering fuel oil at a reduced price.

(b) The study period shows a steady lightening of the mix of oil products used in industry, with light oil (defined as gas/diesel oil and lighter products) accounting for 44 per cent of the total in 2000 and 65 per cent in 2020, as against 32 per cent in 1980. This is in spite of an absolute fall of about 50 per cent in light oil use.

(c) Within light oil use, 'other trades' (which is dominated by the construction industry) is increasingly important. From 48 per cent of light oil used in 1980, this sector's share grows to 77 per cent in 2000 and 89 per cent in 2020. This is the result of competition with gas and

Table 7.8.   *Oil use in industry for different economic growth cases*

	Total oil use (PJ)		
Economic growth case	1980	2000	2020
High	750	374	238
Central	750	338	183
Low	750	273	125

electricity in the premium heat market. The use of light oil in other trades is fairly stable; increased fuel use efficiency almost cancels the effect of the 74 per cent increase in construction industry output.

Table 7.8 shows the effects of the different economic growth cases on total oil use. The sharp decline is, of course, observed in all cases, though the levels of oil use in 2000 and 2020 (dominated as they are by the engineering and 'other trades' sectors where oil continues to have a significant share in fuel choice for new plant) are determined by the level of industrial output.

7.6   Gas use

Gas use, shown for the central case in figure 7.8, may be divided into three categories. Some 24 per cent in 1980 was used, mainly for direct process heating, in the iron and steel and building materials sectors, including china, pottery and glass. Steam-raising in the remaining sectors accounted for 43 per cent, while 33 per cent went to premium heat applications in these sectors.

Gas use in the iron and steel and building materials sectors remains fairly stable up to around 1995 and then declines. The main users are iron and steel (where much of the gas used is produced locally as a coke-oven by-product) and the china, pottery and glass sector; we assume that coal is unable to compete successfully in the latter sector due to the requirement for cleanliness. On the other hand, gas use in the bricks sector is quickly ousted by coal.

A similar pattern is seen for steam-raising uses of gas, with a rapid fall after 1995 as gas-fired plant installed in the 1970s is retired. By 2020, this category of gas use has fallen to 19 per cent of its 1980 level and is largely confined to the engineering and 'other trades' sectors, where the poor prospects for coal have already been noted.

Gas continues to be the preferred fuel for premium heat applications for much of the period, its share in this category of fuel use rising from 35 per cent in 1980 to 56 per cent in 1995, falling slowly thereafter due to competition from

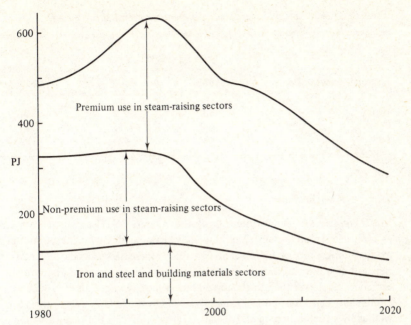

7.8 Industrial use of gas, 1980–2020 (central case). Gas use for feedstock is excluded

electricity. By 2020, premium gas use falls to slightly over its 1980 level, but at that time represents 67 per cent of all gas use. The key sector is engineering, whose share of premium gas use rises from 59 per cent in 1980 to 74 per cent in 2020. The distinction between premium heat uses and the use of fuels for steam-raising creates an area of application for gas in which it is largely protected from competition from coal. As a result, the role of gas in the later part of the period is considerably more important than it would be if all the fuels were in direct competition in a homogeneous market.

We have implicitly assumed that, apart from some gas use in iron and steel, all gas is obtained from public supply, and may towards the end of the period be partly manufactured from coal. On-site or local manufacture of lower calorific value gases (see chapter 11) could provide a cheaper alternative in some circumstances. Detailed examination of this issue is beyond the scope of this study, but key factors are likely to be the existence of a premium process heating application with a high load factor (preferably continuous) and/or a local concentration of industry to justify a shared gas plant.

The effects on total gas use of the different assumptions on economic growth and industrial output are shown in table 7.9.

Table 7.9. *Gas use in industry for different economic growth cases*

Economic growth case	Total gas use (PJ)		
	1980	2000	2020
High	485	572	364
Central	485	515	276
Low	485	424	184

7.7   Electricity use

Electricity use is shown for the central case in figure 7.9. Uses which are specific to electricity (motive power, lighting etc.) grow steadily over the period, at an average annual rate of 2.3 per cent. The rate of increase of specific electricity use per unit of industrial output, however, is only 0.5 per cent per annum. This is considerably slower than the historical rate, which averaged about 2 per cent per annum between 1960 and 1980, and was aided by the fall in private generation as well as by structural change. The slower growth reflects both conservation and saturation, though it should be noted that the assumed electricity price (figure 7.4) suggests that the incentive to conserve electricity use will not increase significantly. Saturation is likely to occur both because opportunities to replace manual labour by machinery are becoming exhausted, and because further progress is likely to involve the introduction of electronic control systems which use very little energy, and may indeed save energy by optimising the production process. Engineering is the most important sector for specific electricity use, accounting for about one-quarter of the total throughout the period.

It is in process heating that some of the most promising opportunities for electricity use lie. Heat uses for electricity are projected to grow by a factor of 7.5 over the period as a whole, rising from 24 per cent of the total in 1980 to 32 per cent in 2000 and 49 per cent in 2020. A particularly steep rise occurs from around 2005 as the relative prices of gas and electricity approach parity on a useful energy basis. Table 7.10 shows that electricity becomes the preferred fuel for premium uses in new plant in different sectors between 1992 and 2009 (though never in iron and steel or 'other trades'). As a proportion of total heat fuel, electricity is of major importance by the end of the period in engineering, chemicals and china, and it achieves a dominant role in the premium heat market in most sectors.

The diversity between sectors illustrates the importance of structural change for overall electricity intensity, both for specific and heat uses. This has been

Table 7.10. *Switching to electricity for premium heat uses (central case)*

Sector	Threshold year[a]	Electricity/total heat fuel (%)				Electricity/total premium (%)	
		1980	2000	2010	2020	1980	2020
Iron and steel	-	3.6	9.1	10.3	15.8	N/R[b]	N/R
Engineering etc.	2003	9.8	17.0	27.6	41.1	17.6	61.1
Food etc.	1992	1.2	6.3	9.1	13.1	7.1	86.1
Chemicals etc.	1997	7.1	18.7	21.4	36.7	19.2	86.2
Textiles etc.	2001	2.2	6.4	10.5	21.1	7.6	75.7
Paper etc.	2009	0.5	1.1	2.4	4.8	3.5	51.8
China etc.	2006	3.6	8.7	27.8	63.6	N/R	N/R
Other trades	-	0.1	0.1	2.2	8.5	0.2	17.7

Notes: Specific uses of electricity are excluded throughout, apart from electrochemical applications which are classed as premium heat.

[a] The threshold year is the year in which electricity becomes the dominant premium fuel in new plant installations. Projected use of electricity as a heat fuel in bricks and cement is very small.

[b] Not relevant (sectors where premium heat is not distinguished from total heat).

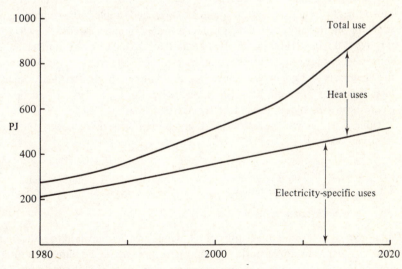

7.9 Industrial use of electricity, 1980–2020 (central case)

Table 7.11.   *Electricity use in industry for different economic growth cases*

	Total electricity use (PJ)		
Economic growth case	1980	2000	2020
High	277	578	1315
Central	277	517	1016
Low	277	429	698

studied for the past by Hankinson and Rhys (1983) and will continue to be important. Structural change within sectors, such as the future of aluminium production within the engineering sector, may also be particularly relevant to electricity use.

The apparently good prospects for electricity as a heat fuel depend on the high efficiency with which heat can be generated in, and confined to, the product itself. This involves the use of a range of technologies, in which further development may be expected. They include induction heating, in which the electrically conducting product (such as a molten metal) is heated by currents induced by an external coil; dielectric heating, in which the molecules of a non-conducting substance are set in motion by a radio-frequency or microwave electromagnetic field; infra-red heating, where a controllable and pollution-free radiant heat is required (e.g. for paint stoving); and simple resistive heating, in which the electrically conducting product is heated by allowing electricity to flow through it directly. Heat pumps may be used for drying (e.g. for timber) and in some circumstances for space heating. Electrochemical processes – important in the chemicals and engineering sectors – are another specialised field which is included under premium heat use of electricity. For a detailed introduction to electroheat technology, the reader is referred to Barber (1983).

Table 7.11 shows the effect of the different growth scenarios on total electricity use.

7.8   Steam-raising technology

Conventional systems

As noted earlier, some three-fifths of all fuel at present delivered to industry is used for steam-raising. Historically, this proportion has been falling, due to the growth in premium fuel uses, but the projections discussed above (table 7.5) suggest that steam-raising will remain a very important fuel use. It is also the key end-use for substitution from oil and gas to coal. The technology of industrial boiler plant is therefore of particular importance to the future of fuel use in this sector.

Industrial boilers are of two main types. In firetube (or shell) boilers, the combustion chamber is surrounded by a shell (usually a horizontal cylinder) containing water. Finer tubes containing the combustion gases usually also pass through this shell before connection to the flue. Boiler capacity is usually measured in pounds of steam/hour (1000 lbs steam/hr from a low pressure boiler is equivalent to an hourly heat output of about 1 GJ). Firetube boilers are made in sizes up to 80 000 lbs/hour, but most are between 2000 and 20 000 lbs/hour, with an average for the UK as a whole of 7400 lbs/hour (Chesshire and Robson, 1983).

A watertube boiler consists of a (usually large) combustion chamber within which are suspended the tubes containing water or steam. Though the size ranges for the two types of boiler overlap, watertube boilers are generally much larger, with an average capacity (excluding those in the electricity supply industry) of some 48 000 lbs/hour. Watertube boilers also generally produce steam at much higher pressures than firetube boilers, which represents an opportunity for electricity generation.

We have already discussed the possible return to coal use, on the basis of the results of the simulation model. This question can also be examined from an engineering perspective using the costs and technical characteristics of different types of boiler, and this is the basis of modelling work by Skea (1981) and Cattell (1983).

Coal-fired boilers are substantially more expensive than oil- or gas-fired boilers, their ancillary equipment is also more costly, and they generally have higher labour and maintenance requirements. Detailed discussion is found in Skea (1981) and Chesshire and Robson (1983). The industrialist contemplating investment in new boiler plant will seek to offset these extra costs with the savings resulting from the fuel price difference, which since 1974 has favoured coal over oil. This trade-off is also affected by the boiler load factor, since a higher load factor will generate savings more rapidly. Other things being equal, coal is therefore more likely to be chosen in industries dominated by process heating and continuous operation than in industries where the heat load is purely seasonal.

The other key issue is the industrialist's investment criterion, since the excess costs are mainly in the form of capital and the savings accrue as revenue. Experience since the oil crisis has shown that most industrialists require a payback period (the ratio of excess capital cost to net annual saving) of two to three years for energy-related investment. Bearing in mind the 5 per cent real discount rate applied to projects in the public sector (equivalent for a project of twenty-five-year life to a simple payback period of fifteen years or more), this seems a highly restrictive criterion. Factors which contribute to this cautious attitude among industrialists include the overall economic uncertainty (which imposes short time horizons), the risks associated with a high level of external debt and the effects of inflation, which, while not damaging the overall economics of a project, may make the early years of the project's life unattractive (see section 6.7).

The choice between different steam-raising fuels also depends, of course, on the fuel price differences. From a small price disadvantage against fuel oil in 1973, coal gained an immediate advantage of 80p/GJ in 1974 (in 1980 terms; the price ratio was almost exactly 2:1), but this was reduced during the later 1970s by general inflation and the strengthened bargaining power of the miners (see chapter 12), falling to a minimum of 49p/GJ in 1978. By 1980, the differential had again reached over 80p/GJ as a result of the 1979 crisis. Against gas, the situation has been more complex, as gas has been sold for steam-raising on interruptible tariffs, sometimes at substantial discounts. In terms of average gas prices, coal was at a disadvantage up to 1976, and by 1980 its price advantage had risen to 39p/GJ. The overall effect of recent price history has been to present confusing signals for potential coal users, with coal's price edge rarely being sufficient to justify investment in coal-fired boilers for most users.

In some circumstances it may be possible to convert boilers from one fuel to another. Conversions from coal to oil or gas (or between oil and gas) are usually straightforward, requiring capital investment only for new burners and fuel-handling plant and reducing the need for maintenance, coal transport and stocking and ash disposal. Such conversions have contributed to the rapid move away from coal since the 1950s (see figure 7.2), and the land previously used for coal stocking has in many cases been used to expand production capacity.

Conversion from oil or gas to coal is often more difficult. The fuel stocking and handling facilities represent a substantial extra cost, and may be physically impossible for many factories; this of course applies equally to investment in new coal-fired plant. In some cases, boilers originally designed for coal but converted to oil or gas may be converted back to coal with little loss of performance. Similarly, large watertube boilers, because of the large combustion chamber, can often be converted to firing by pulverised coal with little loss of output or efficiency. However, horizontal firetube boilers designed for oil or gas often present major conversion problems, both from reduced output and from problems of ash disposal and heat exchanger fouling. The return to coal is therefore likely to be rather slower than the historical growth of oil and gas use.

Coal/oil and coal/water mixtures

One way of using coal in boilers designed for oil is to prepare a suspension of finely-ground coal in oil, which can then be handled as a liquid fuel. In some systems the coal/oil mixture (COM) is maintained by continuous stirring, though with smaller particles and/or the use of additives a stable suspension – known as coal/oil dispersion (COD) – can be achieved. Proportions of coal up to around 50 per cent are feasible. The resulting fuel has high viscosity, may cause abrasion in pipework and deposition in passages through which the combustion gases flow. It will usually be necessary to make provision to deal with the increased particulate load carried by the flue gases. Despite these possible disadvantages, the technique, with which both the NCB (National Coal Board) and British Petroleum are concerned in the UK, can be an economic alternative to fuel oil, particularly in larger industrial boilers. Long-term economics depend on the continuing price advantage of coal, and are necessarily very uncertain.

Another route for coal utilisation is the use of coal/water mixtures, primarily as a storage and transport medium. Most of the water would be removed prior to combustion, the remainder giving rise to some loss of boiler efficiency. This option seems at present to be attracting little interest.

Fluidised bed systems

In a fluidised bed boiler, a bed, usually comprising crushed coal with ash and/or mineral particles, is held in suspension by an upward current of high-velocity air. Combustion is started in the bed, and the rapid motion of the particles (the bed resembles a boiling liquid) leads to very fast and efficient combustion and very efficient heat transfer. Most current systems operate at or near atmospheric pressure, but the use of higher pressures results in faster combustion and therefore a smaller boiler size for a given output. Heat is extracted either from the hot combustion gas above the bed, or through heat exchanger tubes within the bed itself, where the agitation of the particles greatly increases the heat transfer rates.

A particular feature of fluidised bed systems which is of interest for both industry and power generation is the use of limestone or dolomite in the bed as a sulphur removal mechanism. This is probably cheaper than the flue gas desulphurisation systems which may be needed for conventional boilers, and the dry calcium sulphate waste product is more easily disposed of than the slurry produced by wet sulphur removal systems. With current UK pollution regulations and low-sulphur UK coal, this is not a major issue, but could be important in the future.

The NCB are very active in fluidised bed combustion research (Grainger and

Gibson, 1981). Watertube boiler geometry is often well suited to fluidised bed systems. The conventional horizontal firetube boiler geometry, however, is less easy to adapt to this technique, and the most promising development work has been on vertical firetube boilers or boilers combining features of vertical and horizontal geometries. The present position is that the technology for atmospheric pressure designs is fairly well-proven, but has not yet become significant in the market. The recession, together with uncertain fuel prices, has undoubtedly contributed to this, and manufacturers appear unwilling to make a commitment to a technology of which there is little experience. A stronger interest in coal in general, or more stringent sulphur controls, could bring these systems into prominence.

Pressurised fluidised bed systems are at an earlier stage of development than atmospheric systems. Major experimental facilities in the UK are at the Coal Utilisation Research Laboratory at Leatherhead, and at Grimethorpe (2 MW and 80 MW thermal respectively), but commercialisation is not expected until the 1990s. Potential advantages are the high density of heat production and the direct use of the combustion gases in a gas turbine.

Combined heat and power

In 1980, industry (here including coal mines, refineries and gas works) generated 17.8 TWh of electricity, or 18 per cent of their overall consumption. The absolute level of private generation rose up to 1976 and has since fallen; as a fraction of total consumption, it has been falling throughout the period from 1955 as economies of scale have made centralised electricity generation more competitive. Table 7.12 gives a detailed breakdown. It may be seen that chemicals and engineering dominate the picture. Within the latter sector, the aluminium industry is of key importance, and the electricity is produced mainly in condensing turbines (i.e. without heat as a by-product). This element is likely to continue for most of the period covered by the study, but there is little scope for further expansion of electricity generation in engineering. The electricity produced in the chemicals sector will fall as the Magnox nuclear reactors reach the end of their lives, but a substantial output from the oil-refining and other chemicals industries is likely to remain. The importance in this sector of large watertube boilers and continuous processes provides a setting in which CHP is likely to be economic; future trends will depend on structural change within the sector.

Industrial CHP was covered by a report prepared for the government by the Combined Heat and Power Group (1979). This included the results of a survey of actual and potential CHP users. Of fifty-six companies which had considered the use of a CHP scheme, twenty-six had rejected it, with the dominant reasons

Table 7.12.   *Electricity generation by industry (TWh, Great Britain)*

Sector	1960	1965	1970	1975	1980
Iron and steel	2.74	3.03	2.70	1.66	0.86
Engineering etc.	1.32	1.50	1.51	3.32	3.30
Food etc.	0.42	0.42	0.38	0.44	0.55
Chemicals etc.[a]	6.41	8.10	10.29	11.16	10.90
Textiles etc.	0.58	0.56	0.56	0.41	0.23
Paper etc.	2.35	2.75	2.97	2.11	1.62
Other[b]	1.66	1.36	1.21	0.69	0.32
All industry	15.47	17.72	19.61	19.78	17.77
All industry consumption[c]	61.27	78.00	92.60	95.12	98.46

Notes: [a] Includes oil refineries and Calder Hall, Chapelcross and Dounreay
nuclear reactors. The breakdown in 1980 was: nuclear power stations
3.56 TWh, refineries 2.28 TWh, others 5.05 TWh.
[b] Includes coal mines, gas and water works.
[c] Partly estimated for 1970 and earlier.

being overall economics and capital shortage. The tariffs and 'buyback' provisions offered by Electricity Boards were also quoted as an obstacle; legislation in
the 1983 Energy Act may improve this situation. It was clear from the survey
that a high plant load factor was a necessity for CHP to be economic.

The price regime shown in figure 7.4 implies a falling ratio of electricity to coal
price, which will discourage CHP. The continuing trend in industrial structure
away from basic materials and towards high value-added products is also likely
to limit the scope for this technology.

7.9   Industrial energy conservation

It is widely recognised that opportunities for energy conservation in industry are
diverse and substantial, and that less progress has been made than might be
expected on economic grounds. The Department of Industry Energy Thrift
Scheme, and the joint Industry and Energy Departments' Energy Audit
Scheme, have greatly extended our knowledge of the pattern of industrial fuel
use and the scope for conservation. An early Thrift Scheme report (Clarke,
1977) suggested that 15 per cent of energy could be saved with existing
technology and the present mix of products. Table 7.13 lists the options
considered, in order of typical simple payback period. Implementation of these
measures is hindered by the low target payback periods usually used for

Table 7.13. *Opportunities for energy saving in industry*

Payback period^a less than 1 year:
Turn off idle equipment, improve production scheduling
Improve or re-adjust thermostats/timeclocks
Control heat loss through doors, loading bays etc.
Improve maintenance of fuel-using plant
Use waste products (if available) as fuel
Improve boiler and process plant control, and insulation of plant and pipework

Payback period^a more than 1 but less than 2 years:
Use localised air extraction/intake
Improve and maintain compressed air system
Minor modifications of process plant and other equipment
Heat recovery from air vented to the outside
Boiler improvements such as condensate return or the use of flash steam
Major rescheduling of the production process
Waste heat recovery for space or process use
Major maintenance e.g. relining of furnaces

Payback period^a more than 2 but less than 5 years:
Replace lighting system, improve switching
Replace existing boilers or heating units
Clean luminaires, re-paint walls etc.
Improve insulation of building structure

Note: ^a Assessed at 1976 prices; present payback periods would be somewhat less for most options. Note that the payback periods vary widely from one establishment to another.
Source: Clarke, 1977.

energy-related investment (see section 7.8), and by lack of knowledge; the latter problem is being tackled in several ways by the government and by fuel industries.

More recently, the Armitage Norton report (1982) has reviewed the opportunities for, and barriers to, industrial energy conservation. The report was based mainly on a detailed study of twenty-nine companies (not randomly selected) and concluded that savings since the first oil crisis average around 10 per cent, with a marked increase in activity since 1979. If 'conservation potential' is defined as the saving which can be achieved with a payback period of three years or less, then it appears that in these companies about half the potential has been realised, and the scope for further reductions is around 14 per cent of current energy use. The most important barriers to energy savings are lack of knowledge, management approach, capital budgeting procedures and investment appraisal.

There is general agreement that the government should promote energy conservation by publicity, training and education, and technical information and advice, as well as by technical research and development (R&D). The place of grants and subsidies, and the use of statutory measures, are in some degree subject to political controversy. These and other policy issues are discussed in chapter 13.

8

Energy use for transport

8.1 The transport sector in UK energy use

Structure

In 1980, the transport sector consumed one-quarter of the total energy delivered to final consumers (this and other statistics are from Department of Energy, 1983a; Department of Transport, 1981; Central Statistical Office, 1983 and earlier editions). This share has increased over the period from 1960, as shown in table 8.1, as a result of the 60 per cent increase in the absolute level of transport energy use. The role of the transport sector in oil consumption is particularly important. Transport's use of energy is dominated by oil (67 per cent in 1960, rising to 99 per cent in 1980). Through the 1960s its share in total oil use declined as oil penetrated other sectors, reaching a minimum of just over 40 per cent in 1970. Since that time, however, its share in total oil use has increased, owing to the scope for substitution away from oil in other sectors, to reach 56 per cent in 1980. Thus future trends in transport energy use are of great importance for UK energy prospects, and particularly for the use of oil products.

The growth in energy demand for transport has been largely due to the rise in the ownership and use of private cars. In 1980, private transport (cars and motorcycles) accounted for 51 per cent of transport energy, compared with 15 per cent in 1955. Over this period, both energy use and passenger-kilometres (a convenient measure of passenger transport activity) increased by a factor of more than five, while other transport energy use has remained nearly stable. There has also been a steady but slower growth in freight transport: freight tonne-kilometres grew by 65 per cent between 1955 and 1980. At present, traffic by air (including international flights) is growing faster than any other transport mode, increasing by a factor of 2.8 between 1970 and 1980.

Table 8.2 summarises transport energy use as disaggregated for this study. Note the dominance of road transport for both passengers and freight, and the importance of private cars in passenger transport. Of the total energy use, only

124

Table 8.1. *UK transport in total energy use*

Year	Transport energy use[a] GJ	Ratio of transport energy/ total energy[b] %	Ratio of transport oil use/ total oil use[b] %
1960	0.93	17.4	47.4
1965	1.00	17.6	42.6
1970	1.18	19.3	40.5
1975	1.29	21.9	47.2
1980	1.49	25.0	56.4

Notes:[a] Excluding ships' bunkers.
[b] Totals refer to total energy delivered into final consumption.

0.7 per cent is electricity (all used for railways), and all the remainder consists of petroleum products.

Passenger transport

The growth and structure of passenger transport since 1955 is shown in figure 8.1. The average annual growth rate in transport activity has been 3.8 per cent over this period, compared with 2.25 per cent for GDP. All this growth has come from private car transport. Rail passenger transport has been stable, while public service vehicles (buses, coaches and taxis) have seen a steady and substantial decline. Motorcycles and bicycles have increased their role since 1974, but are still of very minor importance. Car transport dropped noticeably in the wake of the 1973/4 oil crisis, and to a lesser extent in 1979, but in both cases the historic upward trend was quickly restored. These responses represented a fall in passenger transport as a whole; there was no significant substitution to either public service vehicles or rail.

Energy intensities for different modes of passenger transport are shown in table 8.3. The figures take account of actual operating conditions and vehicle load factors. It may be seen that energy intensity for long-distance travel varies by a factor of ten between an express coach and a domestic aircraft, with car and train in an intermediate position. Rural services have generally high energy intensities because of their low load factors.

Although the overall energy efficiency of passenger transport would be improved by transferring traffic to the more efficient modes and by improving vehicle load factors, scope for doing so is limited by the dominant role of the car,

Table 8.2.   *Energy consumption by UK transport, 1980*

Mode	Delivered energy (PJ)		Percentage of total	
Passenger (inland):				
Cars[a]	754		47.2	
Motorcycles	11		0.7	
Buses[b]	36	859	2.3	53.8
Taxis[b]	6		0.4	
Rail[c]	40		2.5	
Air[d]	12		0.8	
Freight (inland):				
Lorries[e]	234		14.7	
Vans[e]	124		7.8	
Rail[c]	10		0.6	
Ships[f]	52	423	3.3	26.5
Pipeline	2		0.1	
Air[d]	1		0.1	
International:				
Air[g]	207		13.0	
Ships (bunkers)[h]	107	314	6.7	19.7
Total	1596		100.0	
Sector:				
Road	1165		73.0	
Rail	50		3.1	
Water	159		10.0	
Air	220		13.8	
Pipeline	2		0.1	

Notes:[a] All cars and vans for private use.
[b] Public service vehicles with more than eight seats are buses, others are taxis.
[c] The passenger/freight split is estimated from British Railways data.
[d] Energy estimated from tonne-kilometres flown.
[e] Over 1.5 tons unladen weight are lorries; others are vans.
[f] All coastal and inland freight; also includes 12 PJ for fishing.
[g] International airlines fuelled at UK airports, aircraft industry own use, armed services.
[h] International shipping fuelled in the UK.

Table 8.3. *Energy intensity of inland passenger transport, 1980*

Mode	Energy intensity (MJ/pass.-km)
Car	1.7
Motorcycle	1.2
Long distance:	
Express coach	0.4
Inter-city train	1.4
Aircraft	4.1
Urban:	
Bus	0.7
Underground	2.1
Rural:	
Bus	1.3
Train	1.8

Source: Statistics of traffic and energy use cited in the text. Energy use for rail transport has been adjusted to take account of electricity generation efficiency.

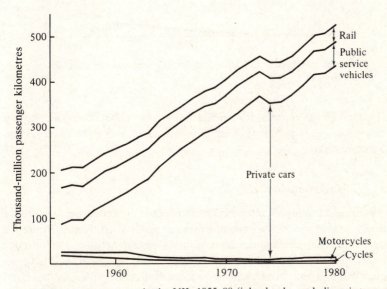

8.1 Passenger transport in the UK, 1955–80 (inland only, excluding air transport)

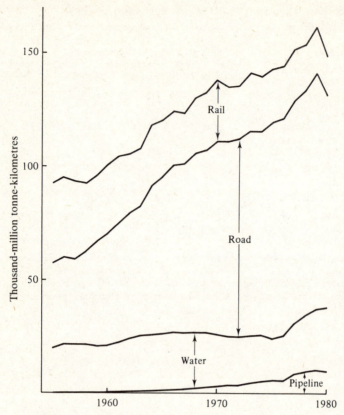

8.2 Freight transport in the UK, 1955–80 (inland only, excluding air transport, partly estimated)

and by the clear preference for private rather than public transport. Further developments in this sector will therefore depend mainly on the efficiency and use of private cars.

Freight transport

In 1980, freight transport consumed 26.5 per cent of the energy delivered to the transport sector, and 85 per cent of this was used in road freight. Figure 8.2 shows the changing size and structure of the freight market since 1955. Freight transport by road is dominant, its share rising from 41 per cent in 1955 to 63 per cent in 1980. Rail, in contrast, has shown a steady decline both in absolute terms and in market share. Inland and coastal water transport (within which the

Table 8.4. *Freight transport energy intensities, 1980 (delivered MJ/tonne-kilometres)*

Mode	Energy intensity
Lorry	02.51
Van	47.20
Rail	00.54
Water	00.70
Pipelines	00.18

Note: Vans are defined as goods vehicles with unladen weight up to 1.5 tons; others are lorries. Energy split between vans and lorries is partly estimated.
Source: See table 8.3.

contribution of inland waterways is very small indeed) rose slightly until the mid-1960s, fell during the following decade and may now be rising again. Pipelines (which exclude gas) are making a small but steadily increasing contribution. Over the period as a whole, freight transport activity rose at an average rate of 1.9 per cent per annum (2.3 per cent per annum to 1979). However, figure 8.3 shows that the tonnage of freight lifted reached a peak in 1973 and has since declined. Up to the late 1960s, the freight tonnage closely followed TIP.* Since that time, though still showing the effects of the business cycle, it has fallen relative to industrial output, probably reflecting a change in the structure of industry away from the heavier raw materials and products towards higher value manufactures.

Comparison between figures 8.2 and 8.3 clearly indicates that average journey length has increased since the mid-1960s. More detailed analysis shows that this change has occurred mainly in road freight and pipelines, with no overall trend in the other modes.

The energy intensities of freight transport in 1980, taking into account actual operating conditions and load factors, are shown in delivered energy terms in table 8.4. The very high energy intensity of vans reflects their very low load factors. The figure for lorries is an average of a very wide range, which overlaps the range for rail freight (ACEC, 1977a).

* TIP (Total industrial production) is here defined as the output of manufacturing industry plus construction. The energy industries and, in particular, MLH 104 (oil and natural gas) are excluded. Inclusion of these industries would substantially increase TIP towards the end of the period. However, the rapid growth of the oil industry has not greatly increased inland freight, since transport of oil products has not followed the output of MLH 104, and therefore inclusion of this industry would distort the analysis.

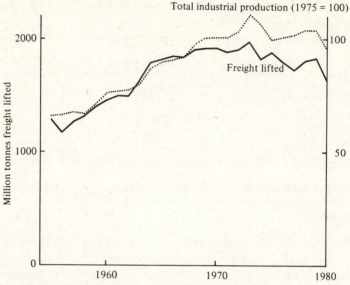

8.3 Freight tonnage and industrial production, 1955–80

International freight

International transport accounted in 1980 for 19.7 per cent of UK transport energy use. Two-thirds of this was for international airlines, and the remainder for ships' bunkers. In this study we shall adopt a simple approach to the estimation of future fuel requirements for international transport, which will be discussed in section 8.6 below.

8.2   Future passenger transport – private cars and motorcycles

Background

The private car offers flexibility and convenience as a mode of passenger travel, especially in suburban and rural areas. For commuters, parking difficulties and congestion may favour public transport, but in 1978/9 journeys to and from work were only 20 per cent of all passenger journeys (Department of Environment, 1980).

The period from 1950 to 1975 saw a steady rise in personal incomes and a fall in the cost of driving. It is not surprising, therefore, to find an increase in the car fleet from 3.6 million in 1955 to over 16 million in 1980 (Department of Transport, 1981), with a similar increase in the distance driven. Tables 8.5 and 8.6 show respectively the changing costs of motoring and the size and use of the

Table 8.5. *Trends in motoring costs per vehicle, 1962-80*

	Annual rate of increase (%)			Percentage of total costs, 1980
	1962-67	1967-73	1973-80	
Car purchase	−5.3	−0.7	3.3	39
Licences	−0.8	−1.6	−2.8	5
Petrol and oil	0.8	−0.4	3.0	33
Other running costs	−0.9	−1.5	2.2	23

Note: Costs deflated by retail price index.
Sources: Tanner, 1977 and 1981; and Central Statistical Office, 1981.

Table 8.6. *Private car activity in the UK, 1955-80*

Year	Number of cars (thousand)	Cars per person	Kilometres per car (thousand)
1955	3 609	0.071	11.7
1960	5 650	0.108	12.1
1965	9 131	0.168	12.8
1970	11 802	0.213	13.8
1973	13 804	0.247	14.2
1975	14 061	0.252	13.8
1980	16 369	0.293	14.1

Note: The basis for the estimation of the number of cars was changed in 1977.
Sources: Department of Transport, 1981; Department of Employment, 1980.

car fleet. Prior to 1973, all elements of motoring costs were falling in real terms. Since the oil crisis, not only has the cost of oil and petrol risen, but so also have other running costs (e.g. maintenance) and the costs of car purchase. Only licence costs have continued to fall. The data in table 8.6 suggest that purchases of new cars have been affected by the 1973/4 oil crisis, and that vehicle utilisation has also been reduced.

The car fleet

The future size of the car fleet is estimated using the car ownership model developed at the Transport and Road Research Laboratory (Tanner, 1977 and

Table 8.7. *Projections of the UK car fleet*

Year	Population (millions)	Petrol and oil prices (1980 = 100)	Overall motoring costs (1980 =100)	GDP per capita (1980 = 100) High	Central	Low	Private car fleet (millions) High	Central	Low
1980	55.9	100	100	100	100	100	16.4	16.4	16.4
1985	56.3	129	110	106	106	102	18.6	18.5	18.4
1990	56.9	157	119	119	116	107	20.8	20.6	20.4
2000	58.2	244	148	153	142	121	24.7	24.4	23.8
2010	58.8	309	169	196	173	137	27.8	27.2	26.4
2020	60.0	350	183	248	208	154	30.5	29.7	28.6

1981) and used by the Department of Transport in its road traffic forecasts (Department of Transport, 1980). The number of cars per person is assumed to follow a power growth curve towards an ultimate saturation level, with the rate of growth modified by income (measured as GDP per capita) and motoring cost. Specifically, we model

$$y = \frac{s}{1 + \{\alpha + at + b \log i + c \log p\}^{-n}}$$

where y is the number of cars per person, s is the specified saturation level, t is the time measured from a base year, i is GDP per capita, and p is the real cost of motoring. The parameters a, b, c and n are chosen by fitting to historical data for given value of saturation level s, and α is chosen to give the correct value of y in the base year. The values used for s are 0.64, 0.60 and 0.56 cars per person for the high, central and low economic growth cases introduced in chapter 4.

The petrol and oil price – a component of motoring costs – is assumed to rise in a fixed ratio with the sterling price of crude oil (see chapter 11), the ratio being based on the average over the period 1974 to 1980. Since the proportion of the price due to tax has fallen since 1979, this implies some catching up of the tax element, as well as substantial future adjustments as the price of crude oil rises. We shall later consider the effects of a lower price for motor fuel. We also assume that car purchases are influenced by petrol costs per gallon rather than per mile, so that improving car efficiency (see below) is not reflected explicitly in perceived motoring costs. Reversal of this assumption would, however, lead to only a very slight increase in the car fleet projections. Other components of motoring costs are assumed to remain constant in real terms. Income, like the saturation level, varies between the three economic growth projections. Table

8.7 shows the results obtained. Note that the size of the car fleet increases by about 50 per cent between 1980 and 2000, but that saturation effects become more important later. The effects of different rates of economic growth are fairly small.

Projections of car usage

Table 8.6 above shows that the annual distance driven per car rose from 11.7 thousand kilometres in 1955 to around 14 thousand kilometres at present (the peak, in 1978, was 14.5 thousand kilometres). This increase is thought to be mainly due to the rise in personal incomes. The effect of petrol prices is difficult to identify prior to 1973, but changes since that date appear to have influenced car usage. For projection purposes, we use a simple constant elasticity model

$$K = K_0 \left(\frac{i}{i_0}\right)^\alpha \left(\frac{c}{c_0}\right)^\beta.$$

where K = average kilometres per car per year, i is GDP per capita, c is car running costs (fuel and other running costs, but not purchase or licence costs), and α and β are parameters determined by fitting to historical data. The subscript 0 denotes a base year. The values obtained for α and β, using data for the period 1965 to 1980, were 0.35 and -0.20 respectively, both statistically significant.

It has been postulated that multiple car ownership by future households will hold down the annual distance driven per car, but cross-sectional data for the UK and US (Tanner, 1981) suggest that this effect is small. In this study we assume that the income and price elasticities α and β remain constant over the projection period.

As for car ownership, petrol prices are based on crude oil prices (see table 8.7 and chapter 11) and other running costs are assumed to remain constant in real terms. The resulting car usage projections, for the three economic scenarios used in the study, are shown in table 8.8. The net effect of the conflicting pressures of fuel prices and income is to yield almost constant car usage rates. As for the car fleet projections, we do not take increasing car efficiency into account in the definition of car running costs. To do so would lead to a 12 per cent increase in usage by 2020 (in the central case) compared with the figures shown.

Energy efficiency for private cars

Improvements in the fuel efficiency of private cars probably represent the most important factor in the future development of the transport sector. The subject

Table 8.8. *Projections of car usage*

Year	Running costs (1980 = 100)	Average car usage (thous. km/yr)		
		High	Central	Low
1980	100	14.1	14.1	14.1
1985	117	13.9	13.9	13.7
1990	134	14.0	13.9	13.5
2000	186	14.2	13.9	13.1
2010	225	14.9	14.2	13.1
2020	250	15.7	14.8	13.3

is discussed in detail in section 8.3, and the assumptions used in this study are included in table 8.14 below. In this important part of the transport sector, different assumptions are made for each economic growth case. Since motoring costs rise faster than GDP and consumers' expenditure in the low case (see table 8.7), we associate this case with the most rapid efficiency gains – a 26 per cent fall in energy intensity by 2000 and a 50 per cent fall by 2020. For the high economic growth case, motoring costs fall relative to GDP and there is less pressure for conservation; we assume a 38 per cent fall in energy intensity by 2020.

Motorcycles

Motorcycle use, though growing, is at present very small (7.4 billion kilometres in 1980 compared with 231 billion kilometres for cars). We make the simple assumption that the distance travelled remains constant in the low economic growth case, and rises to 9.0 and 10.7 billion kilometres in 2020 in the central and high growth cases respectively. We also assume that energy intensity falls (a resumption of the trend between 1950 and 1970, caused mainly by the growing proportion of smaller motorcycles), as shown in table 8.14.

The long term

For the long term, attention is focussed on the use of alternative fuels for private cars. Conventional engines can be adapted fairly easily to use hydrogen (probably using a metal hydride as a storage medium) or ethanol. The latter could be of biomass origin (e.g. from sugar cane) and is in use, as an additive or as a gasoline substitute, in several countries, notably Brazil. Though it has been considered in some countries in Europe, we do not make explicit allowance for the use of ethanol as a road transport fuel in the UK. Hydrogen is relevant only in a very long-term context in which energy supply is dominated by nuclear electricity (from fission or fusion) and hydrogen, produced by electrolysis, fulfils the need for a portable transport fuel.

With some extra technical costs (because of problems of corrosion and toxicity), internal combustion engines can be run on methanol. This could be of biomass origin, or based on natural gas. Methanol can also be converted chemically to a direct gasoline substitute (see chapter eleven).

Electric cars are often advocated as an opportunity to reduce dependence on oil products. Such systems are, however, severely limited by the low energy density of lead-acid batteries and the resulting stringent range and speed limitations. The primary energy efficiency of an electric car is around 18 per cent (largely due to the low efficiency of electricity generation), comparable to that of a diesel engine and rather better than a spark-ignition engine. However, battery weight limits the payload of an electric vehicle, and on an equal payload basis the efficiency is about half that of a diesel car (Francis and Woollacott, 1980). The electric vehicle does, however, depend on relatively plentiful primary fuels.

Advanced battery developments (e.g. sodium-sulphur, zinc-chlorine) may improve energy densities by as much as three times. However, it could be well into the next century before payload efficiencies for electric vehicles catch up with the improving performance of internal combustion engined cars.

Payload efficiency is not, of course, the only relevant criterion for an electric car, and there may be a market for a small electric car of limited range, suitable for use as a 'second car'. The economic appeal of such a vehicle would lie in its dependence on an untaxed fuel available on an off-peak tariff. A further technical possibility is a hybrid vehicle using a small internal combustion engine at high efficiency, with a battery/motor system to provide flexibility. Substantial overall fuel savings have been claimed, but such systems are far from proven, either technically or commercially.

Fuel use for private passenger transport

The combined fuel use for cars and motorcycles is projected for the three economic scenarios in figure 8.4. For the central scenario, total fuel use peaks in the late 1990s at about 12 per cent over current (1980) consumption; thereafter, improvements in efficiency more than compensate for increased travel. In the high scenario, energy use almost stabilises, reaching nearly 30 per cent over current consumption by 2020. In the low scenario, a peak is reached around 1990, after which fuel use falls sharply.

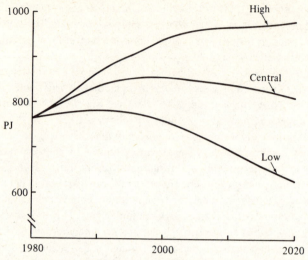

8.4 Projections of delivered energy use for cars and motorcycles

8.3   Private car fuel efficiency

Energy use and losses

Figure 8.5 shows the fate of the energy content of the fuel used in a typical car (Leach, 1979, quoting a US source). Note that only about 12 per cent is available at the wheels, with most being lost in the engine itself. There is substantial scope for improving fuel-use efficiency, which we discuss in four categories:

(a) Changes in driving style and in the driving environment.
(b) Improvements in engine efficiency.
(c) Reduction of losses caused outside the engine itself.
(d) Reduction of the energy required at the wheels.

Driving style

Useful savings can be made by driving with a 'light foot' on the accelerator, by the avoidance of excessive braking and by correct use of gears (generally to keep engine speed as low as possible consistent with the power required). Devices to encourage careful use of the accelerator, and warning lights or other metering devices to indicate high petrol consumption, are now making an appearance in new cars. The total impact of such changes is difficult to assess, but a 'round figure' of 5 per cent improvement would probably be realistic. A similar

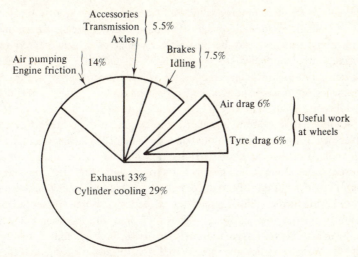

8.5 Energy flows in a typical car

improvement is available from better maintenance (ACEC, 1977b – it is likely that up to 60 per cent of cars have significant faults in ignition or valve timing or in air–fuel ratio control).

The potential benefit from improved traffic control is likely to be mainly the time saved, but there should be a useful by-product in energy saving.

Engine efficiency

The fuel efficiency of cars using existing engine designs can usually be improved significantly. Fuel use in a cold engine is up to twice that in a warm engine, and it has been estimated that 10 per cent of total fuel use is an excess due to cold running. This loss can be reduced substantially by effective automatic choke control. Electronic ignition can also yield useful savings (mainly by eliminating the maintenance problems of electromechanical systems), and direct fuel injection reduces pumping losses.

Changes in engine design are likely to yield major savings. Under ideal conditions (low engine speed and high torque), efficiency of current engines may be up to 30 per cent, but it is likely to be only 15 per cent at 10 per cent load (Leach, 1979; Francis and Woollacott, 1980), largely due to throttling losses. Reliable ignition is ensured in practice by the use of an over-rich fuel mixture, leading to low efficiency and pollution by unburnt hydrocarbons. In general, a high compression ratio leads to high efficiency, but the compression ratio is limited in conventional engines by the need to avoid pre-ignition of the fuel charge. These shortcomings would be overcome in a lean-burn, high-compression (LB-HC) engine, and much development work is being carried out to this end. Some progress may be possible with engines of generally conventional design, but a stratified-charge engine (in which ignition occurs in a small region of rich mixture which then ignites the weaker main charge) seems the most promising option, with potential energy savings of up to 25 per cent (Francis and Woollacott, 1980).

An alternative route to a higher compression ratio, and therefore to higher efficiency, is to use a conventional diesel engine. The efficiency gain in a private car, compared with current spark-ignition engines, is up to 20 per cent with current diesel engines, and modification to use direct fuel injection (the norm in larger engines but difficult to implement in the high-speed engines used in cars) would bring further gains. Against the efficiency gains must be set the increased cost, weight and noise of diesel engines compared with spark-ignition engines of equivalent power (though the cost penalty is likely to fall as spark-ignition engines themselves become more complex). It is also probable that the energy cost of producing diesel fuel at the refinery is greater than that for gasoline, and that developments in LB-HC engines will eat into the efficiency advantage of diesels, so that the long-term position is not clear. It is noticeable that current developments in both diesel and spark-ignition engines are along converging lines, so that the possibility exists of a highly efficient and fuel-flexible composite engine.

Other losses

The use of a thermostatically controlled cooling fan reduces the accessory load on the engine as well as shortening the warm-up period; the potential savings are around 3 per cent.

The role of the gearbox is to maintain the operating conditions of the engine in spite of changing speed and load at the wheels. Conventional transmission systems do not fulfil this role very effectively. Provision of a fifth gear or overdrive for high-speed cruising saves some fuel. However, an automatic continuously variable transmission system (CVT), probably using a microprocessor to keep the engine as close as possible to its ideal operating conditions, would yield energy savings of about 25 per cent. Such systems are the subject of current research.

Energy at the wheels

The energy available at the wheels is divided about equally (under typical driving conditions) between tyre friction and aerodynamic drag, with the latter becoming more important at high speed.

Reduction of aerodynamic drag is now becoming an important design feature of new cars, with 'best' designs having a drag coefficient of about 0.3 compared with the UK car fleet average of 0.45. A reduction of this order of magnitude would probably yield energy savings of about 7 per cent.

Reduction of body weight produces a proportional reduction in both rolling friction and braking losses. The use of new lightweight construction (e.g. plastic body panels and ceramic engine components) could reduce vehicle weight by 30 per cent, yielding around 10 per cent fuel saving.

Other tyre energy losses result from deformation of the tyres under load, and are lower for radial than for cross-ply tyres. Further research is likely to bring about additional gains in efficiency.

Market penetration

It is clear from the above discussion that there is very substantial scope for improved vehicle efficiency. There is also evidence that car manufacturers now see energy efficiency as a marketable feature of their products. Once new design features are taken up by manufacturers, penetration into the vehicle fleet can be fairly rapid, since the average life of a car is only around ten years. The efficiencies used in this study are shown in table 8.14 below.

8.4 Future passenger transport – buses, taxis and rail

The public passenger transport sector, with the exception of domestic air travel, has shown a steady decline, almost unaffected by changes elsewhere in the UK economy. In 1980 it represented just under 10 per cent of all passenger transport energy use. Because of the social need to maintain a public transport service, the scale of the services offered has declined more slowly than their total use, so that there is a falling trend in vehicle load factors.

For this study, public road and rail passenger transport is projected independently of economic growth. Bus and coach traffic, expressed in terms of vehicle-kilometres, is assumed to decline at first at the rate experienced during the 1970s, but with the decline becoming less marked later owing to the need to provide a basic service for those without access to private transport. Within this total, express coach traffic (which has grown by a factor of three over the last decade) is assumed to continue to grow up to 1990 and then level off. A modest improvement in the energy efficiency of buses and coaches is assumed, as shown in table 8.14 below.

In the light of past trends, passenger demand for rail services is assumed to fall slowly, but with inter-city services growing (Department of Transport, 1981). It is assumed that load factors on inter-city services will improve, but that load

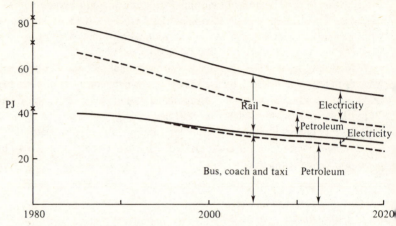

8.6 Projections of delivered energy use for public passenger transport

factors elsewhere will fall slowly. Underground traffic is assumed to remain constant in terms of train-kilometres. The energy efficiency of rail passenger transport is assumed to increase by 18 per cent over the period to 2020 (table 8.14).

Taxi mileage is assumed to grow in line with the central scenario car mileage figures, and efficiency increases are similar to those for private cars.

Figure 8.6 gives the projected structure of fuel use in this sector up to 2020, in delivered energy terms. In the rail sector, electricity use grows to reach about two-thirds of delivered energy by 2020, compared with about one-quarter in 1980; this reflects continuing electrification of both commuter and inter-city services. Electricity also begins to penetrate passenger road transport, for short-haul bus services. Total delivered energy falls by 42 per cent between 1980 and 2020, though, due to the increased use of electricity, the fall in primary energy is only some 17 per cent.

8.5   Future freight transport

Total demand

Figure 8.3 showed that the tonnage of goods lifted since 1975 has been falling relative to TIP, but this has been offset by a rise in the average journey length. We assume in this study that the trend in journey length slows down, under the influence of higher energy costs, so that there is a slight fall in the ratio of freight tonne-kilometres to industrial output as industrial structure continues to move away from heavy basic industries.

Table 8.9. *Projections of freight demand (billion tonne-kilometres)*

	Road			Rail					Total		
Year	High	Central	Low	High	Central	Low	Water	Pipeline	High	Central	Low
1980	95.7	95.7	95.7	19.8	19.8	19.8	19.7	9.9	145.1	145.1	145.1
1985	103	103	96	21	21	21	19	12	155	155	148
1990	116	110	98	24	23	22	19	13	172	165	151
2000	134	119	96	29	26	25	18	14	195	177	153
2010	162	134	100	30	28	26	17	15	224	194	158
2020	198	155	109	31	29	27	15	16	261	215	168

Table 8.10. *Rail freight, 1965-79 (million tonnes; percentages in brackets)*

	1965	1970	1979
Coal and coke	140.5 (60.5)	114.3 (54.8)	93.5 (55.2)
Iron and steel	46.7 (20.1)	40.2 (19.3)	25.1 (14.8)
Petroleum	8.5 (3.7)	18.4 (8.8)	16.3 (9.6)
Others	36.5 (15.7)	35.8 (17.1)	34.4 (20.4)
Total	232.5	208.7	169.3

Table 8.9 shows the projections of freight tonne-kilometres for the three economic scenarios, together with the modal split as discussed below. Note that the demand for freight transport is very sensitive to the level of economic growth.

Rail freight

The different modes of freight transport have widely differing characteristics (speed, cost, flexibility etc.) and tend to serve different markets. We project the modal structure of freight transport by considering first the market-specific modes (rail, water and pipeline), estimating the small contribution from air freight, and then treating road haulage as a residual.

In 1979, three commodities – coal and coke, iron and steel and petroleum products – accounted for 80 per cent of all goods moved by rail (Department of Transport, 1981). Table 8.10 shows how the structure of rail freight has changed since 1965. The decline in coal and steel has reduced total traffic considerably, though future growth in coal output is likely to reverse this trend (71 per cent of coal moved in 1980 was carried by rail). The traffic generated by oil products is likely to be linked to future oil use in the economy as a whole. Tonnage of other goods appears to be fairly stable. These considerations show that total rail freight traffic is likely to increase in the future. From its 1980 value of 19.8 billion tonne-kilometres, traffic is expected to rise by 2020 to 31.0, 29.0 and 27.0 billion tonne-kilometres in the high, central and low scenarios respectively. A 13 per cent fall in energy intensity over the same period is also assumed (see table 8.14 below). An increase in the importance of electricity is expected for rail freight, though to a lesser extent than for rail passenger transport. The fuel-use implications of these projections are included in figure 8.7 below.

Water transport

Water transport in the UK is almost entirely via coastal shipping. This mode of transport is slow, and there are few suitable ports, so that there is little scope for diversification. In 1980, 81 per cent of the tonnage carried consisted of petroleum products, with coal at 8.5 per cent. The levelling off of indigenous oil production and greater use of pipelines are expected to lead to a gradual decline.

Inland water traffic is generally uneconomic with the existing system of waterways, though very energy efficient. Continuing decline is expected.

Pipelines and air freight

In 1980, there were well over 3000 kilometres of pipelines in the UK, carrying crude oil and refined products (James, 1980). Pipelines are highly energy efficient (see table 8.4 above), and traffic grew by a factor of three between 1970 and 1980. Further growth will at first be linked to North Sea output, but growth is likely to continue after the North Sea production peak as petroleum products are transferred from other modes.

It may in the future be possible to transport solids such as coal and mineral ores by pipeline, but this is assumed to have negligible impact in the UK within the period of the study.

Domestic air freight is of very minor importance in the UK and is expected to remain so, though some growth is anticipated up to the end of the century.

Road haulage

Road haulage is assumed to account for all the freight traffic not covered by the other modes. It is divided between vans (defined as having an unladen weight not greater than 1.5 tonnes) and lorries. In 1980 there were more than twice as many vans as lorries in the UK, but vans carried only 3 per cent of the total goods moved. However, about one-third of the total energy used for road freight was used in vans as a result of the very low average load of 0.12 tonnes. Energy use in vans is therefore related to vehicle-kilometres rather than the load moved. (Statistics on the energy split between vans and lorries are very limited, and the values used in this study are estimated from various sources.)

The use of vans is historically related to the output of the services sector, and possibly to oil product prices. We use the formula

$$v = v_o \left(\frac{s}{s_o}\right)^\alpha \left(\frac{p}{p_o}\right)^\beta$$

where v is the van fleet use (vehicle-kilometres), s is the output of the services sector, p is the pump price of petrol, the subscript o denotes a base year, and α and β are elasticities to be determined. Applying this formula to the period 1965 to 1980 gives values of α and β equal to 0.70 and -0.02 respectively, of which only the former is statistically significant.

For forecasting, the same formula is used with an additional factor (1.0 up to 2000, 0.95 in 2010, 0.90 in 2020) to allow for saturation.

The projections of van-kilometres (v) are converted to freight tonne-kilometres assuming the current average load of 0.12 tonnes. The remainder of the total road freight traffic is then assigned to lorries. From the 1980 value of 2.8 per cent of road freight traffic, the figure for van tonne-kilometres rises to 3.3 per cent by 2020 in the low scenario and falls to 2.4 per cent in the high scenario; these differences reflect the different economic structures of the scenarios.

The efficiencies of vans, in terms of delivered energy per tonne-kilometre, are assumed to improve substantially, though rather less than for cars (see table 8.14). This is in part the result of a switch to diesel-engined vehicles. In 1980, 94 per cent of vans had gasoline engines (ACEC, 1981a), but the short-haul delivery work for which many vans are used is particularly suited to diesel engines and it is assumed that higher fuel prices will promote this change. We also foresee significant growth for electric traction in this sector of the market, with electricity gaining 19 per cent of delivered energy by 2020.

The scope for improving lorry efficiency is lower. Vehicle weight and shape are largely determined by the nature of the load, the diesel engines which dominate this sector in the UK are already designed for fuel efficiency, and the transmission systems in use allow much better matching between engine and wheels than is the case for private cars. Nevertheless, bolt-on or designed-in aerofoils can reduce aerodynamic drag, and the general trend towards larger lorries leads to gains in overall fuel efficiency. The assumptions used are shown in table 8.14.

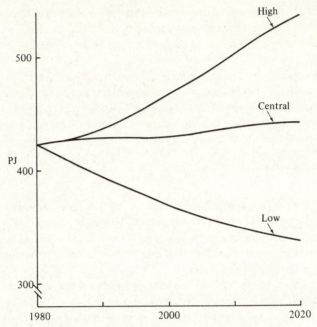

8.7 Projections of delivered energy use for freight transport

Total freight energy use

Figure 8.7 shows total freight energy use (in delivered energy terms, including 1.2 PJ for air freight) for the three economic scenarios. Comparison with figure 8.4 shows the absence of saturation effects in the freight sector. This arises because of the explicit saturation built into the projections of car ownership, the fuel price dependence of both car ownership and use, and the lower scope for energy savings in lorries – the dominant freight transport mode – compared with cars. The average annual growth rates in delivered energy between 1980 and 2020 are 0.6, 0.09 and −0.6 per cent in the high, central and low scenarios respectively.

The structure of freight energy use for the central scenario is shown in figure 8.8. The dominance of road freight becomes more marked, and lorries remain by far the most important single energy use. Though total delivered energy is almost static, total primary energy use rises by about 14 per cent due to the growth of electricity use. Table 8.11 shows the fuel mix in freight transport for this scenario. Note the increasing dominance of diesel fuel, and the growing, but still small, role of electricity.

Table 8.11. *Freight transport fuel mix, central scenario (percentage of delivered energy, excluding air freight)*

Year	Gasoline	Diesel	Electricity
1980	30.9	69.0	0.1
1990	25.6	73.7	0.7
2000	21.7	77.0	1.3
2010	16.9	80.7	2.4
2020	11.4	84.1	4.5

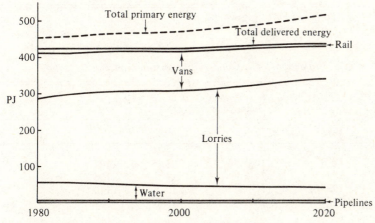

8.8 Modal split of freight energy use, central scenario

8.6   Future international transport

The future of international air and sea transport depends on developments in the world economy as well as in the UK, and for this study we adopt a simple approach based on projections of air and sea traffic and improvements in energy efficiencies.

For international air traffic, British Airways project a 7 per cent growth rate in combined passenger and freight tonne-kilometres up to 1986 and a slower rate thereafter (ACEC, 1979). This view is broadly consistent with government projections (Department of Trade, 1978). It is likely that a high proportion of journeys will be for leisure rather than business, so that traffic is likely to depend on both the level of fares and personal disposable incomes.

Table 8.12.   *Projections of air traffic[a] and energy use*

Year	Traffic (tonne-km) (scaled to 1980 = 100)			Delivered energy (PJ)		
	High	Central	Low	High	Central	Low
1980	100	100	100	220	220	220
1985	145	140	130	296	286	266
1990	185	180	160	345	336	299
2000	280	270	230	430	415	354
2010	350	335	300	461	441	396
2020	390	370	300	428	406	363

Note:[a] Domestic and international.

Table 8.13.   *Projections of UK energy use for international shipping*

Year	Delivered energy (PJ)		
	High	Central	Low
1980	107	107	107
1985	114	114	108
1990	124	119	110
2000	138	126	108
2010	156	135	110
2020	177	147	114

Table 8.12 shows the projected air traffic and fuel use for the three economic scenarios. Domestic air travel, which is very much smaller than international air travel in energy terms, is included. Note the very substantial increase in traffic in all scenarios.

There is major scope for improved fuel efficiency in this sector (ACEC, 1979). For existing aircraft, better load factors and lower cruising speeds have already brought about significant improvements, and these will be reinforced by the trend towards larger aircraft. High bypass ratio turbofan engines – as used in the Boeing 747, Lockheed Tri-Star and DC-10 – yield fuel savings of some 30 per cent over earlier designs. Other technical developments, in both engine and aircraft design, are likely to produce further gains in energy efficiency. The results of these gains are evident from the fuel-use projections in table 8.12.

Table 8.14.   *Indices of transport energy intensity (1980 = 100)*

		1980	1990	2000	2010	2020
Based on MJ/vehicle-km:						
	High case	100	90	81	71	62
Cars	Central case	100	88	77	66	56
	Low case	100	86	74	61	50
Motorcycles		100	85	75	71	67
Taxis		100	88	77	66	56
Buses		100	98	94	90	88
Passenger rail		100	97	91	87	85
Vans		100	86	76	68	60
Based on MJ/tonne-km:						
Lorries		100	95	90	85	80
Rail freight		100	96	92	89	87
Aircraft		100	85	70	60	50
Ships		100	98	96	94	92
Pipeline		100	100	100	100	100

Like air traffic, international shipping will depend on world developments. We make the simple assumption that changes in the level of shipping fuelled in the UK will follow changes in UK inland freight traffic. Allowing for some improvement in efficiency, we obtain the energy projections shown in table 8.13. Energy use stays nearly constant in the low case, but rises substantially in the other two cases.

8.7   Total transport energy use

Figure 8.9 shows the projections of total delivered energy for transport, excluding ships' bunkers, for the three scenarios. Total energy use reaches a peak in all the scenarios, and in the central and low scenarios is well in decline by the end of the period. This results from saturation in car ownership, and increasing energy efficiency (especially for cars); modal changes and fuel substitution are relatively unimportant.

The modal structure and fuel mix are shown for the central scenario in tables 8.15 and 8.16. Modal structure is fairly stable. Fuel mix shows a steady decline in the relative importance of gasoline, matched by growth in diesel and aviation fuels.

Table 8.15. *Modal structure of transport energy use, central scenario (percentages of delivered energy)*

Year	Private passenger	Public passenger	Road freight	Other freight	Air[a]	Ships' bunkers
1980	47.9	5.2	22.4	4.0	13.8	6.7
1990	46.6	4.1	20.5	3.4	18.7	6.7
2000	45.8	3.3	19.5	3.0	21.8	6.6
2010	44.2	2.8	20.1	2.7	23.1	7.1
2020	43.8	2.6	21.2	2.6	21.9	7.9

Note: [a] Includes domestic and international, passenger and freight traffic.

Table 8.16. *Fuel mix in the transport sector, central scenario (percentages of delivered energy)*

Year	Gasoline	Diesel	Fuel oil	Aviation fuel	Electricity
1980	56.3	24.7	4.6	13.8	0.7
1990	51.1	24.9	4.5	18.7	0.8
2000	47.2	25.5	4.5	21.8	1.0
2010	42.9	27.8	4.8	23.1	1.4
2020	40.1	30.6	5.4	21.9	2.0

Note: Includes ships' bunkers.

8.8   Fuel pricing policy

Throughout the foregoing analysis we have assumed that transport fuel prices reflect *pro rata* the rising level of crude oil price. In fact, crude oil contributes only about one-fifth of the retail price of gasoline, most of the remainder being made up of VAT (value-added tax) and excise duty. Thus transport fuel prices depend substantially on government policy.

Though the nominal price of gasoline has risen considerably since 1973, the large tax element, together with general inflation, has cushioned the effects of world oil price rises, and the real price of gasoline in 1979 was below its 1973 level. Thus the price signals, to both drivers and vehicle manufacturers, have not been clear.

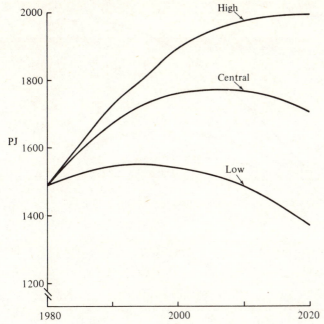

8.9 Total delivered energy for transport (excludes ships' bunkers)

A similar lack of clarity has characterised the relative prices of diesel fuel and gasoline. The price per gallon of diesel fuel in 1975 was 77 per cent of that of gasoline, but had risen to 107 per cent of the gasoline price by mid-1981. As a result – in contrast to many European countries – the share of diesel-engined cars in new car purchases has remained very low in the UK (CACI, 1981). Earlier objections to the promotion of diesel cars, based on the argument that it would encourage imports, are no longer valid as at least two UK manufacturers (Austin-Rover, Ford) are now producing suitable engines.

An issue closely related to fuel pricing is that of the vehicle excise duty, currently levied at a fixed rate for all private cars. In 1978, it was proposed to abolish the duty and to make up the lost revenue through increased fuel tax. This would have several advantages. It would shift the tax burden towards larger cars and towards those who drive further, it would encourage the development of fuel-efficient cars, and it would make drivers more aware of the real costs of private, as opposed to public, transport. At the time, the move was opposed on the grounds that it would discriminate against rural drivers, who drive further than those in urban areas. However, the small difference in distance is more

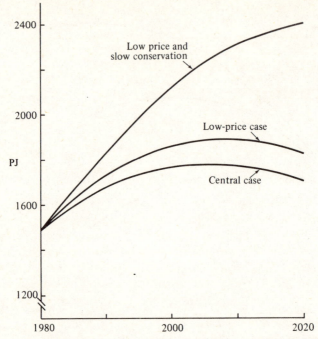

8.10 Projections of total delivered energy use for transport: effect of low fuel prices
and reduced conservation

than offset by the greater fuel efficiency of rural driving (Cousins and Potter,
1982), so that this argument is largely mythical.

We analyse the effect of more lenient fuel taxation policies by considering an
alternative scenario in which the difference between gasoline price and crude oil
price is held at its real 1980 level (giving a gasoline price increase of 55 per cent
between 1980 and 2020, which may be compared with our earlier assumption,
table 8.7, of an increase by 250 per cent) with the central scenario for economic
growth. Such a situation could also arise if world oil prices rise much more
slowly than is assumed in this study. The results are shown in figure 8.10. If
technical improvements in efficiency are assumed to be unaffected by the lower
fuel prices, then the extra fuel for the transport sector as a whole (excluding
ships' bunkers) is 5 per cent in 2000 and 7 per cent in 2020, showing that the
behavioural effects of fuel price changes are small. Figure 8.10 also shows the
effect of low prices combined with slower gains in fuel-use efficiency (specifically, we assume that the gains assumed for 2000 are in this variant delayed to
2020). The extra fuel use from the combined changes is 20 per cent in 2000 and
over 40 per cent in 2020, confirming that technical conservation is the key factor
for the future of transport energy use.

9

Energy use in services and agriculture

9.1 Background

In this chapter we consider the consumption of energy in the services sector and in agriculture. Services include public administration (including schools, hospitals etc.), commercial buildings and other miscellaneous uses of energy, though most non-manufacturing industry is included in the 'other trades' subsector of industry (see chapter 7). We deal separately with agriculture because its pattern of fuel use is very different from that of the services sector.

Shares of services in UK fuel use

In 1981, public administration accounted for 6.4 per cent of the energy delivered into final consumption, while commercial and other uses consumed 6.1 per cent (Department of Energy, 1983a and earlier editions). Both these figures have shown a gradual rise over the last two decades. In the sector as a whole, the dominant fuel is oil (a share of 35 per cent in 1981, most of it in public administration). This represents 10 per cent of total oil use, or 25 per cent of oil use outside the transport sector. The sector also accounted in 1981 for 13 per cent of natural gas use, and 24 per cent of electricity use, with most of the latter in the commercial sector.

Fuel mix

Figures 9.1 and 9.2 show the historical fuel shares in the public administration and commercial sectors respectively. Both sectors show the familiar shift away from solid fuels towards oil and, later, gas, with a steadily increasing share for electricity. In both cases, the substitution of gas for oil has been only partial, reflecting the higher price of gas in these sectors compared with that in industry. Note, however, that the move away from coal has been more rapid and more complete in the commercial sector than in public buildings, and that electricity is a very important fuel in the commercial sector.

151

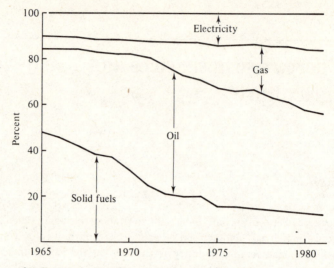

9.1 Fuel shares in public administration, 1965–81

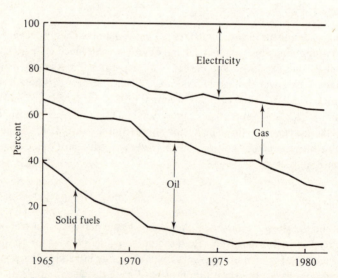

9.2 Fuel shares in the commercial and miscellaneous sector, 1965–81

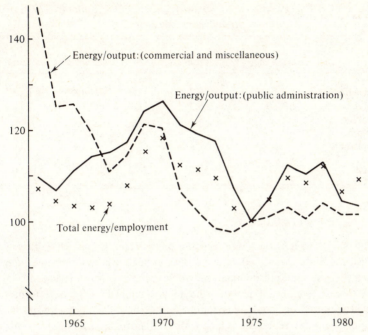

9.3 Energy intensities in the services sectors. Scaled to 1975 = 100

Energy efficiency

Figure 9.3 shows recent changes in the energy/output ratio for the two subsectors (economic data are from Central Statistical Office, 1983 and earlier editions). Both sectors show a downward trend, though it is very slight in public administration. In both cases the curve shows substantial short-term variations, especially around 1970 and 1974/5. In neither case can a response to the oil crises of the 1970s be discerned with confidence, and the post-1973 behaviour seems to be characterised by a slower fall in energy intensity than was seen in the earlier period. The figure also shows the ratio of energy to employment for the sector as a whole. This shows similar short-term variations, but no overall trend, suggesting that the downward trends in the energy/output ratios have resulted mainly from an increase in output per employee. This is a heterogeneous sector, covering such very different establishments as offices, shops, schools, hospitals and places of entertainment, and analysis at a more disaggregated level would be needed to explain more fully the detailed changes in energy intensity.

Table 9.1.   *Energy end-uses in commercial and public buildings, 1976 (percentages of total, in delivered energy terms)*

	Solid fuels	Oil products	Gas	Electricity	Total
Space heating	8.4	35.2	12.3	4.4	60.3
Water heating	2.3	6.0	6.0	1.7	16.0
Cooking	-	0.3	5.9	1.3	7.5
Lighting	-	-	-	10.6	10.6
Appliances	-	-	-	5.6	5.6
Total	10.7	41.5	24.2	23.6	100.0

Energy end-uses

Table 9.1 shows how fuels were used in commercial and public buildings in 1976 (Bush and Matthews, 1979). Space and water heating account for three-quarters of all fuel use, and are dominated by oil products. Gas use is also substantial, and there is significant use of solid fuels, mainly in schools, hospitals and government offices. Cooking is dominated by gas, while electricity-specific uses (mainly lighting) represent a larger share than in the household sector (see chapter 6).

Energy use in agriculture

In terms of energy use agriculture and forestry form a small sector, accounting in 1981 for 1 per cent of energy delivered into final consumption and 4 per cent of non-transport oil use. Figure 9.4 shows historical fuel use in the sector. There are three main end-uses: mobile motive power, which is oil-specific; heaters and driers, which were at one time dominated by solid fuels but are now mainly oil-based; and uses of electricity. In both the fossil fuel end-uses, there was a sharp peak in 1973 and rapid falls in 1974 and 1980–1, suggesting a response to the oil price rises. The erratic behaviour of the historical data is due to the dependence of agricultural output on the weather, and also on the use of a monetary measure of output which is influenced by changes in commodity prices.

The ratios of fossil fuel use and electricity use to output are shown in figure 9.5. For fossil fuels, a slow downward trend in energy intensity has accelerated since 1973 (the trends are similar from 1965 for heaters and driers and for motive power). Electricity intensity was climbing prior to 1970, then levelled off, and has also been falling since 1973.

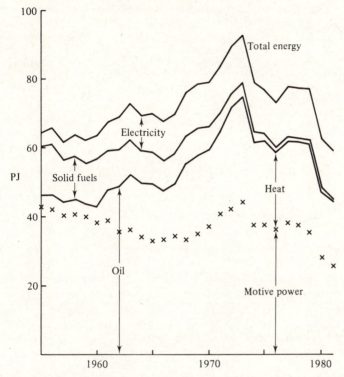

9.4 Fuel use in agriculture, 1955–81

9.2 Future energy use in public administration

Method

Projections of energy use in the services sectors are based mainly on qualitative arguments rather than on a detailed formal model. We divide energy use into three categories: space and water heating, cooking and specific uses of electricity (the latter comprises lighting – the dominant element – air conditioning and miscellaneous appliances). The 1980 base year split between categories is based on provisional estimates by the Energy Technology Support Unit (ETSU) at Harwell.

For each category, we project the ratio of fuel use to sector output, taking into account likely technical changes in efficiency. In the services sectors, fuel use is more readily related to employment than to ouput, and will therefore fall relative to output if productivity rises. As a result of the way output is defined in the public administration sector, the ratio of output to employment is very

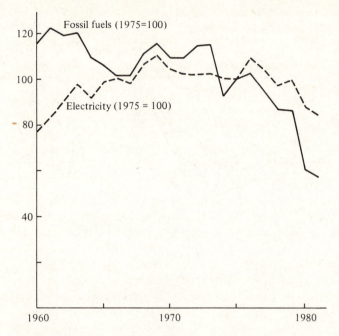

9.5 Fuel use/output ratios for agriculture, 1960–81

nearly constant, and the productivity effect on energy use is unimportant. (In much of the sector, in particular education and medical services, which in 1980 accounted for 63 per cent of employment, fuel use is related to the number of users of the service rather than employees; we make the implicit assumption that the user/employee ratio remains nearly constant.) The output projections for the three economic growth scenarios (see chapter 4) are used to calculate future energy use, and fuel shares in each category are assessed qualitatively in the light of expected fuel price changes and technical developments. The projected energy/output ratios are shown in table 9.2 and discussed below.

Space and water heating

Technical conservation in space and water heating will occur mainly as a result of improvements in the building stock. The links between the government and public administration, and in particular the established role of the Property Services Agency in encouraging energy conservation, prompt an optimistic view of future prospects, and we assume a 30 per cent fall in energy intensity between 1981 and 2020. Table 9.2 shows the detailed figures.

Table 9.2. *Energy/output ratios in public administration (PJ/unit output, with 1975 output scaled to unity)*

Year	Space and water heating	Cooking	Lighting etc
1980	286	31.4	38.1
1985	268	30.5	39.6
1990	251	29.9	40.8
2000	226	28.9	40.0
2010	206	28.3	37.3
2020	197	27.7	34.3

Figure 9.1 above shows that coal has retained a small but significant share of this sector, mainly in large schools, hospitals and government offices. Overall, however, the sector does not look promising for coal, with a purely seasonal heating load and an average boiler size of only 6000 lbs steam/hour (Chesshire and Robson, 1983; see chapter 7 for a discussion of boiler technology and coal use). We assume that coal's share of space and water heating fuel use rises from its 1980 value of 16.2 per cent to 22 and 25 per cent respectively in 2000 and 2020. Of the remaining fuels in this sector, natural gas and gas oil are both more important than fuel oil (most of which is used in hospitals), which suggests that scope for fuel switching will be limited. We assume some movement away from fuel oil and gas oil (with shares of 10 and 19 per cent respectively in 2020 compared with 20 and 36 per cent in 2000), and an increase in the share of gas from 24 per cent in 1980 to 31 per cent in 2020. In view of the narrowing price difference between gas and electricity (discussed more fully in chapter 7), we anticipate a growing role for electricity in space and water heating, its share rising from 4 per cent in 1980 to 15 per cent by 2020.

Cooking

We postulate a 12 per cent reduction in the energy/employee ratio for cooking, rather less than the fall anticipated in the household sector (chapter 6) since improvements which have yet to become general in domestic cookers are already common in commercial systems. At present, five-sixths of fuel use for cooking is in the form of gas. By analogy with the household sector, we assume a moderate shift towards electricity, which achieves a 25 per cent share by 2020.

Lighting etc.

The ratio of total electricity use to output in the public administration sector rose steadily up to 1970, but has since increased much more slowly and

Table 9.3.   *Output projections for the services sectors (1975 = 100)*

Year	Public administration			Commercial and miscellaneous		
	High	Central	Low	High	Central	Low
1985	109.0	109.0	108.2	117.6	117.6	113.4
1990	116.8	115.7	112.6	132.9	131.3	121.3
2000	139.6	134.3	125.6	176.3	167.4	142.6
2010	166.9	154.3	138.7	232.7	213.7	168.3
2020	197.5	175.6	151.7	303.1	269.0	196.3

erratically; part of the recent increase is also due to penetration of electricity into space and water heating and cooking. There is substantial scope for conservation in lighting, though experience to date suggests that this potential may be only slowly realised. We assume that specific electricity use/employee continues to rise slowly until around 1990, after which conservation causes a fall to 90 per cent of the 1980 value by 2020. With a moderate or high nuclear programme, we expect electricity prices to be relatively stable in the long term, so that the incentive for continuing conservation comes from technical development rather than from price rises.

Total fuel use

The economic growth scenarios introduced in chapter 4 include output projections for the services sector as a whole, and we need first to derive separate series for public administration and commerce. Between 1960 and 1975 the outputs of these two sectors grew at nearly the same rate; since 1975 the rate of growth of public administration has been about half that of commerce. This is largely a process of short-term adjustment, and we expect some recovery in public administration. Nevertheless, saturation in the long term is more likely in the latter sector than in commerce. The output series for the two sectors are summarised in table 9.3.

The implications for fuel use of these output series, together with the foregoing discussion on energy intensity and fuel shares, is shown in table 9.4. In absolute terms, energy use rises by between 5 and 37 per cent over the period 1980 to 2020, while the energy/output ratio falls by around 28 per cent. Electricity's share of delivered energy rises from 15 to 26 per cent. Gas remains the dominant fossil fuel, with a rising share of total fuel use. Coal use rises substantially, but still accounts for less than one-fifth of all fuel use in 2020.

Table 9.4.   *Projections of fuel use in public administration (delivered energy, PJ)*

Year	Solid fuels	Fuel oil	Gas oil[a]	Gas	Electricity	Total
1980	48.6	58.9	109.8	100.0	56.6	373.9
High economic growth:						
1990	52.9	47.0	92.5	110.6	73.2	376.2
2000	69.3	41.0	78.8	133.1	89.1	411.3
2010	80.7	39.5	75.5	144.9	114.5	455.1
2020	97.3	38.9	74.0	161.7	139.7	511.6
Central economic growth:						
1990	52.3	46.5	91.6	109.6	71.2	371.2
2000	66.7	39.4	75.8	128.1	85.7	395.7
2010	74.6	36.5	69.8	134.1	103.7	418.7
2020	86.5	34.6	65.8	143.8	116.0	446.7
Low economic growth:						
1990	50.9	45.3	89.2	106.6	70.5	362.5
2000	62.4	36.8	70.9	119.7	80.2	370.0
2010	67.0	32.8	62.7	120.5	93.2	376.2
2020	74.8	29.9	56.8	124.2	107.4	393.1

Note: [a] Including all oil products lighter than fuel oil.

9.3   Future energy use in the commercial and miscellaneous sector

Method

We adopt the same approach in this sector as was used for public administration, projecting the ratios of fuel use to sector output for space and water heating, cooking and specific electricity use. As before, energy use per employee is a more natural measure of energy efficiency than energy/output, and the latter ratio falls with increasing productivity quite independently of any technical energy conservation. The number of employees per unit output fell sharply up to about 1972, but since then the improvement has been much more gradual. On the basis of the period 1971 to 1981, we assume a future annual fall of 0.64 per cent.

Space and water heating

The procedure is the same as for the public administration sector. Improvements in the stock of commercial buildings are the main source of technical

Table 9.5. *Energy/output ratios in the commercial and miscellaneous sectors (PJ/unit output, with 1975 output scaled to unity)*

Year	Space and water heating	Cooking	Lighting etc.
1980	223	25.7	70.4
1985	210	24.1	70.9
1990	198	22.9	69.7
2000	176	20.8	63.2
2010	156	19.1	54.6
2020	138	17.5	46.3

conservation. Though the technical potential is probably similar to that in the public sector, there are several reasons to expect performance to be rather worse:

   (a) The commercial sector is fragmented, lacking any focus for conservation analogous to the Property Services Agency and therefore dependent on government publicity and market price signals.

   (b) Energy costs are small (around 3 per cent) in relation to total output, and there is widespread ignorance of energy-saving opportunities.

   (c) Much commercial property is leasehold, so that energy conservation investment is impeded by conflicts of interest between landlords and tenants.

In view of these obstacles, we assume only a 20 per cent fall in non-premium energy use per employee between 1980 and 2020. The detailed results are shown in table 9.5. The aggregate conservation appears to be large, but more than half of this is due to higher employee productivity.

The prospects for a return to coal use in this sector are very poor. The 1980 share of solid fuels in space and water heating energy was only 5 per cent, with no real sign of an upturn (see figure 9.2). Average boiler size is very low at about 3600 lbs steam/hour (Chesshire and Robson, 1983). We assume that the share for solid fuels rises, under the influence of favourable prices, to 12 per cent by 2020. The upward trend in the share of gas continues at the expense of both fuel oil and gas oil up to 2000, but is reversed towards the end of the period due to competition from electricity. Electricity had a 15 per cent share in this category of fuel use in 1980, and is clearly in a favourable position for further penetration; we assume that its share rises to 30 per cent by the end of the period.

Cooking

As in public administration, we assume that there is a 12 per cent fall in technical energy intensity for cooking, which is additional to the fall in energy/output due to increasing employee productivity. In this sector electricity already has a 45 per cent share in fuel use for cooking, and we assume that this increases to 55 per cent by the end of the period.

Lighting etc.

The rapid increase in electricity use per employee over the last two decades (some 6 per cent per annum) cannot provide a basis for long-term projections. As noted for public administration, there is substantial scope for conservation, even with stable long-term prices. Specific electricity uses accounted for about 22 per cent of energy use in 1980 (compared with 11 per cent in public administration), and probably more than 40 per cent of energy expenditure. This suggests that there should be a greater awareness of the need to use electricity efficiently than in other sectors. We assume that specific electricity use per employee rises up to 1990 and then falls, reaching 15 per cent below its 1980 value by 2020. Relative to output, of course, the fall is substantially greater.

Total fuel use

The output projections given in table 9.3 are combined with the energy intensities in table 9.5 and the foregoing discussion on fuel shares to produce the overall fuel use in the commercial and miscellaneous sector shown in table 9.6. Over the period as a whole, total energy use rises by between 13 and 74 per cent, corresponding to a fall in the energy/output ratio of 37 per cent, of which more than half is the result of increased output per employee. Electricity grows in importance, its share rising from 36 per cent in 1980 to 48 per cent in 2020. Gas remains the dominant fossil fuel; coal accounts for less than one-tenth of all energy use in 2020, while the share for oil products falls from 27 to 13 per cent over the period.

9.4   Future energy use in agriculture

We project energy use in agriculture by considering the three categories separately: mobile motive power, heaters and driers and electricity uses. In each case we postulate future trends in the ratio of energy use to output, and use the output series introduced in chapter 4 to infer the levels of fuel use.

All the energy/output ratios show a sharp fall in 1980 and 1981 (see figure

Table 9.6.   *Projections of fuel use in the commercial and miscellaneous sectors (delivered energy, PJ)*

Year	Solid fuels	Fuel oil	Gas oil[a]	Gas	Electricity	Total
1980	12.9	30.8	63.3	117.4	128.2	352.6
High economic growth:						
1990	19.8	27.9	57.7	129.4	152.1	386.9
2000	27.9	27.9	55.7	154.9	191.3	457.7
2010	38.1	27.2	54.4	173.8	241.0	534.5
2020	50.3	27.2	54.5	185.3	295.3	612.6
Central economic growth:						
1990	19.5	27.6	57.0	127.9	150.2	382.2
2000	26.5	26.5	52.9	147.1	181.6	434.6
2010	35.0	25.0	50.0	159.5	221.2	490.7
2020	44.6	24.2	48.4	164.4	262.2	543.8
Low economic growth:						
1990	18.0	25.5	52.6	118.0	138.9	353.0
2000	22.5	22.5	45.1	127.0	156.3	373.4
2010	27.6	19.7	39.4	125.7	174.3	368.7
2020	32.6	17.6	35.3	120.0	191.3	396.8

Note: [a] Including all oil products lighter than fuel oil.

9.5), and in the absence of a physical explanation for this it seems prudent to treat it as a transient effect. Instead of basing the projections on the absolute level of fuel use in these years, therefore, we fit a regression to each ratio over the period 1973 to 1981, and use the fitted 1980 value as a starting-point for projections.

For mobile motive power (all provided by gas/diesel oil), we assume a 30 per cent fall in the ratio of energy to output over the period 1980 to 2020. Part of this is the result of technical improvements in tractor efficiency, part the result of changed agricultural practice such as reduced cultivation or direct drilling methods.

Other fossil fuel uses, broadly characterised as 'heaters and driers', range from crop drying to greenhouse heating for horticulture. The requirement is often highly seasonal, and the resulting low load factor discourages capital investment. We assume a 20 per cent fall in energy intensity. In the early 1960s this end-use was dominated by fuel oil, but the share of gas oil increased to around 50 per cent by 1973 and has since remained fairly close to that figure. We assume a continuing 50:50 split between fuel oil and gas oil. The availability of

Table 9.7.   *Projections of fuel use in agriculture (delivered energy, PJ)*

Year	Fuel oil	Gas oil (heat)[a]	Gas oil (traction)[b]	Electricity	Total
1980	8.2	12.0	28.1	14.4	62.7
High economic growth:					
1990	12.0	12.0	33.1	16.0	73.1
2000	13.0	13.0	34.7	17.5	78.2
2010	13.8	13.8	35.7	19.0	82.3
2020	14.7	14.7	36.8	20.6	86.8
Central economic growth:					
1990	12.0	12.0	33.0	15.9	72.9
2000	12.9	12.9	34.4	17.3	77.5
2010	13.6	13.6	35.0	18.7	80.9
2020	14.3	14.3	35.8	20.0	84.4
Low economic growth:					
1990	11.9	11.9	32.8	15.9	72.5
2000	12.7	12.7	33.8	17.1	76.3
2010	13.3	13.3	34.2	18.2	79.0
2020	13.8	13.8	34.6	19.4	81.6

Notes: [a] Includes all fuels other than fuel oil used for heating, in particular a small
        amount of solid fuels (1.05 PJ in 1980).
     [b] Includes all fossil fuels used for mobile motive power.

gas for agriculture is severely limited by problems of distribution; LPG
(liquefied petroleum gases) use is included under the heading 'gas oil'.

The agricultural sector is unusual in that the electricity/output ratio is in
decline. We assume a further fall of 15 per cent between 1980 and 2020.

The implications of these assumptions for future fuel use are shown in table
9.7. The differences between the different economic growth scenarios is very
slight. In absolute terms, energy use rises by about 35 per cent over the period,
corresponding to a 14 per cent fall in the energy/output ratio. This low figure is
to some extent the result of the anomalously low fuel use in 1980; relative to a
1980 'trend' value the fall is about 24 per cent. Fuel shares remain generally
stable.

9.5   Technology and policy issues

Agriculture

Direct energy use in agriculture is a small element in the national energy scene,
though energy efficiency is clearly important to farmers themselves. Indirect

energy use in this sector (e.g. the energy embodied in fertilisers or machinery) is greater than direct energy use (see, for example, Leach, 1975). Savings of indirect energy, by improving machinery utilisation or reducing fertiliser inputs, are questions of agricultural economics which are beyond the scope of this study.

Energy efficiency in buildings

The techniques required for energy conservation in public and commercial buildings are generally straightforward and readily available. The work of the Property Services Agency in the public sector has already demonstrated that substantial savings can be achieved. Policy effort in this context needs therefore to be concentrated in two areas. First, owners and users of buildings need to be aware of both the cost of fuels and the opportunities for savings. Clear fuel price signals are very important, as are the decision-makers' criteria of cost-effectiveness. The latter are, of course, very much influenced by the economic environment as a whole (capital shortage, long-term economic viability for commercial firms etc.), and what to the energy analyst seems an unduly strict investment criterion may be wholly rational to the decision-maker himself. Second, institutional obstacles to conservation investment need to be considered. These include conflicts of interest between landlords and tenants, which at present often prevent the benefits of energy conservation from reaching the investor. In the longer term, the quality of the building stock, particularly its thermal performance and use of daylight, will be influenced by changes in the building regulations. These issues are discussed further in chapter 13, and are summarised in Select Committee on Energy, 1982.

Commercial and public buildings often provide a good opportunity for energy saving through electronic control systems, particularly for lighting control, and the control of heating systems to reflect more fully the external conditions and the pattern of occupancy of the building. The use of microprocessors can provide a useful monitoring service to inform managers about the patterns of energy use as well as permitting more sophisticated control. For further details, see Fisk, 1979 and 1981; and Crisp, 1983.

Small-scale CHP systems are sometimes recommended for public or commercial buildings (or groups of buildings), and these would certainly save energy. However, in view of the difficulties in implementing straightforward and cost-effective energy-saving measures, the prospects for small-scale CHP do not seem very promising in the short to medium term. In addition, the benefits of such schemes would be somewhat reduced if they replaced power station coal or nuclear fuel by gas or oil products.

Fuel switching

The fuel use projections for commercial and public buildings (tables 9.4 and 9.6) imply a continuing major role for gas, significant penetration of electricity into non-specific markets, a steady decline in the use of oil products and only modest growth in coal use. Prospects for coal in this sector are very limited. The small average boiler sizes have already been noted, and the absence on most sites of facilities to store and move coal is a further obstacle. Coal users would in general be dependent on small-scale deliveries by road, implying a higher delivered price than that for larger industrial users; furthermore the network of local coal merchants which existed when coal was the dominant fuel in final consumption is now too limited to support a major switch to coal.

Methods of transporting, storing and using coal which increase its resemblance to a liquid fuel may aid substitution. Coal/oil or coal/water mixtures may replace fuel oil in some circumstances, especially in larger establishments. These techniques are discussed more fully in chapter 7.

An alternative route away from short-lived fuels is through substitution to electricity as a heat source, and in the analysis we envisage significant progress in this direction. The anticipated relative prices of coal, gas and electricity (especially with a significant nuclear component) support this view. In addition, the often low capital cost of electric heating systems can do much to offset the higher running cost, especially in highly insulated buildings.

10

Electricity supply and nuclear power

10.1   The electricity supply industry

The electricity supply industry in England and Wales and Southern Scotland was brought under public ownership by the Electricity Act of 1947. Existing undertakings, which then numbered 560, were integrated into new statutory area Electricity Boards set up by the Minister of Fuel and Power. These boards, twelve in England and Wales and two in Southern Scotland, shared responsibility for the retail distribution of electricity for consumers. Generation and transmission on the main grid system became the responsibility of the British Electricity Authority. Also under the 1947 Act the North of Scotland Hydro-Electric Board (NSHEB), which had been formed in 1943, became responsible for all public generation, transmission and distribution throughout Northern Scotland. In 1955 the electricity supply in Southern Scotland was again re-organised with the formation of an autonomous body – the South of Scotland Electricity Board (SSEB) – which, unlike the Electricity Boards in England and Wales, was made responsible for generation and main transmission as well as distribution. At the same time, electricity supply in England and Wales became the responsibility of the Central Electricity Authority. The next step came with the 1957 Electricity Act which re-organised the industry in England and Wales to introduce greater decentralisation: the Central Electricity Authority was replaced by two new statutory bodies – the Electricity Council and the Central Electricity Generating Board (CEGB); in addition, the twelve Electricity Boards were given greater autonomy. For a review of the period 1947 to 1962, see Hannah, 1982.

The CEGB owns and operates the power stations and main transmission network, and is responsible for the bulk supply of electricity to the twelve Electricity Boards in England and Wales, for onward distribution to consumers. The CEGB is also responsible for the planning and construction of new generating and transmission capacity.

The Electricity Council, which includes representation from the CEGB and each Electricity Board, provides a forum where general policy of the electricity supply industry can be discussed and reviewed. In 1978/9 the Council stated its main corporative objective as: 'To maintain and develop supplies of electricity to meet the needs of customers in England and Wales on a continuing basis as cheaply as possible.'

In 1972 the Electricity Supply (Northern Ireland) Order set up a new structure for the electricity supply industry in Northern Ireland. The Northern Ireland Electricity Service (NIES) was established to take over the combined functions of the Northern Ireland Joint Electricity Authority, the Electricity Board for Northern Ireland and the electricity departments of the Belfast Corporation and the Londonderry Development Commission. Thus the NIES became responsible for generation, transmission and distribution of electricity to consumers throughout Northern Ireland.

During the 1970s there was considerable discussion, within the industry and in government, about further re-organisation with a view to strengthening the role of the Electricity Council so that it had greater control over general policy and planning, including some functions now carried out by the CEGB, and at the same time broadening the responsibilities of the Electricity Boards to include a role in electricity generation and transmission. Political uncertainty at the time, including disagreements between the industry and the political parties about some aspects of the proposed changes, prevented the re-organisation from taking place.

In 1983 a new Energy Act changed the conditions for the private generation and supply of electricity. The Act requires Electricity Boards to offer to purchase electricity from private generators or suppliers, to allow them to use the Boards' transmission system and to publish tariffs. It also extends the rights of private generators or suppliers to obtain supplies from an Electricity Board, either for their own use or their customers' use. The Act imposes a duty on the Boards to adopt and support CHP and similar schemes, provided any expenditure involved meets their normal financial criteria. It also gives statutory status to the Electricity Consumers' Council.

Up to this time (1983), in addition to the public supply, some 7 per cent of total electricity had been produced and used by industrial companies, often in the form of CHP. It seems unlikely that the new freedom to sell surplus electricity to other consumers on the public supply system will have more than a marginal effect.

The financial criteria under which the Electricity Boards operate may be illustrated by those for the CEGB. It is required at least to break even on its revenue account taking one year with another. It must fix its tariffs only after consulting the Electricity Council, and, again after consulting the Council, obtain the approval of the Secretary of State for Energy for its capital expenditure programme. The CEGB must also aim to control its costs and set the overall level of its tariffs to achieve whatever return on its assets the Secretary of State may require. Its current financial target is to achieve a trading profit representing a net return on its assets of 1.7 per cent per annum averaged over three years from 1980/1 to 1982/3 (this is based on the value of net assets in accordance with current cost accounting excluding work in progress and a working capital adjustment). The government also requires the electricity supply industry as a whole to work within specified external financing limits. These requirements are supplemented by criteria setting physical standards – electricity supply regulations under the Act require the Boards to maintain a supply of electricity sufficient for the use of all consumers entitled to be so supplied, and they specify narrow limits on permissible voltage and frequency variations.

Thus the CEGB's obligations to minimise electricity costs do not permit them the choice of particular supply systems or fuels to satisfy public preferences or general policy considerations. However, under the 1957 Act the Secretary of State may, after consulting the Electricity Council and the CEGB, give the Board directions of a general character which he considers to be in the national interest (no such directions have been made up to the time of writing). There are, of course, a variety of obligations on the CEGB concerning safety in their operations and protection of the environment.

Before constructing new generating plant, the CEGB must go through a number of planning procedures and obtain the necessary statutory and other consents. The latter include consent from the Secretary of State for Energy for the proposed station, and approval also for the financial expenditure involved. In the case of a nuclear station, the Board must receive also a site licence from the Health and Safety Executive. The process of obtaining consent involves discussions with a variety of statutory bodies, including local authorities, and it will normally involve an extended Public Inquiry chaired by an Inspector who then reports to the Secretary of State for Energy. Thus there is, inevitably, a long lead-time from the initial site search to commissioning, typically ten to twelve years. We shall consider the resulting problems when we discuss electricity planning in section 10.7.

10.2   The electricity supply system

England and Wales

At the end of March 1983, there were one hundred power stations in England and Wales operated by the CEGB, with total net capacity of nearly 55 GW (these and other statistics are from CEGB, 1983a). A summary of these stations and their output is given in table 10.1. The supply of electricity was dominated

Table 10.1 *Power stations and electricity supply in England and Wales, 1982-3*

Number of stations	Type of station	Net[a] generating capacity GW	Electricity supplied TWh	Average load factor[b] %
	Steam:			
57	coal	33.0	157.6	54.0
12	oil	10.1	7.0	8.0
1	coal and oil	0.2	0.6	30.0
1	coal or oil	1.9	7.7	46.0
2	coal or gas	1.6	4.6	32.0
73	Total steam	46.8	177.5	43.0
	Nuclear:			
8	Magnox	3.5	22.7	75.0
1	AGR[c]	1.0	6.4	70.0
9	Gas turbine	2.7	0.1	0.3
7	Hydro-electric	0.1	0.2	23.0
2	Pumped storage	0.6	⌈ 0.4 ⌊ −0.6	- -
100	Total	54.7	206.7	43.0

Notes:[a] Net of own use (GW sent out).

[b] Average load factor is the number of units supplied divided by the number of hours in the year times the net generating capacity.

[c] AGR = advanced gas-cooled reactor.

by coal-fired steam units, which produced 83 per cent of the total generated (50 per cent of the total was produced by only ten coal-fired stations). Nuclear power stations produced 11 per cent, with the remainder coming mainly from large oil-fired units.

The average load factor, based on declared net capability (see note b table 10.1), was 74 per cent for nuclear power stations, 53 per cent for coal-fired stations and 8 per cent for the large oil-fired stations, but only 0.3 per cent for gas turbines. These average load factors reflect the operating costs of the different types, which are dominated by fuel costs. These are relatively small for nuclear power, averaging 1.42 p/kWh, with total nuclear operating (works) costs of 1.75 p/kWh. For fossil fuel units, the average fuel cost in 1982/3 was 2.00 p/kWh giving total operating (works) costs of 2.31 p/kWh. Gas turbines using refined oil products would have cost about three times the average, and are used only for meeting peak demand.

The average thermal efficiency of all stations on the CEGB system in 1982/3 was 32.9 per cent; for fossil-fuelled stations alone it was 34.1 per cent. For the top twenty of the latter, the average was 35.6 per cent, with the highest (Rugeley B in the Midland region) operating at an average efficiency of 37.6 per cent. These figures may be compared with the historical values for average efficiencies of conventional thermal stations – only 17 per cent in 1932, and 22 per cent in 1952, reaching 31 per cent in 1972.

South of Scotland

The South of Scotland Electricity Board (SSEB) operated sixteen power stations in 1982/3 with net capacity totalling 6.3 GW (SSEB, 1983). This capacity was in excess of requirements (table 10.2) and corresponded to an average load factor of only 31 per cent. Thus the total effective capacity was reduced by placing 1.5 GW in indefinite storage. Of the remaining total of 4.8 GW, there was 1.3 GW of nuclear power (Hunterston A and B) but, because of its low running costs and its consequent high load factor, nuclear power provided 44 per cent of the total electricity generated.

North of Scotland

The North of Scotland Hydro-Electric Board (NSHEB) maintain and operate more than fifty hydro-electric power stations in the highlands and islands of Scotland (NSHEB, 1983). These range in size from a few megawatts to over 100 megawatts with a total capacity of 1.1 GW, and in addition there is 0.7 GW of pumped storage. The output from hydro-electric power is supplemented by fossil fuel stations with 1.3 GW operating at low load factor, and by purchases of electricity from the UKAEA (United Kingdom Atomic Energy Authority) and others. This left a small net surplus of 0.3 TWh in 1982/3 which was sold to the SSEB (table 10.2). In previous years there had been a substantial import from the SSEB averaging nearly 5 TWh per annum, but the recession (in particular the closure of the Invergordon aluminium smelter) meant that total demand on the NSHEB system fell by nearly 25 per cent between 1980 and 1983. Furthermore, supplies of cheap North Sea gas for the Peterhead power station reduced any need for imports.

Northern Ireland

The Northern Ireland Electricity Service (NIES) operates five main power stations and several transportable gas turbines (NIES, 1983). Its net capacity in 1982/3 was 2.3 GW. Nearly 90 per cent of this capacity is oil fired and, mainly as

Table 10.2. *Power stations and electricity supply in Scotland and Northern Ireland, 1982-3*

Board	Type of station	Net[a] generating capacity GW	Electricity supplied TWh	Average load factor[b] %
SSEB	*Steam:*			
	coal	4.1	9.5	26
	oil	0.6	0.3	6
	Nuclear	1.3	8.5	72
	Gas turbine	0.2	-	-
	Hydro-electric	0.1	0.3	31
	Total	6.3	19.3	35
	Net purchases[c]/ interchange		−0.1	
NSHEB	*Steam:*			
	oil and NGL[d]	1.2	2.9	26
	Gas/diesel	0.2	0.3	20
	Hydro-electric	1.8[e]	3.6	40[f]
	Total	3.2	3.5	32
	Net purchases[c]/ interchange		−0.2	
NIES	*Steam:*			
	coal	0.2	1.0	51
	oil	1.7	4.1	28
	Gas turbine	0.3	-	-
	Total	2.2	5.1	

Notes: [a] Net of own use (GW sent out).
[b] Average load factor is the number of units supplied divided by the number of hours in the year times the net generating capacity.
[c] Including purchases from the United Kingdom Atomic Energy Authority (UKAEA) and British Nuclear Fuels Ltd. (BNFL).
[d] Natural gas liquids.
[e] Including pumped storage 0.7 GW.
[f] Excluding pumped storage.

Table 10.3. *Main transmission lines, 1983*

	Operational voltage	Length in operation	
		Overhead	Underground
	kV	km	km
England and Wales:			
CEGB	400	5 088	126
	275	1 693	526
	132	241	202
	66[a] or less	37	30
Scotland:			
SSEB	400	336	nr[b]
	275	1 492	nr
	132	1 527	nr
	33 or less	17 426	nr
NSHEB	275 and 132	5 097	nr
Northern Ireland:			
NIES	275	400	3
	110	809	28

Notes:[a] Not including distribution lines operated by Electricity Boards not by the CEGE
[b] Not reported.

a result of this oil dependence, total electricity costs are about 20 per cent higher than in other regions of the UK; prices in 1982/3 were kept to the general UK level through a government subsidy of £54 million. The possibility of developing indigenous coal deposits or of importing coal from Scotland is currently under discussion. The NIES system is too small for nuclear power to be an economic option. The only remaining alternative would be an interconnection with one of the other UK Electricity Boards, though this may be ruled out on general security grounds.

Transmission and distribution

The main transmission systems operated by generating boards in the UK are based primarily on 400 kV and 275 kV overhead transmission lines. The lengths of line in operation in the four main systems are summarised in table 10.3. Many of these high voltage lines in the 'super-grid' system have been in operation for almost thirty years and a programme of refurbishment and renewal has recently been started. In addition research and development programmes are under way to introduce more advanced control systems, for example using computer-assisted scheduling of generating plant to meet variable consumer demand.

10.3   Nuclear power development

The initial development of nuclear power on a commercial scale in the UK was based on a programme of Magnox reactors. These are graphite-moderated and use carbon dioxide gas under pressure as coolant. Proposals in a government White Paper (Cmnd 9389, Ministry of Power, 1955) indicated a programme to introduce nuclear generation totalling between 1.5 GW and 2.0 GW over the next ten years. The programme was subsequently increased and by 1971 a total of 3.4 GW (declared net capability or DNC) was in service. This was less than the design capacity of 4.5 GW due to the need to limit corrosion of mild steel components in the reactors, but apart from this reduction and extended outages, due to technical problems at Dungeness and Bradwell, the Magnox reactors have generally achieved high load factors.

In 1964 the government announced a second nuclear power programme which would be based on the advanced gas-cooled reactor (AGR) (Cmnd 2335, Ministry of Power, 1964). Five AGR stations were ordered, four for the CEGB and one for the SSEB. Each consisted of twin reactor units of 600–625 MW output capacity. The resulting programme met severe delays, arising partly from design problems due to the large extrapolation from the 30 MW prototype and the dispersion of expertise between three different design companies, partly from the failure to clear all significant design and safety measures before the start of construction, and partly from management and labour problems on construction sites that were endemic to large-scale construction projects in the UK at that time. In their submissions for later nuclear development the CEGB take the view that these serious planning and management problems will be largely overcome by an increase in advance planning and by new types of site agreement with the labour unions involved. This view influenced the decision in 1979 to order two more AGR stations, one for the CEGB and one for the SSEB and construction experience to date (1983) on the two new sites has been favourable. This order replaced an earlier decision in 1974 to proceed instead with a 4 GW programme of steam-generating heavy water reactors (SGHWR) for which a prototype was in operation by the UKAEA; this is no longer considered a viable option. Nuclear stations ordered prior to 1983 are listed in table 10.4.

In 1978, Mr Tony Benn, Secretary of State for Energy in the Labour government, confirmed the cancellation of the short-lived SGHWR policy and

Table 10.4. *Nuclear power stations in the UK*

Station	Capability[a] MW	Type	Date of commissioning
Berkeley	276	Magnox	1962
Bradwell	245	Magnox	1962
Calder Hall	200	Magnox	1956
Chapelcross	200	Magnox	1959
Dounreay	250	FBR	1976
Dungeness A	410	Magnox	1965
Dungeness B	(1100)	AGR	1983
Hartlepool	(1100)	AGR	1983
Heysham I	(1100)	AGR	1983
Heysham II	(1255)	AGR	1988
Hinkley Point A	430	Magnox	1965
Hinkley Point B	1150	AGR	1976
Hunterston A	300	Magnox	1964
Hunterston B	1150	AGR	1976
Oldbury	434	Magnox	1967
Sizewell	420	Magnox	1966
Torness	(1240)	AGR	1987
Trawsfynydd	390	Magnox	1965
Winfrith	93	SGHWR	1968
Wylfa	840	Magnox	1971

Note: [a] Capabilities are shown net. Those in parentheses are provisional.
Source: National Nuclear Corporation and others, see the UK National Energy Data published by the World Energy Conference (1983).

stated a new policy of support for a dual programme using AGRs and PWRs (pressurised water reactors). The latter would be based on a design developed in the US and in use there and in other countries. This policy was endorsed in 1979 by Mr Benn's Conservative successor, Mr David Howell.

An introduction to the technical basis of nuclear energy is given in Eden et al. (1981), and Williams (1980) and Burn (1978) review its history.

The Sizewell Inquiry

During 1982 the CEGB applied for planning permission to construct a PWR nuclear power station at Sizewell on the coast about seventy miles north-east from London. Their application (CEGB, 1982) was referred by the Secretary of State for Energy to a Public Inquiry, chaired by an 'Inspector', a distinguished lawyer Sir Frank Layfield, who was aided by four Assessors covering economic questions, safety (engineering) and safety (radiation), and nuclear fuel transport. If approved, this would be the first PWR to be constructed in the UK so the Inquiry (still in progress at the time of writing) represents an important step in UK energy policy. The CEGB have based their case mainly on: (i) economic savings from the proposed power station, (ii) fuel diversity by displacing some need for fossil fuel in electricity generation and (iii) capacity needs – to replace plant that is to be retired and also to help meet any increase in demand. In addition they point to the benefit from creating an option for building future PWRs elsewhere in the UK, subject to the minister's approval in each case but not involving further assessment of a new reactor type.

It is this last point that most worries opponents of the Sizewell proposal – they fear that it will permit a major expansion of nuclear power based on the PWR. They question the estimates of costs made by the CEGB, and express doubts about other parameters such as future electricity demand. They also challenge the proposal on safety grounds and on environmental issues.

The Sizewell Inquiry is likely to last for two years, the Inspector's report is expected in the spring of 1985, with a final decision by the minister later that year. Thus, on the CEGB's central estimate of ninety months' construction time, if the proposal was approved the power station would not be in full operation before 1993. This is close to the onset of a period when major replacement of older power stations will be required. If the Sizewell PWR proposal is not approved, the CEGB would need to choose between a possible option of ordering further AGRs, provided site permissions can be obtained, or ordering new coal-fired power stations. The CEGB takes the view that these alternatives would be more costly than the PWR.

10.4   Electricity demand and supply

The long lead-times for planning and constructing power stations create formidable problems for planners. Up to 1965 the growth rate for electricity demand in the UK was very high, averaging nearly 8 per cent per annum over the previous fifteen years. For individual Electricity Boards the problem was to provide enough capacity to meet maximum demand. Over the period 1950–5 the maximum demand supplied on the CEGB system had to be restricted so that it fell below the estimated potential maximum demand in every year, with an average shortfall of 8 per cent. During the next five years, the maximum demand was met, but during the 1960s and into the early 1970s restrictions were again required in most years due to poor availability of the new 500 and 660 MW units.

By 1972–3 the CEGB had capacity with a gross capability of 61.1 GW, and net capability (after subtracting own works needs) of 56.4 GW. In that year the total electricity generated on CEGB plants was 221 TWh of which 205 TWh was available for supply. Net imports from the SSEB and EdF (Electricité de France) amounted to 3 TWh, transmission and distribution losses were nearly 17 TWh. Thus 191 TWh was supplied to customers. The total supplied from the other UK Electricity Boards in that year amounted to 30 TWh.

Already by 1973 there had been a marked reduction in the growth rate of electricity demand in the UK. The average of nearly 8 per cent per annum prior to 1965 fell to 5 per cent in 1965–70 and was slightly lower again in 1970–3. This change can be attributed primarily to the development of natural gas from the North Sea and its rapid penetration of premium heating markets where electricity had previously enjoyed considerable growth. After 1973 the shock to the energy market of a quadrupling of oil prices, coupled with low and erratic economic growth in the UK, led to a zero average growth rate for total electricity demand over the next ten years, a small rise up to 1979 being more than lost in the subsequent recession. The electricity intensity (total electricity demand divided by real GDP in 1975 pounds sterling) had increased from 4.8 MJ/£ in 1954 to 9.6 MJ/£ by 1970, but by 1982 it had fallen to 9.2 MJ/£.

The rapid growth in total electricity demand prior to 1973 was matched by similar growth in the estimated maximum demand potential (i.e. the maximum demand if no restrictions had been applied). In 1972/3 there were no such restrictions and, for the CEGB system, the maximum demand supplied was 40.64 GW, though it was a mild winter and under average conditions a maximum of 42.60 GW would have been expected. The system load factor was 58.3 per cent. This is defined as the total supply on the system averaged over the year and divided by the maximum demand. If average climatic conditions had prevailed the estimated system load factor would have been 55.7 per cent. The estimated system load factor under these conditions, and assuming no supply restrictions, had steadily increased from 43.8 per cent in 1950/1 to 55.7 per cent in 1972/3 and it reached 57.4 per cent in 1981/2.

The system load factor represents the average effect of variations or fluctuations in total demand for electricity. These are illustrated for 1982/3 in figure 10.1 which shows the variations in demand over each of four days (CEGB, 1983b). A typical winter day has an average electricity demand equal to about 1.5 times that for a typical summer day, but the peak demand amounts to more than four times the lowest demand.

It is evident that the total capacity required on the system would be less, and total electricity costs would be lower, if these wide variations in demand could be reduced. In the next section we shall discuss how this is encouraged by pricing and enhanced by technology. The reader will have noted that the figure given earlier for a net capability of 61.1 GW in the CEGB system in 1972/3 is 43 per cent greater than the estimated maximum demand for that year. This does not

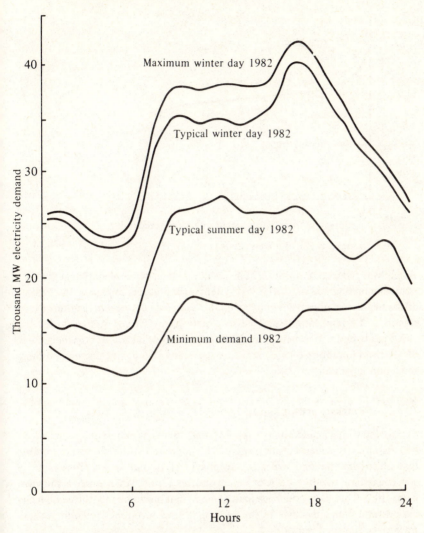

10.1 Summer and winter demands on the CEGB system

mean that the CEGB had a 43 per cent over-capacity as, in any supply system, a margin is required to ensure security of supply. In the CEGB the planning margin is currently set at a level which would be expected to result in disconnection through shortages of generating plant under climatic conditions corresponding to 3 or 4 winter peaks in 100. This leads to a planning margin of 28 per cent, and between 1972/3 and 1982/3 the excess capacity on the CEGB

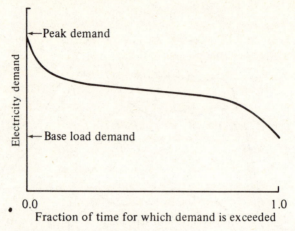

10.2 Example of load duration curve

system was reduced to this level. The resulting plant/demand margin at the time of maximum demand on the CEGB system is, in practice, much less than 28 per cent due to the non-availability of plant due to faults or on long-term cold standby. The implications of excess capacity in the CEGB system during the 1970s has been further considered by Evans (1981) who showed that the greater flexibility of operation due to excess capacity allowed a significant compensating reduction in running costs.

10.5   Electricity pricing and load control

The way in which an electricity supply system utilises its generation capacity can be illustrated by a load duration curve. This curve shows the proportion of time that electricity demand exceeds any given value, and such curves may be constructed for an entire year, or for any shorter period. An example is shown in figure 10.2. This shows the base load demand that has to be met throughout the period, and demands close to the peak that have to be met for only a small fraction of the total period.

An electricity system is operated at lowest cost by using plant that has the lowest running cost to meet the base load – in the case of the CEGB this is met as far as possible by nuclear plant, which is supplemented by the most efficient coal-fired steam plant. Successive blocks of demand, requiring successively shorter periods of operation, are met by plants chosen from the merit order so that those with the highest running costs are used only to meet demand near the peak. In the CEGB system this peak demand is met mainly by gas turbines, but is supplemented by pumped storage. The control of the system to provide electricity at least cost is computer-assisted and requires information on the operating costs and status of all plant – whether it is undergoing maintenance, usable but cold, ready to supply power or on load. It is also necessary to estimate short-term variations in demand (see figure 10.1, for example), using past experience, weather forecasts and knowledge of special circumstances such as television programme schedules. A spinning reserve must be maintained that is sufficient to cover the loss of (at least) the largest generator.

Electricity pricing was traditionally based on *average costs*. The tariff level was determined by the supply industry's financial targets and annual costs; the tariff structure is intended to ensure that each consumer pays his 'share' of the cost of supply in capacity costs and fuel used. Thus average cost pricing is related only to past expenditure and current average costs; future needs are ignored.

In recent years, *marginal cost* pricing has been introduced to overcome this defect, and it is applied in the UK as in most power utilities elsewhere (Turvey and Anderson, 1977; see also Berrie et al., 1983). In marginal cost pricing, past costs are of no significance, only uncommitted capital and running costs provide the current 'signal' to consumers making additional demands for electricity.

Marginal capacity-related charges (per kW) are determined mainly from the capital costs of installing new plant, or delaying the scrapping of old plant by increasing maintenance, to meet an increase in demand at the time of the system peak. With marginal cost pricing, capital charges on additional demand which occurs near times of peak demand are higher than those for off-peak demand. Marginal energy-related charges include fuel costs, plus the operating and maintenance costs of the system to meet an incremental kWh at any particular time and system location. Marginal consumer-related charges are for connections, metering and billing. Sales of electricity from the CEGB to the Electricity Boards of England and Wales are governed by the Bulk Supply Tariff (Electricity Council, 1983), which incorporates all the above elements.

In practice it is not feasible to operate marginal cost tariffs in full detail for final consumers. For example, at system peak they would be many times those at off-peak and it would be both costly and politically difficult to apply them widely to small users. Also, marginal cost tariffs do not guarantee that financial targets will be met, nor do they incorporate the consumer response to them – they are based on the past and on forecasts of current demand rather than on actual current demand. Marginal cost pricing is still the subject of considerable debate among economists.

One of the consequences of marginal cost tariffs is that they assist in *load management* by discouraging consumption at peak periods when electricity prices are high. Other aspects of load management involve special off-peak tariffs. However, their complexity, and the special metering involved, limit the application of the more sophisticated tariffs to large consumers.

Load management may also be introduced by direct physical control. In simple forms, this has existed for some years, for example by an automatic cut-out when a consumer's demand reaches a certain level. In more sophisticated forms using low-cost modern electronics this can be extended to interactive load control whereby three separate tariff options could be made available to consumers (Berrie et al., 1983):

(a) a continuous electricity supply charged at a high rate,
(b) a programmed interruptible (off-peak) rate,
(c) non-programmed interruptible (day and night) rates.

Consumers could have the facility to program their loads to a selected tariff and flexibility to vary the program. The supply system could communicate varying spot prices to the consumer, reflecting actual marginal costs at that time, and the information could lead to an appropriate response by the consumer's program and control system. By this type of approach to load management, it is expected that there will be a gradual but steady decline in the magnitude of peak demand compared to the average.

A general review of power system economics is found in Berrie (1983).

10.6   Power plant options

Base-load conventional thermal power

In order to assess the economic merits of different types of generating plant it is necessary to make estimates of capital cost, construction period, lifetime and availability of service, all of which are relevant to the overall value of the plant. The main options in the near future, for which a comparison of costs is important, are coal-fired plant and two types of nuclear plant – the AGR and the PWR. Central estimates by the CEGB of their capital costs, construction time, lifetime and availability are set out in table 10.5. Availability is shown both as an annual average and as an average during the winter peak period, since these affect system requirements in different ways. These estimates by the CEGB are based on experience with past power stations excluding some cases where there were special circumstances that delayed construction or increased costs in ways that are unlikely to be repeated (CEGB, 1982).

In addition to coal, AGR and PWR stations, which represent base-load options, there is a need for gas turbine plant, with low capital costs and high fuel costs, that can be brought quickly to full power to meet peak demand. There is also an option to convert existing oil-fired stations to coal-firing for base load. This is an expensive option, though its costs would be at least partly offset by savings on fuel costs and the siting of many oil-fired stations would permit the

Table 10.5. *New generating plant options: cost and performance estimates*

				Availability (%)	
Plant type and output[a]	Capital cost (1982 £ per kWso)	Construction period (months)	Life (years)	Average annual	Winter peak
Coal: 3 × 660 MW 1875 MWso	664	80	40	72	86
AGR: 2 × 660 MW 1230 MWso	1293	90	25	65	85
PWR: 1 × 1200 MW 1110 MWso	1033	90	35	64	81

Note: [a] Power sent out, excluding use by power station.

use of imported coal. Whether they would be fully offset or not would depend on future costs of coal and oil and on the amount of nuclear power in the system.

Alternative methods of electricity generation

The types of power station listed in table 10.5 are likely to provide the main options for electricity supply during the medium-term future. Other developments may become important in the longer term:

- *Advanced coal-fired plant* could involve gasification and the use of combined cycles to give higher conversion efficiencies, and/or atmospheric or pressurised fluidised bed techniques. These are unlikely to be economic compared with conventional plants unless environmental requirements on sulphur emissions become much more restrictive (Grainger and Gibson, 1981).
- *Combined heat and power (CHP)* is already widely used by private industry and its use may be extended by the 1983 Energy Act. A government study of CHP district heating development (the Marshall Study, Combined Heat and Power Group 1977 and 1979) concluded that its development could become economically worthwhile if fossil fuel prices were to rise substantially in real terms. However, the long lead-times for changing domestic heating systems on a wide scale mean

that CHP/district heating could not become substantial for several decades. On such a time-scale it is likely that energy conservation measures and improved design of dwellings will have reduced heat loads so that other methods still offer both lower costs and greater flexibility for domestic heating.

- *Nuclear fast breeder reactors (FBR)* are likely to be required in any long-term nuclear programme, as they use uranium much more efficiently than thermal reactors such as the AGR and PWR. The UK experimental FBR at Dounreay has established its viability, and a commercial prototype is under construction in France. However, the slow-down of the growth in world electricity demand and reduced orders for nuclear power plant have postponed, probably until beyond 2020, the time when uranium scarcity could necessitate the use of FBRs on a large scale. This need could be further delayed by the modification of conventional thermal reactors to give a higher uranium burn-up than with current systems.

- *Nuclear fusion* has almost been established on a laboratory scale as a potential source of energy. It seems unlikely that it will be available on a commercial scale before the middle of the twenty-first century. It might then be viewed as a preferred source of electricity to the FBR in view of the latter's use of plutonium and the associated risks, for example, of weapons proliferation. In the very long term nuclear fusion could provide an option available for many thousands of years using the vast quantities of energy stored by deuterium in the oceans. However, on that kind of time-scale, artificial photo-synthesis might provide fuels based on hydrogen and oxygen provided from water and sunlight.

Renewable sources of energy

The prospects for renewable energy sources in electricity generation are reviewed by Taylor (1983).

- *Windpower* is currently considered to be economic on hill-top sites, though these could meet environmental opposition. By the 1990s commercial prototypes for large-scale land-based wind 'farms' should be available, and they could be economic if the development of nuclear power was limited. Offshore wind farms would be more acceptable on environmental grounds, but the costs would be higher. As an order of magnitude, by 2020 the UK might have 5 per cent to 10 per cent of its electricity generated by the wind, or 20 to 40 TWh annually.

- *Wave-power* has been shown to be technically feasible on a small scale. Its large-scale development would require a costly programme and it is unlikely to proceed unless nuclear power is limited on policy grounds.

- *Tidal power* from a barrage in the Severn estuary is thought to be an economic investment if nuclear power is limited and the cost of generation from fossil fuels shows some increase. Such a scheme would take fifteen to twenty years to complete, so it could be in operation soon after the end of the century, giving 13 TWh per annum.
- *Geothermal* aquifers and hot rocks could provide pre-heated water for use in power stations, but the question of economic viability in the UK is unlikely to be answered before the 1990s.
- *Solar electricity* generated by photo-voltaic cells is unlikely to be an economic option in the UK in the foreseeable future.

10.7   Electricity investment planning

The objectives of the electricity supply industry include the provision of future supplies to meet expected consumer demand as cheaply as possible. Uncertainty about future levels of demand, and the long lead-times for construction of new power stations, means that the planning programmes must accept a risk of over-capacity if shortages are to be avoided. As we have already noted, there was over-capacity in the CEGB system during the 1970s, even though construction times for new (AGR) nuclear power stations proved to be much longer than had been expected. The excess capacity arose because growth rates for electricity demand of 5 per cent or more had been expected to continue, and new capacity would have been required to meet this additional demand. It is now generally expected that demand growth will be lower. The demand sector analyses presented in this study, which are based on a fuel price regime favourable to electricity and on fairly healthy long-term economic growth, indicate an annual rate of demand growth in the range 1.7 to 2.7 per cent; other studies have pointed to a growth rate of 1 per cent or less.

Even very low growth prospects, however, do not imply that no new power stations are required. Stations completed during the 1960s will be reaching the end of their useful lives in the 1990s – their maintenance costs will be increasing and their reliability will be falling – so replacements will be needed. The magnitude of this task can be seen from the fact that a total of 23 GW of plant was commissioned between 1960 and 1969 and 17 GW between 1970 and 1974. With an expected economic life of between twenty-five and forty years for each power station, it is clear that a major construction programme will be needed, with completions beginning in the 1990s, even if total electricity demand does not increase.

Even when additional capacity is not immediately required there may be an economic case for new station construction. For example, the increased cost of

Table 10.6. *Components of net effective cost (1982 £/kW per annum)*

	No new nuclear background	
	Sizewell B	Coal-fired station
Capital	91	52
Decommissioning	1	0
Other operating costs	10	9
Fuel costs	35	126
Savings from reduced use of other stations[a]	−230	−177
Total NEC	−93	10

Note: [a] Under a high nuclear background, the savings from reduced use of other stations would be smaller.

fuels, particularly oil, means that a new station with higher efficiency than some old stations, or using cheaper fuel, could provide a net economic gain even if it was not needed on capacity grounds. This has been put forward by the CEGB as one of the key arguments for constructing a PWR nuclear power station at Sizewell (CEGB, 1982). With their estimates of costs, they find that there would be a saving of fuel costs on the CEGB system, for a wide range of future scenarios, that would more than offset the costs of the nuclear power station – thus the 'net effective cost' (NEC) would be negative.

The NEC depends on the 'background' assumed, namely other stations in the CEGB system, including future stations (as well as on other parameters). The resulting NEC if no other new nuclear stations are built is shown in table 10.6.

The CEGB also pointed to the value of opening up the option to build future PWR stations as a result of going ahead with one such station at Sizewell. They did not themselves seek to quantify the economic benefit of this future option, but one approach to such an assessment was provided by the work of Evans (1984; see also Evans and Hope, 1984). This evaluated the net decision benefit (NDB) to the CEGB system as a whole, using a decision tree analysis with probability distributions for each uncertain variable. Due to the uncertainties, in general the decision tree will not be symmetric – it will be skewed in favour of building a first station. If this proves to be uneconomic, no further stations of that type would be built. However, if it is economic, and gives a net financial saving, further stations could be built, each of which would also give a net gain. Thus the downside risk would be limited to a loss on one station whilst the upside benefit would accrue from a sequence of similar stations. The results from an analysis of the NDB, like those for the NEC, are of course dependent on the input assumptions about costs, future electricity needs etc.

Modelling future options

The calculation of the NEC of a new power station is evaluated by means of a system planning model, based on a linear program to minimise future system costs discounted back to present-day values. The objective function to be minimised includes the following elements:

- capital costs for each type of plant, annuitised with an appropriate discount rate;
- fuel costs, taking account of fuel prices, plant efficiencies, power generated and the duration of operation;
- non-fuel running costs including operating costs and maintenance charges.

The total system costs are minimised subject to a number of constraints including:

- power demand must be met at all points of the load duration curve;
- plant availability for each type and vintage of plant is reduced below full capacity by an 'availability' factor to allow for outages, maintenance etc.;
- system security: the available system capacity is required to exceed the expected peak demand by some fraction – the planning margin;
- capacity construction: the rate of construction of new capacity is limited and allowance must be made for lead-times.

Input data for the model include information on the age and type of existing plant on the system, using past experience to indicate how availability of older plant declines and maintenance costs increase with age.

The model evaluates system running costs by simulating its actual operation, with plant brought into production in a 'merit order', the plant with lowest running costs first, and including successively higher-cost plant until the required level of power demand is met. The resulting running costs are combined with the capital costs of plant to be constructed to give the objective function for total system costs that needs to be minimised.

The need for fuel diversity may provide an additional constraint. Each type of plant carries its own risks for future 'unexpected' changes in costs – notably illustrated for fossil fuels by the rise in oil prices – and future environmental controls on sulphur emissions could lead to new costs in fossil fuel plants. Similarly, public anxiety about nuclear power has led to increased costs in

Table 10.7   *UK public electricity supply 1980-2010: Department of Energy (1982) Scenario BL*

	1980	1990	2000	2010
GDP index	100	113	136	159
Electricity demand[a] (TWh)	231	248	285	324
Generating capacity (GW)	68	73	79	86
New capacity commissioned during ten-year periods (GW)		16	15	41
Of which new nuclear plant for a least-cost system (GW)		6	10	22
Giving total nuclear capacity (GW)	6	11	18	35

Note: [a] Net of distribution losses.

construction and control systems to meet more rigorous safety requirements. Alternatively, excessive dependence on coal-fired plant may lead to a substantial need for coal imports whose costs would be found to vary in the future (as with all traded commodities).

10.8   Meeting future electricity needs

In their evidence to the Sizewell Inquiry (Department of Energy, 1982), the Department of Energy have provided estimates of future capacity requirements for UK electricity generation for a variety of scenarios. They also give results on the types of plant to meet these requirements that were derived on a least-cost basis (i.e. not taking account of possible policy choices, and assuming that future costs are known). Their projections are summarised in table 10.7 for one of their scenarios (BL) which is towards the lower end of their four 'middle' scenarios. This scenario assumes economic growth that averages 1.6 per cent per annum over the period 1980–2010. The corresponding growth in electricity demand averages 1.1 per cent per annum over the same period.

   Our own projections for UK electricity demand are summarised in table 10.8 and our estimates for the associated electricity capacity are given in table 10.9. We have also shown alternative projections for nuclear power capacity.

   It will be noted that the demand projections arising from this study are significantly higher than those given by the Department of Energy. They reflect an average growth rate of about 0.4 per cent per annum in the electricity/GDP

Table 10.8.   *Authors' projections for UK electricity demand*

	1980	2000	2020
Low growth:			
GDP index	100	121	154
Electricity demand[a] TWh	231	331	452
Central growth:			
GDP index	100	142	209
Electricity demand[a] TWh	231	371	577
High growth:			
GDP index	100	153	248
Electricity demand[a] TWh	231	386	666

Note: [a] Net of distribution losses.

Table 10.9.   *Authors' estimates of UK electricity capacity requirements (public supply)*

	1980	2000	2020
Total generating capacity GW[a]:			
Low growth	68	85	113
Central growth	68	96	144
High growth	68	100	166
Of which total nuclear GW:			
Low nuclear case			
Low growth	6	10	17
Central growth	6	10	22
High growth	6	10	26
High nuclear case			
Low growth	6	13	38
Central growth	6	15	48
High growth	6	15	55

Note: [a] Based on 28 per cent planning margin.

ratio compared with −0.4 per cent for the Department's scenario BL. This difference arises for two reasons:

(a) In view of the fairly stable outlook for electricity prices created by the growing proportion of electricity produced by nuclear stations, we have been somewhat cautious in our assumptions on the degree of conservation likely to be achieved in the main uses of electricity, motive power and lighting.

(b) We see a growing role for electricity as a heat fuel, particularly in the early years of the next century, as gas prices rise towards parity with coal-based SNG (substitute natural gas).

The considerable uncertainty of forecast electricity demands (which is discussed in more detail in chapter 14, particularly sections 14.8 and 14.9) illustrates the difficulty of planning in an industry where plant life and construction time may together approach half a century.

A key issue for the electricity supply system is the future role of nuclear energy. Up to around the end of the century, there is little scope for expansion. The existing Magnox stations will have been retired by 2000, but some 8 GW of AGR capacity should be operational. An additional tranche of PWRs may be coming into use at that time (depending on the outcome of the Sizewell Inquiry), and total capacity in 2000 is likely to be between 10 and 17 GW (Evans, 1983). Beyond the end of the century the constraints are much less certain; with high growth in electricity demand, nuclear capacity in 2020 could be 60 GW or higher. In the high nuclear variant (which is the main case considered in the discussion of the UK energy outlook in chapter 14), we assume a positive outcome to the Sizewell Inquiry and a substantial, though by no means extreme, follow-on programme. The capacity growth in the first two decades of the next century is at most 2 GW per year, somewhat less than the commissioning rates achieved for fossil fuel fired plant in the 1960s and early 1970s. In this case by 2020 nuclear energy would account for some 43 per cent of electricity output. The low nuclear variant is consistent with a negative outcome of the Sizewell Inquiry or substantial delays in the follow-on programme, and for this the nuclear energy contribution to electricity in 2020 amounts to only 20 per cent.

Most of the rest of electricity generation will be coal-based. As a proportion of capacity (see table 10.9), this appears larger than its relative contribution to output, because the shape of the load duration curve (figure 10.2) leads to a lower load factor for fossil fuel fired plant than for nuclear plant. The contribution from oil-fired plant is likely to fall rapidly, though a small quantity of oil will be required for start-up in coal-fired stations and for gas turbine use.

Refinery economics may also lead to the availability of some very heavy fuel oil at low prices.

As noted earlier, the contribution from renewable sources and CHP/district heating is unlikely to be large over this time-scale. If the high levels of demand projected in this study are realised, however, it is probable that nuclear capacity will, for most of the period, be constrained below its value in a least-cost system. In this situation it may well be proper to assess the economics of renewable electricity sources against new coal plant rather than against nuclear power.

10.9   Environmental and social factors

The generation and use of electricity, like all forms of energy, has environmental and social consequences which may well be relevant to energy policy questions. Generation from oil or coal involves air pollution, particularly from sulphur dioxide, which has been blamed for 'acid rain' in Germany and Scandinavia. In addition, the release of carbon dioxide in the combustion process is believed by many analysts to pose a threat to the stability of the world climate by raising average global temperatures. To these problems must be added the possible safety, health and ecological hazards associated with the extraction and transport of oil and coal. Since all these environmental issues are common to all uses of the fuels concerned, they are discussed further in chapters 11 and 12.

For the electricity supply system, the reduction of sulphur emissions (which may be necessary if regulations currently being considered by the EEC (European Economic Community) become law) is not technically difficult, but will make a significant difference to the cost of fossil fuel based electricity.

Unique to electricity are the possible environmental and social problems associated with nuclear energy. A detailed treatment is beyond the scope of this study, and the reader is referred to Roberts (1984), Cottrell (1981), Flowers (1976) and NEPSG (1977). In brief, possible hazards arise in four main areas:

(a) Radiological risks from the normal operation of reactors or fuel reprocessing plants. This is unlikely to be a major problem, though the biological effects of low levels of radiation are not well understood.
(b) Risks from larger releases of active material through accidents in reactors or fuel reprocessing plants. Here the key issues are the probability of an accident of given severity and the subsequent dispersal of the active material; the overall technical risk appears to be small (certainly much smaller than other risks which we accept as a matter of routine) but uncertain. The magnitude of the consequences

of a major accident are such as to cause public concern despite their low probability.

(c) Hazards, to man or to the environment in general, from the disposal of radioactive waste products, including those from spent nuclear fuel. Once again, the quantified risks appear small, though the absence of a generally accepted route for ultimate waste disposal remains a matter of concern.

(d) The diversion of fissile material, by governments or subversive groups, for use in nuclear weapon development. The main focus of concern is plutonium; extensive use would be made of this material in an electricity supply system with a large capacity of fast breeder reactors, though it should be noted that this hazard is still present in a system using only thermal reactors. Many technical and legal mechanisms to reduce this risk are feasible, though it necessarily remains unquantifiable.

From a technical viewpoint, the risks from nuclear power do not appear to be a major obstacle to its development when they are compared with risks from other energy sources or other activities. Nevertheless, public concern on nuclear energy is a real factor limiting its future role. One effect of the debate has been to increase the cost of nuclear energy, both by increased plant complexity and delayed construction. Furthermore, it should be recognised that the widespread rejection of the nuclear option, on a world scale, itself incurs political risk through the increased pressure on other fuels.

10.10   Policy issues

Electricity and the primary energy sources which provide it are often prominent in debates on energy policy. Some commentators wish to minimise the future role of electricity, on the grounds of its low efficiency of generation. Against this view, however, it can be argued that electricity provides the only large-scale avenue for the use of nuclear energy and many of the renewable energy sources. In this study we have allowed market forces to dictate the level of electricity demand, and the resulting projections, though necessarily very uncertain, suggest healthy demand growth.

The future of electricity demand is very dependent on the role of nuclear energy. The cost of nuclear power in the UK remains uncertain due to the long period since the last power stations were commissioned. Fears are still expressed by some over the safety of nuclear energy, possible health hazards and connections with nuclear weapons, and these fears may constrain the deployment of the technology or increase its cost. However, failure to make use of the nuclear option would significantly increase the UK's long-term imports of coal and/or gas. A related issue is the viability of the UK nuclear industry itself. Here we need to ask whether the high cost of nuclear power stations in the UK is linked to the low ordering rate (compare the situation in France), and whether it is appropriate for the UK (which in 2000 is likely to have less than 3 per cent of the total nuclear capacity outside the CPE) to support an independent nuclear industry.

The renewable energy sources, especially wind, tides and waves, are often cited as keys to the future of electricity supply. Our studies suggest, however, that they will be of very limited importance over the next forty years. Nevertheless, development work on these options is clearly justified as an insurance against possible constraints on the contribution from nuclear energy. Furthermore, introduction of these sources into the supply system at a time when nuclear capacity is below its optimum level is likely to improve their relative economics significantly.

The projections of electricity demand which arise from this study imply a continuing major role for coal in electricity generation, to the extent that substantial coal imports are necessary. This suggests that, in the long term, the coal industry should not regard nuclear energy or coal imports as a threat to its own markets.

From a macroeconomic viewpoint, electricity is characterised by its high use of capital, almost all of which is consumed, for a given power station, before any electricity is produced. This is especially true of nuclear energy and the renewable energy sources, where capital is the major element in total costs. The impact of this on the capital market could lead to difficulties unless care is taken to avoid excessively uneven investment requirements by smoothly spreading orders for power stations over time.

11

Oil and gas supply

11.1   History

In 1850 Dr James Young, a Scottish chemist, devised a process by which paraffin-wax, kerosene, and lubricating oil could be obtained from a natural oil which flowed into the workings of a Derbyshire coal-mine, and soon afterwards the technique of boiling off the volatile constituents of the crude oil was sufficiently developed to obtain petrol. A quarter of a centry later, in 1875, Otto constructed his first petrol-motor; ten years later Benz inaugurated the era of motor vehicles by fitting Otto's motor into a car. (From *Power Production* by Hans Thirring, 1954.)

Dr Young's discovery continued to provide liquids from coal, and later in the nineteenth century a substantial oil-shale industry developed in Scotland. However, this indigenous oil production dwindled in the twentieth century under the impact of cheap oil imports. The volume of imported oil was still only 9.5 million tonnes in 1950, but by 1960 it was 45 million tonnes and it reached 102 million tonnes by 1970 (Department of Energy, 1983a and earlier editions). Similarly, through the early 1960s a small amount of indigenously produced natural gas (in the form of colliery methane) was augmented by a growing volume of imported gas.

At this time, exploration for gas was in progress in the southern sector of the North Sea. Figure 11.1 shows the agreed boundaries of the UK Continental Shelf (UKCS), with oil and gas fields in production at the end of 1982 (the 'Brown Book', Department of Energy, 1983b). Gas was discovered in the West Sole field in 1965, and several further substantial discoveries were made in the following years. Production started in 1967, and rose rapidly, reaching 432 PJ (10 MTOE) by 1970 and 1570 PJ (38 MTOE) by 1977. By this time, supplies from the southern sector were being augmented by supplies from the more difficult northern sector of the North Sea including imports from the Norwegian part of the Frigg field; by 1982 the northern sector accounted for 28 per cent of

○ Oil fields in production

× Gas fields in production

Thistle Murchison
Dunlin Statfjord
Cormorant Brent
Heather Ninian
×Frigg
Beryl
Norway
Claymore Piper
Buchan Tartan
Beatrice
Montrose○ ○Forties
Fulmar
Auk
Argyll
Denmark
Germany
Holland
Rough
West Sole
Viking
Indefatigable
Hewett
Leman Bank
France

11.1 The UK Continental Shelf: oil and gas fields in production at end of 1982

total production. Figure 11.2 shows the output of gas from each field up to 1982. Note the rapid rise in total output as production was started in successive southern sector fields. This presented the British Gas Corporation (BGC) with considerable marketing problems, which were solved by maintaining low gas prices, especially for industrial users on interruptible tariffs. Note also that all the southern sector fields (West Sole to Rough) have passed their production peak.

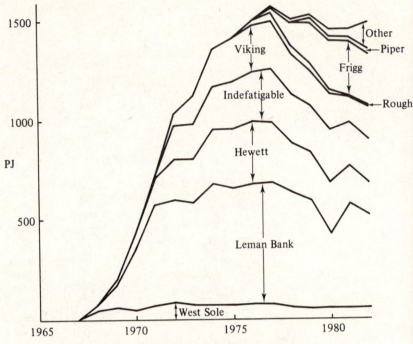

11.2 Gas production from the UK Continental Shelf, 1967–82

Almost all the fields in the southern sector of the North Sea produce only gas. By contrast, most fields in the northern sector produce oil, with associated gas (i.e. gas originally dissolved in the oil, but released from it at atmospheric pressure) as a by-product. The first oil discovery in this sector was the Montrose field in 1969, and this was followed by an accelerating series of discoveries reaching a peak in 1975. Since that date the discovery rate has been slower, though 1981 and 1982 showed a sharp increase over earlier years. For each field in which production has not been deferred for economic reasons, the interval from discovery to production has been around four to six years, with peak production obtained in most cases from two to four years after start-up. Figure 11.3 shows total offshore crude oil production since 1974, classified by year of production start-up in the fields concerned. It will be noted that a production plateau has been reached in most fields brought into production before 1978, so that further expansion depends on the exploitation of new fields. The drop in output from some fields in 1980 and 1981 is probably due to the weak market for oil rather than to resource depletion.

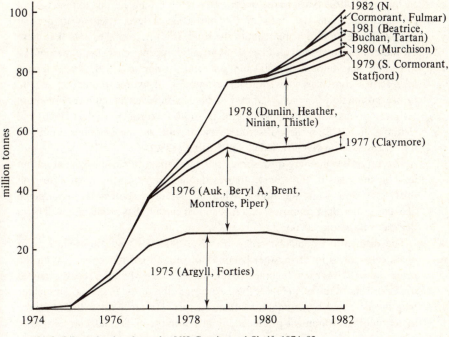

11.3 Oil production from the UK Continental Shelf, 1974–82

11.2 Oil and gas reserves

The discussion of oil and gas reserves is often confused by semantic problems. In this study, we adopt the conventions used in the Brown Book. *Proven reserves* are those which, on the available evidence, are virtually certain to be technically and economically producible; *probable reserves* are those which are estimated to have better than a 50 per cent chance of being technically and economically producible; and *possible reserves* are those which at present are estimated to have a significant but less than 50 per cent chance of being technically and economically producible. These definitions are not free from ambiguity. 'Technically and economically producible' is probably intended to mean producible with the technology available, and under the economic conditions prevailing, at the time of production, which is clearly subject to a great deal of uncertainty. Furthermore, the interpretation placed on the word 'significant' in the definition of possible reserves has a considerable effect on the numerical value obtained.

With these provisos on the terminology, the 1983 Brown Book quotes total proven, probable and possible oil reserves originally recoverable from the UKCS as 2000 to 4200 million tonnes, of which 457 million tonnes had been used by the end of 1982. Most of the uncertainty in this estimate is due to reserves not yet discovered; on the basis of the mid-range values, reserves in present discoveries amount to 62 per cent of the total. It is interesting to note that these estimates of reserves have shown a slight fall in recent years (the upper end of the range was quoted as 4500 million tonnes prior to 1979). These figures represent a consensus view, but the estimation of hydrocarbon reserves and future production is a complex and at times controversial subject. For more technical discussion, the reader is referred to MIT World Oil Project (1976) and Eckbo et al. (1978), while a dissenting view, favouring a more optimistic outlook for oil reserves, is given in Odell and Rosing (1980).

The ratio of remaining oil reserves (all categories) to current annual output lies, on the basis of the reserve figures quoted above, in the range fifteen to thirty-six years. Thus the notional life of UK oil resources is measured in decades rather than centuries, and it is almost certain that production will be in decline well before 2020.

The distinction should be noted between 'reserves' and 'oil-in-place'. For technical reasons involving the dynamics of oil and gas movement within the reservoir rock, it is usual (averaged over the world as a whole) to recover only 25 to 30 per cent of the oil in place; this is known as the recovery factor. This factor may be increased by a range of enhanced recovery techniques, including the injection of gas (often gas produced initially with the oil and difficult to dispose of usefully), the injection of water, the injection of organic solvents, the fracturing of the reservoir rock and partial combustion. Some of these techniques are very expensive, but the simpler methods, such as water injection and gas injection, are already in use in the North Sea, leading to a higher recovery factor. Reserves are the product of oil-in-place and the recovery factor, and reserve estimates take into account anticipated improvements in the recovery factor. Note that the recovery factor is also influenced by the rate at which an oil pool is exploited; too rapid exploitation will reduce the total amount of oil which can be recovered.

We use the same definitions for gas reserves as for oil reserves. The 1983 Brown Book gives a range of 1450–2125 billion m^3 (57 to 83 EJ or 1350 to 1979 MTOE) for proven, probable and possible reserves originally recoverable from the UK Continental Shelf, of which 430 billion m^3 have been used. Most of these reserves are already discovered. Dry gas (which is produced without oil and is gaseous at atmospheric pressure) predominates, but there are also significant quantities of gas condensate (heavier compounds which are liquid at atmospheric pressure) and gas directly associated with oil production. The remaining reserves represent 26 to 43 years of use at the maximum rate of consumption so far recorded (in 1977) so that the notional life of UK natural gas resources is similar to (or slightly greater than) that of UK oil.

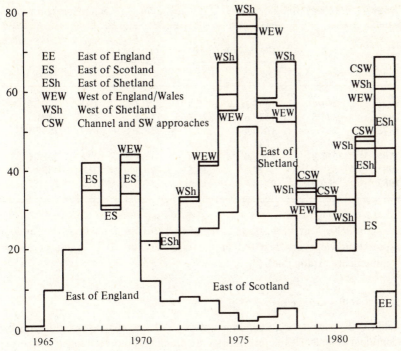

11.4 Exploration wells drilled in the UK Continental Shelf (number per year)

11.3 Exploration

In contrast to the UK coal industry, the exploitation of the UK's oil and gas is in the hands of a large number of private companies based in the UK and abroad. Government control is exercised through the issuing of licences for exploration and production, and the government seeks to obtain revenues from the oil and gas through royalties and taxation and (in the case of gas) via the BGC.

Up to 1983, there had been eight rounds of licensing. The first four were very large, but in later rounds an approach of more frequent licensing of smaller total areas has been adopted; this is intended to achieve stable investment and activity profiles and to optimise the use of human resources.

The number of exploration wells drilled is shown for major areas of the UKCS in figure 11.4. Exploration east of England (i.e. in the southern sector of the North Sea) was concentrated in the late 1960s; it has recently been recommenced in response to more favourable fiscal and gas pricing arrangements. Most exploration through the 1970s was east of Scotland or Shetland, with a small amount in areas to the west of Great Britain. Exploration activity fell in

Table 11.1   *Expenditure on the UK Continental Shelf (£ Million current values)*

Year	Exploration	Development		Operating		Total
		Oil	Gas	Oil	Gas	
1976	301.4	1507.1	373.5	81.3	48.5	2311.8
1977	374.8	1555.6	344.3	158.9	47.7	2481.3
1978	261.2	1690.4	282.9	258.2	87.7	2580.4
1979	240.8	1841.1	191.3	426.6	92.7	2792.5
1980	378.8	2163.0	216.8	618.5	107.5	3484.6
1981	550.2	2477.0	279.5	928.8	124.0	4359.5
1982	860.9	2348.4	612.5	1175.2	162.5	5159.5

the late 1970s, but now shows a rising trend. Thus far, about one in four exploration wells has resulted in the discovery of oil or gas (not always commercially exploitable).

11.4   Oil and gas costs

Table 11.1 shows total recent expenditure by the companies operating on the Continental Shelf. Development costs are dominant, representing in this period the extensive investment in the northern sector of the North Sea. These proportions will, of course, change with time; in the early years, exploration costs will be dominant, with development and operating costs taking an increasing share as oil or gas fields are discovered and developed. Total expenditure, though rising in nominal terms, is more nearly constant in real terms.

The overall cost of North Sea oil is quoted in the 1983 Brown Book as about $12/barrel for fields already in production, and $17/barrel for fields under development (in 1982 terms). This includes exploration, development and operation costs, but excludes royalties, taxes and abortive exploration costs not attributable to individual fields. Though these costs are very much less than world oil prices, there is wide variation between costs in different fields, and the government take is substantial.

The cost of gas to the BGC (after the payment of taxes by the producers) is indicated approximately by the overall cost of prime materials (i.e. purchased gas, oil or coal) per unit of gas sold, shown in figure 11.5 (British Gas Corporation, 1981 and earlier editions; this includes some coal prior to 1975, and is slightly distorted by conversion losses in the small part of gas supply which is manufactured from other fuels). Southern sector costs are very much lower

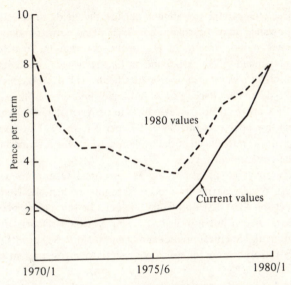

11.5 Cost of prime materials to the British Gas Corporation (per unit of gas sold)

than those for the northern sector, and the introduction of northern sector gas in 1977 (see figure 11.2) led to more than a doubling in the real cost of gas between 1976/7 and 1980/1. The 1980/1 cost was 7.87 p/therm (74.6 p/GJ), approximately equivalent to $11/barrel.

11.5   Institutional structures and taxation

The fiscal environment within which companies active on the Continental Shelf operate is complex and has developed piecemeal over a period of considerable uncertainty. For a detailed discussion, see MacKay and Mackay (1975), Noreng (1980) and Kemp and Rose (1983). Payments to the government arise in (at present) four ways.

Licence fees and royalties accounted for 21 per cent of the total government take in 1982/3. Royalties – the major element – are assessed for most current licences as 12.5 per cent of market value, though no royalties are charged for fields receiving development consent from 1982/3 onwards.

Petroleum revenue tax (PRT) is a tax on profits, designed to create revenues on a larger scale, and earlier, than is possible through corporation tax. The tax is assessed on a field by field basis (so that losses in one field cannot be used to offset profits in another). Operating and capital costs may be offset against revenue; capital costs increased by up to 75 per cent (35 per cent since 1979) to cover interest, which cannot be deducted explicitly. Some allowance may also be made for unsuccessful capital investment outside the fields in question. In addition, an allowance may be made, for each field, corresponding to the market value of 1 million tonnes of production per year up to a total of 10 million tonnes (changed to 5 million tonnes in 1982 but since restored); this is designed to encourage investment in the smaller fields. The overall effect of these deductions is to delay the effective onset of the tax until several years into the field's life. The rate at which PRT is levied was initially set at 45 per cent of profits, and this rose to 60 per cent in 1979 and 70 per cent in 1980. A further increase to 75 per cent was introduced at the beginning of 1983. PRT amounted to 42 per cent of the government take in 1982/3.

Corporation tax is payable at a rate of 52 per cent. Operating costs, depreciation, interest, royalty payments and PRT are fully deductible. Deficits from offshore projects on the UK Continental Shelf can be set against income from other offshore projects, but not against onshore income. Deficits from outside the UK Continental Shelf cannot be set off against North Sea profits (the so-called 'ring fence'). Corporation tax was 6 per cent of total government take in 1982/3.

The 1981 Finance Act introduced a temporary fourth tax, the supplementary petroleum duty (SPD). This was levied at a rate of 20 per cent of the value of the oil and gas produced, and accounted for 31 per cent of the government take in 1982/3. It was replaced at the beginning of 1983 by a system of advanced payment PRT (APRT) with generally similar provisions, and allowable in full against PRT itself. APRT has been opposed by the oil companies, who have argued that it discourages the development of marginal fields, and following the 1983 budget it is to be phased out over a four-year period.

The tax structure outlined above is generally recognised as over-complex and unclear in its effects. The aims of the tax regime should be to create revenue for the government, to encourage commercial participation in the UKCS (particularly for marginal fields), and to prevent losses made elsewhere from being set against UKCS profits. A reasonable degree of stability in tax structure and rates is desirable if taxation is not to add to the already substantial uncertainties faced by operating companies. Some tension between the government and operating companies on the split of oil revenues is inevitable, but there is also considerable common interest, and it is to be hoped that oil companies and the government can cooperate to evolve a simpler and more effective system. The machinery for such cooperation exists, and recent tax changes suggest that it can work effectively.

In addition to direct taxation of oil companies, the UK government has been involved in North Sea oil through the state-owned British National Oil Corporation (BNOC). Established in 1975, BNOC was granted from 1976 the right to purchase up to 51 per cent of all oil production at market prices. From the sixth licensing round in 1978, BNOC was given an equity share greater than 51 per cent in all new developments. BNOC revenues were paid straight into a Treasury account, along with oil revenues from other companies, and BNOC expenditures were financed directly from this account. These arrangements placed BNOC in a somewhat ambivalent position, as the other oil companies did not know whether to regard BNOC as a commercial rival or as an agent of the government. Furthermore, it was not clear that there was equitable treatment between BNOC and private companies in, for example, access to capital funding. In 1982, the exploration and development interests of BNOC were denationalised to become Britoil (a sale which was less successful as a fund-raising exercise than it might have been owing to the depressed state of the oil market at that time).

As a result of the 1975 Petroleum and Submarine Pipelines Act and the 1976 Energy Act, the UK government has extensive rights to control the level of production from established oil or gas fields. This is not welcomed by the operating companies, for whom it represents an additional economic risk. Recognising these problems, the then Labour government issued at the end of 1974 the 'Varley Guidelines' (quoted in the 1975 Brown Book) which limited any delays or production cutbacks, particularly on fields discovered before the end of 1975. Commitment to these guidelines was reaffirmed in 1980, though with the declared intention of making use of the greater flexibility implied by the guidelines for fields discovered after 1975, and for most earlier fields from 1982.

The taxation position is also complex for UK gas. For dry or associated gas in the northern sector, the tax structure is the same as for oil. This tax had not been instituted at the time the southern sector fields were developed. However, this does not imply that the companies operating in the southern sector were able to take all the economic rent created by the energy price movements of the 1970s. Until recently, the BGC was the monopoly purchaser of gas, and was able to hold the purchase price at a low level. At first, this low cost was to a large extent passed on to the users in order to expand the market to match new supplies of gas. Subsequently, as gas prices followed the upward trend in other fuel prices, the net government take from the BGC was increased to reach a peak of just over 25 per cent of turnover in 1977/8, as shown in figure 11.6 (VAT, PAYE and employee's social security payments are excluded from the net government take). The figure also shows how the government take has fallen since 1977/8 as the cost of gas to the BGC has risen. The effect on gas prices has been to smooth out what would have been a very late rise in prices, or equivalently to maintain a fairly stable real price.

As a result of the Oil and Gas (Enterprise) Bill (1982), the rights of the BGC as a monopoly purchaser of gas have been substantially reduced, so that large and many medium-sized customers have the right to purchase gas from any

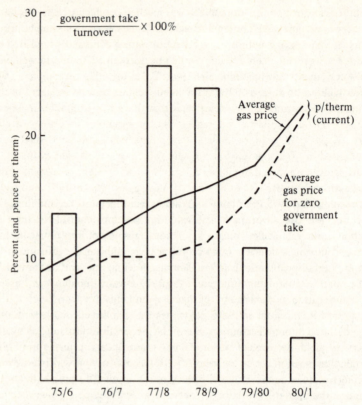

11.6 Net government take from the British Gas Corporation and its effect on gas prices

supplier, with provision for the gas distribution system of the BGC to be used as a common carrier. This is intended to encourage further exploration for gas on the UKCS, an aim which so far appears to have been achieved.

11.6   International trade

Crude oil and oil products are freely traded commodities. Oil from the UKCS is of generally rather higher quality (i.e. low specific gravity and low sulphur content) than that for which UK refineries were designed, and attracts a premium price. In 1980, therefore, just over half the crude oil produced in the UK was exported, and a slightly larger quantity was imported. Taking into account a net export of refined products, overall production was in that year 103 per cent of inland petroleum use, rising to 142 per cent by 1982. This is in marked contrast to the situation in 1975, when production was less than 2 per cent of consumption. The significance of this change may be judged from the fact that the value of net energy imports rose from 2.1 per cent of GDP in 1973 to 5.2 per cent in 1974, and fell to 0.25 per cent in 1980, and in 1982 net exports were 1.6 per cent of GDP.

International trade in gas, on the other hand, is much more restricted. There are three possible mechanisms for such trade:

(a) Overland or submarine pipeline.
(b) Liquefied natural gas (LNG).
(c) Transport of a manufactured product such as methanol.

Imports of LNG to the UK were started on a regular basis in 1964, and have since continued at a low level, about 30 PJ per year; in 1980 this represented less than 2 per cent of total natural gas. The long-term development of LNG trade is a possibility, though the extra transport costs imposed by the need for refrigeration pose a significant barrier. In addition, substantial investment is needed in specialised handling and storage facilities at the ports concerned, which favours long-term bilateral commitments between suppliers and users rather than the flexible pattern appropriate for crude oil.

All gas from the North Sea is brought ashore by pipeline and connected directly to the onshore distribution network; the possibility of an extended gas-gathering pipeline to make better use of associated gas from the northern sector is discussed below. Some of the gas brought ashore in this way is from the Norwegian section of the Frigg field (386 PJ or 21 per cent of the total in 1980) and represents an import into the UK. Pipelines share with LNG trade the general problem of inflexibility.

It has been suggested that the problems of trade in LNG might be avoided by converting natural gas to methanol. The latter could in the medium term be used as a gasoline additive, or in the longer term be converted directly to a gasoline substitute. This route involves fairly heavy energy losses, of course, and is mainly considered as a means of using associated gas (for example from the Middle East) which would otherwise be flared. It is likely to be of only marginal significance in the UK within the period covered by this study.

Apart from the continued imports of Norwegian gas, therefore, depletion policy for gas may be discussed mainly on the basis of UK self-sufficiency, with further expansion of international trade only towards the end of the period.

11.7   Depletion policy and production

The UK government has never adopted a formal, quantified plan for the depletion of UKCS oil and gas resources. In view of the uncertainties of the reserves on the UKCS, their production cost, and the long-term price of, and demand for, hydrocarbons, any such plan would have been self-defeating. In 1974, the Secretary of State for Energy expressed the government's objectives as being to 'ensure that this vital national resource will be used at a rate which secures the greatest long-term benefit to the nation's economy', and this was used to justify widespread government powers to control exploration and production. A further statement was made in 1980 emphasising the need to 'maximise indigenous hydrocarbon production on a long-term basis', which was interpreted to imply the delaying of some production to extend the period of UK self-sufficiency. It is worth noting that a situation in which a substantial oil producer such as the UK chooses to limit its exports to a low level is not encouraging for those nations who are very dependent on oil imports.

In the short to medium term, the aim has been to acquire as much knowledge of the resource base as possible, through the allocation of licences in small areas subject to specified exploration programmes. A rapid build-up in output has also been sought (and achieved) in order to realise from as early a date as possible the fiscal and macroeconomic benefits of the oil resource.

From a theoretical point of view, the optimal rate of depletion depends on the relationship between the rate of appreciation of the value of the reserves in the ground and the return available from investment elsewhere. This is known as the 'Hotelling principle' after the economist who formulated it in 1931. This optimum is difficult to realise in practice because expectations of future prices are very unstable, and because the main control of depletion is through exploration licences, which are issued some years ahead of production (direct control of production is, of course, possible, but can be very expensive). From the point of view of the government, the appropriate value for the rate of return on alternative investment is the social rate of return, which is probably less than the return expected by commercial companies. North Sea resources benefit the country both by creating employment in related industries and through the use made of government revenues. On the other hand, it has been suggested that investment in the North Sea may 'crowd out' investment in manufacturing industry, and oil resources may raise the value of sterling, reducing inflation but at the same time inhibiting exports and encouraging the import of manufactured goods (Forsyth and Kay, 1980). These effects might reduce the net benefit from oil, and favour a slower depletion rate. However, a more recent study (Atkinson et al., 1983) suggests that, on balance, the effects of North Sea oil have been beneficial for GDP, industry and employment.

For the purpose of this study, we assume that oil is exploited as rapidly as possible subject to the constraints of a realistic exploration programme and the technical limits on the rate of production from any given field. For the reference production profile shown in figure 11.7, we take an initial recoverable reserve

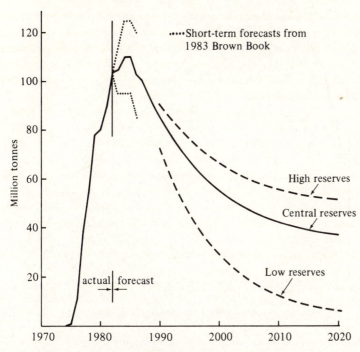

11.7 Oil production profiles for the UK Continental Shelf

figure of 3,500 million tonnes (somewhat above the mid-point of the range quoted in section 11.2 in recognition of the caution usually shown by petroleum geologists), and assume that 80 per cent of the as yet undiscovered oil, including 'possible' reserves in existing discoveries, is found between 1982 and 2020 at a uniform rate of discovery. The 1982 reserves to production (R/P) ratio, here defined as the ratio of remaining proven plus probable reserves to current annual production ratio, was 14.2 years, but the short-term forecasts in the 1983 Brown Book (shown in figure 11.7) suggest that this will drop to around 11.0 years by 1986 as production passes its peak in the mid-1980s. We assume a continuing value of 11.0 years. This shows that oil output is likely to fall fairly rapidly from the mid-1980s. In 2000, the reference profile indicates an output of 55 million tonnes (half the peak output), with a maximum, given high reserves, approaching 70 million tonnes. By 2020, the reference output is less than 40 million tonnes, but is by this time falling only slowly.

As noted above, depletion policy for gas depends on the development of UK gas demand, and the key markets are industrial premium heat, and space and water heating in domestic and commercial buildings. Coal costs, and the economics of coal gasification (see section 11.11 below) will also influence

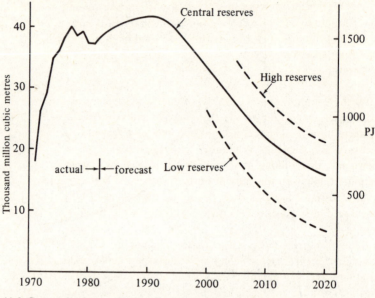

11.8 Gas production profiles for the UK Continental Shelf

gas depletion policy. For a reference production profile, we assume reserves of 1900 billion m³, again somewhat above the mid-point of the range quoted in section 11.2, and a uniform discovery rate of 80 per cent of the as yet undiscovered gas by 2020. The 1982 reserves to production ratio was 24.6 years, well above the technical minimum, which is similar to that for oil, indicating that gas output is at present determined by demand. Figure 11.8 is based on the gas demand for the central economic growth scenario arising from the analysis in chapters 6–9. The reserves to production ratio becomes the determinant of output from around 2000. Production falls fairly rapidly, reaching around 16 billion m³ (below 40 per cent of its peak value) by 2020. The effect on this decline of alternative assumptions on reserves is also shown in the figure.

11.8   Special issues for gas

Flaring and gas-gathering systems

Much North Sea oil is produced in direct association with gas. This gas represents a significant energy resource. There are several options for the disposal of such gas, including:

(a) Use on production rigs as an energy resource.
(b) Transfer to shore by gas pipeline.

(c) Transfer to shore in solution in oil pipeline (mainly for natural gas liquids).
(d) Re-injection into reservoir rock to maintain oil pressure.
(e) Flaring.

Of these options, direct use as an energy resource and injection into an existing oil pipeline are clearly cost-effective and avoid wastage, but the scope for these options is limited. Re-injection into the reservoir rock improves the oil recovery factor and is preferable to flaring from a resource conservation viewpoint; this is done in several North Sea fields. Flaring of excess gas is permitted only with the consent of the Secretary of State for Energy, and the level of flaring has fallen from just under 8 per cent of oil produced in 1979 (measured in terms of the energy contents of the oil and gas) to less than 4 per cent in 1982.

In order to make the best use of associated gas, development of an extensive gas-gathering pipeline has been proposed (Department of Energy, 1978b). This would involve, in addition to the existing gas pipelines from Frigg and Brent, a pipeline from the mainland to T block (close to the UK/Norway line east of Piper, see figure 11.1), with a northward leg to the Brent group and a southern leg to new fields close to Auk. The scheme would allow for an extension of trade with Norway, and (more speculatively) with Denmark. Though the scheme was considered economic, the government chose to rely on private investment, which was not available in sufficient quantities owing to uncertainties in the future price of gas. Accordingly, in September 1981 the government decided not to pursue the integrated gas-gathering scheme, but to rely instead on more localised schemes developed by the North Sea operating companies. FLAGS (Far-North Liquids and Associated Gas System), serving the fields east of Shetland, is an example of successful cooperation in gas gathering.

Whether the government's policy is adequate will depend on future developments in the gas market, and the success of other options in reducing the level of flaring. In principle, the 'leave it to the market' approach adopted by the government may be open to three objections. First, it is not realistic to expect individual companies to adopt the long-sighted approach necessary for an optimal national strategy; they will naturally seek a rate of return on investment higher than that appropriate for long-term social planning. Second, the fragmentation of commercial interests in the North Sea could make the development of an integrated scheme difficult. Third, the companies concerned cannot exercise their commercial judgement as long as the price of gas is determined by a single dominant purchaser; recent legislation makes this objection less relevant.

Gas storage

Because of the importance for gas demand of domestic and commercial heating, the gas market is subject to major seasonal variations. The economic penalties of imposing this seasonal variation on offshore production wells are substantial, and it is therefore desirable to store gas and to make other special arrangements to meet peak demands. Options in use or being developed are:

(a) Load management through interruptible tariffs: this has been important in industry in the past, but is likely to be less so in the future.

(b) Underground storage: two salt cavities at Hornsea in Humberside were in use in 1981 for gas storage, with a total capacity of 2,000 million ft^3 – useful for storage on a daily cycle. Further cavities will be brought into use.

(c) Seasonal production: existing contracts are aimed at seasonal production as far as possible. In addition, the Morecambe Bay field in the Irish Sea (discovered in 1974) is being developed specifically for seasonal production.

(d) Undersea storage: as the southern sector fields are depleted, consideration is being given to their use for seasonal storage of gas; development for this purpose is in progress in the Rough field.

(e) LNG storage: LNG provides a compact but relatively expensive storage medium for meeting peak demands.

(f) SNG: methane may be manufactured, currently from liquefied petroleum gases or naphtha, to meet peak demands.

11.9   Oil and gas prices

Oil is a freely traded commodity on world markets, and the price of crude oil in the UK is assumed to be fixed by the world price. In this study we use a reference oil-price scenario based on the analysis of the world energy scene given in chapter 2. This is not intended as a forecast, but as a reference point for planning purposes which is appropriate if energy supplies are not to limit world economic growth in the long term. The sterling oil price depends, of course, on the real dollar exchange rate. This itself is difficult to predict, depending on (among other things) the perception of sterling as a petro-currency, UK and US interest rates and the balance of trade. We assume a fixed value of $1.5 (based on 1980 values) from 1985. This is well below the peak of $2.33 reached in 1980, but broadly in line with more recent values. It is also necessary to make a small allowance for transport costs. The resulting sterling price is shown in figure 11.9. The exact form of this price trajectory will in practice be very much influenced

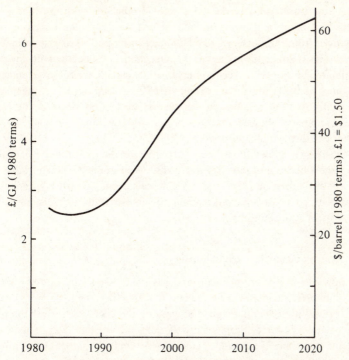

11.9 Crude oil price: reference projection. This curve is intended to indicate a general trend in oil prices. Actual prices are likely to change more erratically

by cyclical factors, political events and changes in the dollar exchange rate. In general terms, it is expected that the period of oil-price stability will end, as the world economy recovers, in the late 1980s and 1990s. The price will then rise at a rate determined by the need to balance the oil market in an environment of world economic growth, reaching around double its present value by the end of the period.

The prices of different oil products depend on refinery costs and technical characteristics, on taxation policies and on the operation of the market. We assume that the relationships which have applied since 1974 generally continue in the future. This is of particular significance for transport fuels, where we are implicitly assuming that the tax element is increased in line with any increases in the price of crude oil. The effect on oil use of relaxing this assumption is noted in chapter 8.

For gas, there is no starting-point analogous to the world traded price of crude oil, though gas trade may become increasingly important towards the end of the period. In the short and medium term, gas prices will be determined mainly by energy policy considerations. As the cost of production from the North Sea rises, this will exert a growing influence on prices, but the cost of SNG, manufactured from UK coal, will, in the longer term, impose an upper limit on gas prices. Gas manufacture is discussed in section 11.11 below: with the coal costs estimated for the central economic growth case (chapter 12), ex-plant costs for SNG are expected to be about 380 and 460 p/GJ in 2000 and 2020 respectively, corresponding to average consumer prices of 525 and 600 p/GJ in the same years. These figures suggest that gas prices will generally remain below oil product prices throughout the period.

Historically, gas prices have been very low for industry relative to other sectors, largely because of interruptible tariffs. We assume that such tariffs will be phased out fairly quickly, and that domestic and industrial prices will converge, with some advantage remaining for industrial users due to the lower specific costs of connecting larger consumers.

11.10   Safety and environmental impact

Exploration and development of oil and gas fields, especially in deep water, inevitably involves danger. Up to the end of 1981, there had been 112 deaths and 509 serious injuries in the course of work on the UKCS. The probability of death per man-year for workers on installations (i.e. excluding ships) is about 0.001, some four times the figure for coal miners. On the other hand, because of the lower labour involvement in oil and gas extraction, the number of deaths per unit of energy is nearly five times as great for coal as for oil and gas.

Much publicity has been given to the ecological hazards resulting from major spillages of crude oil, for example from tanker accidents. In fact, most pollution arises from the much larger number of small incidents, often involving the illegal dumping of ballast water.

The storage of oil and gas may be a source of fire risk. Of particular concern is LNG storage, and anxiety over the siting of LNG tanks near port facilities may be a factor limiting the development of LNG trade.

Air pollution resulting from the use of oil products (and to a lesser extent gas) can be a significant health hazard. UK crude oil is of low sulphur content, but fuel oil consumed in the UK, which may be manufactured from imported crude oil with higher sulphur content, will cause sulphur pollution. This is injurious to health if the local concentration is high, damages buildings and causes 'acid rain', possibly over a very wide area. Local concentrations can be controlled by the use of tall stacks, or the sulphur can be removed from flue gases before it reaches the atmosphere, though at significant extra cost.

A further important cause of air pollution, significant for health because it originates at a low level in populated areas, is motor vehicle exhausts. Here the main pollutants are unburnt hydrocarbons, oxides of nitrogen, carbon monoxide and lead, the latter being due to lead-based anti-knock compounds added to gasoline. These are discussed further in chapter 8, and, for example, in Chem Systems International Ltd (1976).

The more pervasive problem of climatic change, resulting from the change in atmospheric carbon dioxide due to burning fossil fuels, is discussed in chapter 12.

11.11 Manufactured gaseous and liquid fuels

It was noted in section 11.9 that natural gas is likely to be supplemented towards the end of the period by substitute natural gas (SNG), based on coal. Similarly, though in the longer term, coal may be used as a source for liquid transport fuels. For a detailed technical description of the processes involved, the reader is referred to Grainger and Gibson (1981) on which the following outline is based.

Gasification

The manufacture of gas from coal is not new; most gas was supplied in this way before natural gas became available. This 'town gas', consisting mainly of carbon monoxide and hydrogen, would at present be termed medium btu gas (MBG) with a thermal content of around 18 MJ/m^3, compared with 37 MJ/m^3 for natural gas. Such a gas would not be used for public supply in the future owing to its low heat content and toxicity, though it might be used within an industrial complex or on a local basis. Similarly, low btu gas (LBG, which consists of MBG diluted by nitrogen, with a thermal content of around 6 MJ/m^3) may be used within industry. SNG is a direct equivalent of natural gas, manufactured from oil or coal.

Town gas was produced rather inefficiently, often as a by-product of coke. Many more efficient processes now exist or are under development, the main parameters being the pressure used, the gasifying agent (air, oxygen or hydrogen) and the physical form in which the coal is maintained for the reaction to take place. Commercially available systems include the Winkler and Koppers-Totzek reactors, which use oxygen at low pressure, the Wellman-Galusha process (low pressure air) and the Lurgi reactor, which uses oxygen at a pressure of up to 32 atmospheres. The BGC are making good progress with a modified Lurgi gasifier, the 'slagging gasifier', which uses higher temperatures and in which ash is removed as a liquid.

The main combustible products from most gasifiers are carbon monoxide and hydrogen, though some methane is found directly, especially at high pressures and low temperatures. After removal of dust, tar, carbon dioxide and contaminants such as hydrogen sulphide, the gas is suitable for industrial use (as MBG if the gasifying agent is oxygen, or LBG if air is used). If SNG is the desired product, the gas undergoes a shift reaction with steam, in order to obtain the required ratio of carbon monoxide to hydrogen, and finally a methanation stage to produce methane. Both the shift and methanation reactions involve the use of catalysts.

Typical efficiencies of SNG processes are in the range 50–66 per cent (the low end of the range being the Koppers-Totzek process which is optimised for synthesis gas – carbon monoxide and hydrogen – rather than SNG), and for this study we use an efficiency of 64 per cent. Capital cost estimates vary widely, and their implications for SNG costs depend on the method of financing used. We use a capital cost per unit of SNG produced, based on a 5 per cent discount rate over a twenty-five-year life, of 60 p/GJ, together with a non-fuel running cost of 70 p/GJ (based on data in Ormerod, 1980).

Liquefaction

The aim of coal liquefaction is to produce transport fuels and possibly chemical feedstocks, since other uses of oil products are generally open to more efficient fuel substitution mechanisms. There are two routes: synthesis, in which the first stage is gasification; and degradation, where pyrolysis, solvent extraction or hydrogenation are used to convert the coal into a mixture of fairly heavy organic compounds.

The synthesis route is similar to that used for SNG, except that the input mixture and reaction conditions for the Fischer-Tropsch reaction (methanation in SNG production) are varied to produce heavier paraffins or, in one version of the process, methanol. The latter can be converted catalytically to a gasoline substitute (the Mobil process) and was noted in section 11.6 as a possible energy carrier in international trade.

Degradation processes are very diverse, and we cannot in this study attempt a full description. A process favoured by the NCB is supercritical gas extraction (SGE), which uses a pressurised gas (such as toluene) at a temperature of around 400°C to extract up to 40 per cent of the mass of the coal as a mixture of hydrogen-rich compounds. Subsequent recovery of the solvent, and processing of the products, is fairly straightforward, and the coal residue is a useful fuel particularly suitable for gasification.

The economics of coal liquefaction are difficult to assess, both because the processes are under rapid development and because liquefaction is likely to be integrated into a larger system producing gases and other products. The efficiency of existing plants is probably less than 40 per cent, though future developments in coal hydrogenation could raise efficiencies for liquids and gases combined to over 70 per cent. For the simple analysis used in this study, we assume that capital and non-fuel running costs are both 70 p/GJ (based on Ormerod, 1980, with a twenty-five-year life and 5 per cent discount rate) and 60 per cent efficiency. This would yield a product similar to fuel oil or a low-sulphur crude oil; further processing would be needed to produce transport fuels.

12

Coal supply

12.1 The UK coal industry

History

The UK coal industry is the oldest of the major energy industries. Its peak output – 287 million tonnes – was in 1913. With the increasing use of oil and, later, natural gas, the coal industry was in almost continuous decline from 1957 until the energy crisis of 1973. Figure 12.1 shows the pattern of total and deep-mined output over the past thirty years (Department of Energy, 1983a). The difference, which is almost entirely from the output of open-cast mining operations, has always been a small proportion of the UK total (in contrast to the world coal picture as a whole, in which open-cast coal is of major importance). However, its importance in the UK has grown in recent years. In 1980/1, open-cast output was 15.7 million tonnes, or 12 per cent of the total, compared with 7.2 million tonnes – just under 4 per cent of the total – fifteen years earlier. The figure also shows the effects on output of the major industrial disputes in 1971/2 and 1973/4.

In the wake of the 1973/4 oil crisis, coal output has stabilised, due to slack demand, at between 120 and 130 million tonnes. What may have been the first signs of new growth, in 1979/80 and 1980/1, have not been sustained due to the economic recession, but general economic recovery may prompt an upturn in coal demand.

Productivity

Coal mining in the UK is still a comparatively labour-intensive industry. In 1978/9, wage and wage-related costs accounted for 50.7 per cent of total coal costs. Changes in this figure depend on productivity improvements and on the level of miners' wages. Productivity, which is usually expressed in terms of output per man-shift, has risen steadily, mainly as a result of mechanisation of coal cutting and loading, but also through regional restructuring and the closure of less efficient pits. Figure 12.2 shows the change in overall productivity over

214

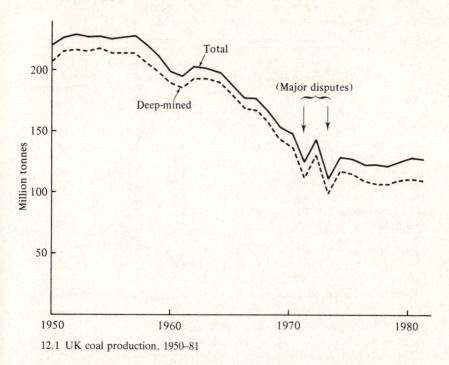

12.1 UK coal production, 1950–81

the last three decades, together with the trend in mechanisation, and further advances in cutting and loading techniques are likely. Productivity has been nearly constant at about 2.3 tonnes per man-shift since the late 1960s, though the commissioning of new mining capacity (as is envisaged by the NCB) should allow a further rise.

Miners' earnings have generally kept ahead of those of comparable workers in other industries, and the disputes of 1971/2 and 1973/4 showed the very considerable bargaining power which, under certain market conditions, the miners can exercise. Past and future wage levels, and their influence on coal costs, are discussed more fully in section 12.3 below.

Structure

Thus far we have considered the mining industry as a whole. For administrative and statistical purposes, the UK industry is divided into twelve areas. Wide differences exist between these areas, both in the types of coal found and in the levels of productivity. Table 12.1 provides some relevant regional statistics for the period between 1963/4 and 1980/1. It may be seen that productivity in 1980/1 varied by more than a factor of two between the most efficient and the

Table 12.1. *Regional statistics for NCB deep-mined coal*

Area	Share in NCB deep-mined production (%)		Output per man-shift overall (tonnes)		Ratio of total 1980/1 output to 1963/4 output
	1963/4	1980/1	1963/4	1980/1	
Scottish	8.79	7.06	1.43	1.92	0.46
North-East	17.29	12.86	1.43	2.07	0.42
North Yorkshire	5.53	7.76	1.94	2.68	0.81
Doncaster	5.25	6.54	1.89	2.18	0.71
Barnsley	6.27	7.60	1.85	2.62	0.70
South Yorkshire	5.95	6.74	1.74	2.17	0.65
North Derbyshire	7.77	7.54	2.13	3.21	0.56
North Nottingham	5.91	10.93	2.51	3.04	1.06
South Nottingham	7.45	8.06	2.69	2.68	0.78
South Midlands	6.76	7.72	2.22	2.36	0.66
Western	12.64	10.21	1.65	2.35	0.46
South Wales	10.39	7.00	1.21	1.46	0.39

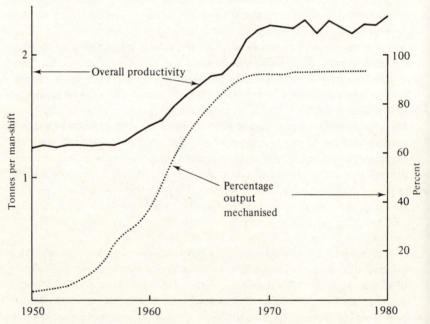

12.2 Productivity and mechanisation: NCB deep-mined output, 1950–80

Table 12.2. *Structure of coal demand, 1960 and 1980*

	1960	1980	Gross thermal content, 1980
Total demand (million tonnes)	200.0	123.5	(GJ/tonne)
Demand shares (%):			
Collieries	2.5	0.6	27.0
Power stations	26.4	72.6	23.8
Gas works	11.5	0.0	31.1
Coke ovens etc.[a]	15.8	11.8	30.5
Industry	17.7	6.3	27.1
Transport	4.7	0.1	31.1
Households	18.0	7.2	30.8
Services and agriculture	3.3	1.4	27.5

Note: [a] Includes all solid-fuel manufacture outside gas works.

least efficient areas, and that all areas except one have seen an increase in productivity. Output has fallen in all areas except North Nottingham, and (with the exception of North Derbyshire) there is a clear correlation between the fall in output and the level of productivity. Areas with lower productivity have seen a faster fall in output, both because the least efficient mines are generally old and close to exhaustion, and because of the financial advantages of concentrating production in the most efficient areas.

When considering the future prospects for the coal industry, it is important to recognise that coal is not a homogeneous commodity. Different types of coal are suited to different uses, and attract different market prices. Table 12.2 shows how the structure of coal demand has changed between 1960 and 1980, and includes average thermal contents of the coal in each market (this is a first indication of quality, though other variables, including volatiles content, ash content, the size of the mined coal and its physical strength when converted to coke, are important in different markets). It may be seen that the demand share has fallen substantially in the premium sectors (gas works, coke ovens, transport and households), and that the share of coal going to power stations has increased from just over one-quarter to nearly three-quarters.

The association of different grades of coal with different markets has important implications for the regional structure of the industry. For example, in 1978/9 in the South Wales area, 37 per cent of output went to coke ovens, 21 per cent to households and only 30 per cent to power stations. The future role of this area is therefore closely related to the output and policies of the steel industry (the major user of coke). On the positive side, the suitability of South

Wales coal for the household and coke oven markets gives it a price advantage which to some extent offsets the low productivity of the area.

12.2   Plans and prospects

Current industry outlook

Through the 1960s, the steady decline of the coal industry was seen by the government as both inevitable and consistent with long-term policy considerations (Ministry of Power, 1967). It was expected that cheap oil would continue to be available, and arguments on supply security and import-dependence were met by plans to develop nuclear power and North Sea gas. The burden of government policy towards the coal industry was to ensure an orderly decline and to offset the undesirable social consequences of pit closures.

Perceptions of the future role of coal changed rapidly in the wake of the 1973/4 oil crisis. 'Plan for Coal', the outcome of a tripartite agreement between the government, the NCB and the coal industry unions (National Coal Board, 1974; Department of Energy, 1974), envisaged a new capacity of 42 million tonnes per year by 1985, comprising 9 million tons by extending the life of existing pits, 13 million tons from major improvement schemes and 20 million tons from new mines. This, it was estimated, would entail capital expenditures of £600 million between 1974 and 1985 (at 1974 prices) in addition to regular annual capital expenditure of £70 to £80 million. In addition, open-cast output would be increased from around 10 million tons to 15 million tons. Taking into account the expected closures of exhausted pits, this would yield an annual capacity of 135 million tons by 1985.

A review of progress with 'Plan for Coal', and an assessment of prospects to 2000, was given in 'Coal for the Future' (Department of Energy, 1977). By the summer of 1976 it had become clear that the capital cost estimates in 'Plan for Coal' had been over-optimistic, and that delays in obtaining planning approval would limit the contribution from new mines. The objective of 135 million tons by 1985 was retained, but the composition of planned output was modified: the main change was to halve the expected contribution from new mines, and to increase the scale of extensions of existing pits.

In current money, the capital expenditure forecasts in 'Plan for Coal' had risen from £1400 to £3150 million. Most of this was due to inflation; the real increase, arising both from early optimism and more detailed costing as 'Plan for Coal' was put into effect, was estimated at 29 per cent.

For the longer term, a planning objective of 170 million tons of annual output (of which 20 million tons would be open-cast) was proposed for the coal industry for the year 2000. This would involve new deep-mined capacity, additional to that in 'Plan for Coal', of some 60 million tons – a commissioning rate between 1985 and 2000 of 4 million tons per annum. The annual capital expenditure (including regular expenditure not associated with new capacity) was expected to be around £400 million at March 1976 prices. This overall aim for the industry was echoed in the Energy Policy Green Paper (Department of Energy, 1978a).

Since the change of government in 1979, the emphasis has changed from long-term expansion to short-term economic viability. As a result of the 1980 Coal Industry Act, the industry was directed to achieve economic break-even (apart from social cost grants) within three years. At the same time, the general recession prompted a fall in coal demand. Coal imports peaked at 7.3 million tonnes in 1980, though political events in Poland created an opportunity to export coal which was taken up from 1981.

In this new atmosphere, the bargaining power of the NUM (National Union of Mineworkers) has been substantially reduced. Up to the end of 1983, wage settlements and pit closures were achieved by negotiation. The prolonged strike of 1984 (still unresolved at the time of going to press) underlines both the social stress arising from pit closures and the political difficulty in achieving rational objectives.

An inquiry into the coal industry by the Monopolies and Mergers Commission was announced in March 1982, and reported in June 1983 (Monopolies and Mergers Commission, 1983).

Reserves and development constraints

In the chapters on oil and gas, it was clear that the long-term supply prospects were very dependent on the level of reserves. This is less so for coal. NCB estimates (Moses, 1981) give a figure of 190 billion tonnes of coal in place in the UK, in seams greater than 60 cm in thickness and at depths of less than 1.2 km. Of this total, a quantity of 45 billion tonnes is considered to be recoverable using current mining technology. This, as has often been pointed out (e.g. Department of Energy, 1977), is more than three hundred times current annual production, which may be compared with the reserves to production ratio for UK oil and gas of less than twenty-five years (see chapter eleven).

Alternatively, we may consider the proportion of recoverable reserves which need to be developed in order to provide the output given in 'Coal for the Future' for the year 2000. If we include extensions of existing mines, this represents a capacity increase, compared with 1976, of 102 million tonnes per annum. Taking the average life of a mine as fifty years (a somewhat arbitrary figure: 'Coal for the Future' uses a figure of twenty-five in a similar assessment, while the average age of mines in the UK – considerably less than their average lifetime to exhaustion – is around seventy years), this capacity increase will require the development of 5.1 billion tonnes of reserves, or eleven per cent of the recoverable total.

There is, clearly, considerable uncertainty in the total level of technically recoverable reserves. In particular, no explicit criterion for the cost of mining the coal is stated. Since in recent years it has been considered proper to extract coal at a substantial financial loss, this is an important omission. Nevertheless, the exhaustion of coal reserves is unlikely to be a key issue in the UK over the period covered by this study.

Of more importance are the practical constraints on the rapid development of mining capacity. The 60 million tonnes of new capacity which according to 'Coal for the Future' would be commissioned between 1985 and 2000, is equivalent to six coalfields the size of Selby, or thirty the size of Park or Thorne. The time-scale for converting known reserves to operational capacity is around twenty years (Moses, 1981). Even for well-mapped reserves at a new site, the time-scale for obtaining planning approval and carrying out the necessary construction work can be greater than ten years, and the recent Vale of Belvoir Public Inquiry has shown that opposition to such development can be widespread and vociferous. Extensions of existing mines can be carried out more quickly, but recent NCB plans suggest that scope for such extensions is limited. In view of these long time-scales for development it would be desirable to be able to predict with confidence the demand for coal at least ten years ahead. This is, of course, impossible in the present uncertain economic situation, and there is a danger that continuing short-term stagnation in coal demand will inhibit development to the extent that the industry is unable to meet a rise in demand later this century.

12.3   Coal costs

History

Figure 12.3 shows the changing structure of coal costs in recent years, excluding interest payable on outstanding debts. The share of wages and wage-related costs fell steadily durning the 1950s and 1960s, due both to improving productivity (see figure 12.2) and to a fall in miners' wages relative to other workers. Depreciation and other overheads increased during the same period as a proportion of the total, while the share of other costs – repairs, maintenance and fuels – remained nearly constant.

Wages

Since wages constitute the largest single element in coal costs, they are of prime importance in any study of future costs. Wage comparisons between different

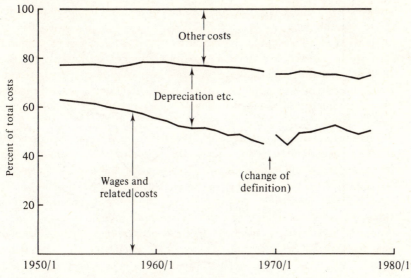

12.3 The structure of coal costs (NCB collieries)

groups of workers are both difficult and emotive. For the coal industry, a detailed account is given by Handy (1981). Figure 12.4 shows the ratio of miners' wages (on an hourly, and for a limited period a weekly, basis) to the average wages for adult male manual workers in all industries (Central Statistical Office, 1983). Hourly rates are more relevant than shift or weekly rates because shift lengths vary between industries and with time in any given industry, though workers' perceptions of their prosperity will be based on relative weekly earnings. The rate for all workers in the coal industry is inferred from published earnings per man-shift using a time-varying weighted average shift length. Allowances in kind (i.e. miners' coal) are included. Some problems of interpretation remain. The data for miners include juveniles and a small number of female employees. On the other hand, they also include foremen, who are excluded from the general manual wage statistics.

It is clear from figure 12.4 that, in terms of hourly rates, underground workers have always received a substantial premium over surface workers and manual workers in general. In weekly terms, these premiums are much less marked, and underground workers were about equal to average manual workers in 1973/4. It was, indeed, partly the failure of the miners to profit from the general growth in prosperity in 1973 that prompted the industrial dispute of 1973/4. The revival of the industry in the mid- to late 1970s, aided by the headroom created by higher oil prices, allowed the miners to improve their competitive position, so that by

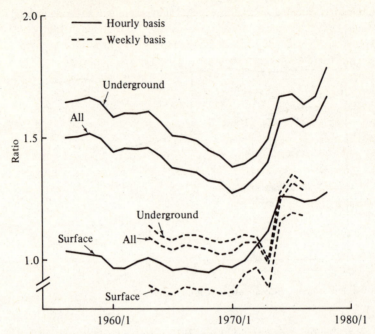

12.4 Ratios of miners' earnings to average earnings for adult male manual workers

1978/9 underground workers were earning, on an hourly basis, 1.8 times the manual worker average.

The wages of surface workers prior to 1974 were close to the manual worker average in hourly terms (lower in weekly terms), but have climbed substantially since that date. Since nearly four-fifths of the hours worked are underground, the average for all workers in the coal industry follows the curve for underground workers.

Extension of the analysis to more recent years is hindered by changes in definitions. However, the weekly earnings ratio for all workers appears to have stabilised at around 1.3 relative to the manual worker average.

It is sometimes suggested that if the rising price of oil creates an opportunity for an economic rent to be obtained for coal (i.e. a revenue over and above its total cost), then this will inevitably be taken by the miners in the form of increased wages. However, it seems more likely that any rise in miners' earnings will be self-limiting. First, the willingness of the miners themselves to support claims for higher earnings is likely to be reduced as their living standards rise and as the financial sacrifices incurred by strike action become more marked. Second, the desire of other workers to maintain comparability with the miners would lead to 'catching-up' claims which would (via inflation) erode miners' real earnings. How these mechanisms would operate in a future industrial, economic and political environment is uncertain. For this study, we assume an upper limit on the ratio of miners' hourly earnings (all workers) to average manual workers' earnings of 1.8, rather above the 1978/9 value. This ratio could be exceeded, but not on a long-term basis. As it is generally recognised that mining is an arduous, unpleasant and sometimes dangerous occupation, we also assume that the ratio will not fall below 1.25. In terms of weekly rates, the corresponding range is approximately 1.0 to 1.4.

For most of the recent period, average manual wage rates have moved in line with GDP, and we assume that this will continue in the future. Thus we expect that all wages, including those of miners, will be higher in real terms if economic growth is higher, and conversely.

Productivity

The effect of miners' wages on coal costs depends, of course, on productivity. Figure 12.2 above shows that overall productivity has levelled off at around 2.25 tonnes per man-shift (it was 2.4 in 1981/2). 'Coal for the Future' predicts average productivity for new pits of over 7 tonnes per man-shift. This seems at first sight an optimistic figure. However, in 1980/1, overall productivity at new mines was 4.25 tonnes per man-shift, and the figure for the best colliery was 5.9 tonnes per man-shift (National Coal Board, 1981).

Data on the distribution of manpower productivity and production costs are given in the Monopolies and Mergers Commission report (1983). Figure 12.5 shows curves of cumulative output against cost and productivity. Note the high-cost, low productivity tail; the worst 10 per cent of output accounts for about 17 per cent of total costs. To bring average costs (excluding interest charges) down to the 1981/2 net proceeds of £35.59 per tonne would require output to be reduced to about 95 million tonnes, with a 20 per cent fall in total manpower.

For this study, we assume that pit closures take place in order of productivity, starting with the least-efficient pits, with capacity being lost at an annual rate of 3 per cent to 1985. Thereafter, we postulate two closure strategies, a 'fast' programme at 4 per cent per annum and a 'slow' programme at 2 per cent per annum. This implies the closure of 21 to 30 million tonnes between 1981 and 1990, and 37 to 56 million tonnes between 1981 and 2000.

New capacity is assumed to take the form of extensions of existing mines (up to a total additional capacity of 30 million tonnes and with a fixed productivity of 3.3 tonnes/man-shift) and new mines with a productivity of 6.5 tonnes/man-shift. In general, mine extensions are assumed to be brought in more quickly

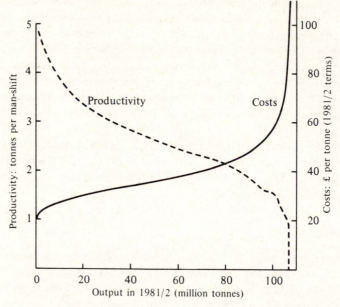

12.5 Cumulative deep-mined output (1981/2) against cost and productivity. Curves show output which can be produced at a marginal cost below the figure shown, or at a marginal productivity greater than the figure shown. Costs are in 1981/2 terms, and exclude interest. Average productivity = 2.40 tonnes/man-shift; average cost = £38.74/tonnes

than new mines. We illustrate long-term trends in manpower and productivity by means of two projections of total output, shown in table 12.3. These are both very much lower than the projections made in 1974 and 1977. Though they are not intended as forecasts, they reflect changed perceptions of the demand for coal, the need for a rationalisation of the industry and the present cost disadvantage of UK coal in the world market. Manpower and productivity implications, for deep-mined coal only, are shown in figures 12.6 and 12.7. Note that a fall in manpower appears unavoidable, though there is a long-term possibility of a stable workforce in conditions of high output growth. Because output growth enhances productivity, the ratio of the outputs in 2020 for the two projections, 1.39, corresponds to a rather lower manpower ratio of around 1.25. The worst manpower problems occur early in the period, when the annual fall in the workforce is nearly 5 per cent. Though this is high in comparison with recent rates (about 3 per cent per annum between 1970/1 and 1981/2), it is very much slower than the decline in manpower experienced throughout the 1960s. The

Table 12.3. *Illustrative projections of coal output*

Year	High projection (million tonnes)			Low projection (million tonnes)		
	Deep-mined	Open-cast	Total	Deep-mined	Open-cast	Total
1985	105.7	14.3	120.0	101.5	13.5	115.0
1990	105.7	14.8	120.0	97.0	13.0	110.0
2000	104.0	16.0	120.0	88.0	12.0	100.0
2010	113.0	17.0	130.0	88.0	12.0	100.0
2020	122.0	18.0	140.0	88.0	12.0	100.0

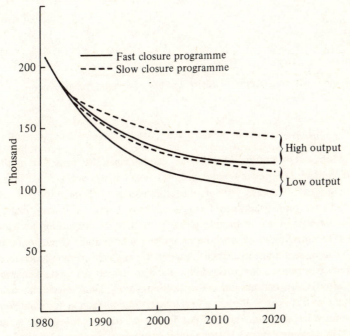

12.6 Manpower implications of different output and closure programmes

reduction in manpower is likely to cause social problems in specific areas; this is discussed further in section 12.7.

Figure 12.7 shows that a substantial rise in productivity may be expected, ranging from about 50 per cent to nearly 100 per cent over the period to 2020. The implications of these results for coal costs are discussed below.

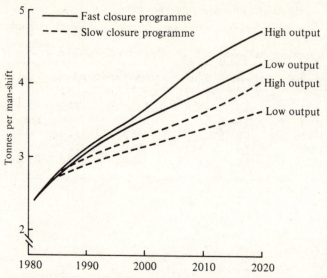

12.7 Productivity implications of different output and closure programmes

Capital costs

For mines already operating in 1979/80, capital costs are reflected in the published figures for depreciation and interest (see NCB accounts for that year), and this figure, estimated as £4/tonne of coal, is assumed to remain fixed in real terms for all coal from such mines. For new mines and mine extensions, capital costs will naturally vary from one project to another according to local conditions. For this study, we use 'round figures' of £125 and £62 per tonne of new mine and mine extension capacity respectively (in 1980 terms). To convert these to costs per tonne of coal produced, we add an element for interest charges incurred during construction, and amortise the resulting figure over a nominal mine lifetime of forty years. We use a real interest rate of 5 per cent throughout (the recommended discount rate for public sector projects) to obtain capital costs, of £8.74/tonne and £3.72/tonne for new mines and mine extensions respectively. Some account is taken of uncertainty by using high and low variants 30 per cent above and below these figures.

No allowance is made for an increase in the capital cost as attention is turned to less attractive reserves later in the period. The industry's current exploration work suggests that many of the deposits being discovered are of very high quality, which supports the simple assumption used in this study. However, it may well be that capital costs will rise beyond the end of the century.

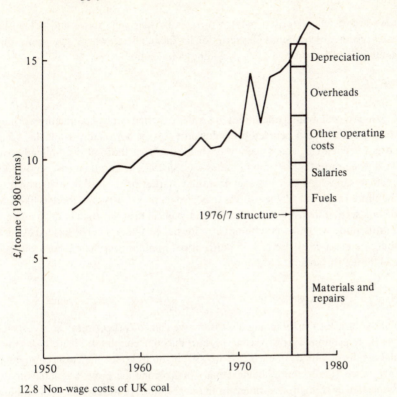

12.8 Non-wage costs of UK coal

Other costs

Figure 12.8 shows how non-wage costs have increased, in real terms, since the early 1950s. Depreciation is included, but, as the breakdown for 1976/7 shows, it is a relatively small item. Interest charges are excluded. The graph has been distorted between 1971/2 and 1973/4 by industrial disputes.

This suggests that in periods of stable or rising output non-wage costs have risen at a rate of between 3.5 and 4.5 per cent per annum, with a slower rise during the period of declining output. This increase in costs is likely to be mainly the result of technical progress (though it includes some largely non-recurring items such as compensation for subsidence), and will continue into the future through any expansion of the industry. We assume a future rate of increase of 2.5 per cent per annum, falling to 1.5 per cent per annum beyond 2000. This is low by historical standards, but reflects the greater opportunities for cost savings associated with new mine developments, and the disappearance of the high maintenance costs associated with uneconomic pits. We also postulate high and low variants characterised by growth rates 0.5 per cent above and below the rates given above. Since depreciation is included elsewhere, we apply this assumption to non-wage costs excluding depreciation.

Open-cast coal costs

Open-cast coal mining operations are usually carried out by contractors working for the NCB, and a detailed breakdown of costs is not readily available. Total costs for open-cast coal have always been less than those of deep-mined coal. This price ratio fell to a minimum of 0.60 in 1973/4, and then rose to 0.73 by 1978/9, showing some influence from the market price of coal. Exhaustion of the more readily available sources may also increase costs, and there is likely to be less scope for cost reduction through technical progress than in deep mining. In this study we make no attempt at a formal cost analysis, but instead assume that open-cast costs rise at 1.75 per cent per annum from their 1980/1 value of £24/tonne throughout the period.

Total costs

On the basis of the foregoing discussion, we can construct overall coal costs for the three economic growth scenarios introduced in chapter 4. Figure 12.9 shows the results obtained. In each case we assume an intermediate closure programme. Since (other things being equal) high economic growth is likely to be associated with high investment in the coal industry, we use the high and low output series for the high and low economic growth scenarios respectively, and an intermediate series for the central scenario. Economic growth affects costs directly through the average manual worker wage, but we also assume different values of the wage ratio (1.66, 1.53 and 1.39 for the high, central and low cases), arguing that high coal demand will increase the miners' bargaining power.

Figure 12.9 shows that coal costs are likely to be stable (and could indeed fall somewhat) up to around 1990. Thereafter, a steady rise may be expected. For the central case, costs rise by 24 per cent between 1980 and 2000, and 61 per cent between 1980 and 2020. The difference between the three cases is not great; cost increases to 2020 in the high and low cases are 72 and 47 per cent respectively.

The figure also shows the highest and lowest cost projections obtained, using high and low variants of the capital cost of new mines and mine extensions and of the other non-wage operating costs. At worst, the cost doubles between 1980 and 2020, while at best it falls significantly up to 1990 and is by 2020 only 23 per cent over its 1980 value.

The structure of coal costs alters substantially over the period. In 1980/1, wages and related items accounted for 46 per cent of deep-mined costs,

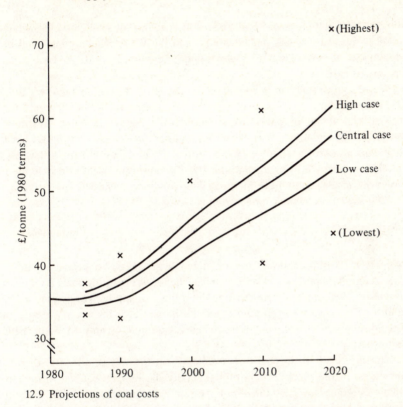

12.9 Projections of coal costs

non-wage operating costs 43 per cent, and depreciation and interest 11 per cent. For the central economic growth projection in 2020, wages etc. represent 30 per cent (the increase in productivity almost exactly balancing the increase in real earnings), non-wage operating costs 60 per cent and capital 10 per cent.

12.4   Coal trade

World coal trade

It is generally expected that, as pressures on world oil increase, a growing trade in coal will develop. At present, this trade is fairly small, and is dominated by metallurgical coal. The WOCOL study (Wilson, 1980) anticipates an increase of a factor of three to five in the volume of world coal trade between 1977 and 2000, with almost all the increase being due to steam coal. In 1980, thirteen of the twenty-one IEA countries were net importers of coal, and eight relied on imports for more than half their coal supplies (International Energy Agency,

1982). Development of this coal trade will, of course, depend on the growth of total energy demand and on oil prices, and the WOCOL study may well be optimistic. Nevertheless, it is clear that international trade in coal is an important issue.

World coal production is dominated by the US, USSR and China (which in 1977 together produced 60 per cent of world output). The UK falls into the second tranche of producers, alongside Poland, West Germany, Australia, South Africa and India. The IEA study quoted above classifies the UK as a high-cost producer among the IEA countries, in contrast to the major low-cost producers Australia, Canada and the US. The lower production costs in these countries result mainly from the geological conditions, which favour open-cast mining as well as low-cost underground mining.

World coal prices

At present, world coal prices are dominated by the low cost of production in the US, Australia, South Africa and Canada. The UK is importing coal (7.3 million tonnes in 1980, mainly from Australia and the US, and bought by the CEGB and the British Steel Corporation), and this is exerting a downward pressure on UK coal prices; some coal is also being exported, mainly to other EEC countries.

The future of world coal prices depends on the way in which coal trade develops. In the short term, with a generally slack energy market, prices are likely to remain low, and the very large resource base may allow low prices to continue. However, if, as is likely, oil prices rise substantially in real terms, an opportunity will exist for coal producers to increase their prices. Furthermore, exploitation of the reserves of the current major producers, on the scale needed to support the level of world demand anticipated in the early years of the next century, may be prevented by social and environmental pressures. Substantial reserves also exist in developing countries, but the investment needed to develop them may favour bilateral agreements between exporting and importing countries, leading to some diversity of coal prices.

The UK in world coal trade

A growing world trade in coal is likely, though the long-term price prospects are far from clear. Although port constraints limit the participation of the UK in such trade in the short term, the lead-time for expanding port facilities is similar to that of other major investments in the energy field, and this cannot be viewed as a permanent constraint.

It is sometimes suggested that coal imports should be controlled in order to protect the UK industry. However, it seems likely (e.g. Monopolies and Mergers Commission, 1983) that, apart from the low-productivity 'tail', NCB production costs would allow the UK to compete against imported power station coal particularly as new, highly efficient capacity, such as Selby, is brought into use. Key issues are inland transport and shipping costs; the latter depends on the size of vessel, port constraints and the distance travelled. Within the EEC, UK production costs are lower than those of Belgium, France and West Germany. With the growth of stocks due to low demand the NCB has recently found opportunities to export on a significant scale. The social problems created locally by the closure of uneconomic pits are, of course, real and important, but import controls are not an appropriate response to them.

In the short to medium term, UK access to world traded coal should have a stabilising influence, tending to moderate pressure for excessive wage increases, and (as recently) allowing excess stocks to be cleared. In the longer term, the fairly modest growth in production costs forecast for the NCB (see above), together with the increase in coal demand projected in this study (see chapter 14), suggest that the NCB need not feel threatened by access from world trade, particularly if world prices rise above the cost of the cheapest coal.

Because of the difficulty of predicting both world coal prices and the sterling exchange rate, we do not take world prices explicitly into account in the determination of UK prices.

12.5   Coal prices

Competition with other fuels and imported coal

The price of world-traded coal, and the competition in various markets between coal and other fuels, will place an upper bound on the price of coal in the UK. Port capacity may constrain this mechanism, and it may also be influenced by government action through, for example, the taxation of oil products or assistance in replacement of oil-fired plant by coal-fired plant.

It has been pointed out already that, unless world recession is permanent, a world coal price substantially below UK production costs is unlikely in the long term. Competition with other fuels is more complex. We suggest a hierarchy of markets which may open to coal as the difference between coal costs and oil (or gas) prices widens:

(a) Metallurgical uses – coal is the preferred fuel for technical reasons.
(b) Electricity generation – coal is currently preferred on economic grounds.
(c) Industrial steam-raising – coal is preferred to oil now in some circumstances; the size of the market is sensitive to price differences.

(d) SNG – for domestic use and industrial processes.
(e) Synthetic liquid fuels – for transport.
(f) Chemical feedstocks – a diverse market in which the economics of coal use depend very much on the route employed and the end-product.

It is also possible that market forces may allow coal prices to rise above production costs. This would create an economic rent, some of which would be likely to go to the miners (though subject to the constraints noted in section 12.3) and some could be taken as a tax by the government, just as oil is taxed at present.

Government support

Since 1978/9, the coal industry has been running at an increasing deficit, which has been made up through government grants. In 1981/2, the sum involved was £428 million, equivalent to nearly £4 per tonne of deep-mined coal. We assume that this is a temporary situation, and that the combination of new investment and the closure of uneconomic pits will ensure the industry's viability without ongoing government support. Prices will therefore be related to total production costs.

Price variations

Coal prices vary between different sectors in the UK, reflecting both differences in coal quality and different distribution costs. On the basis of statistics for the past decade, we adopt the following empirical relationships for the future:

Coal price for electricity generation or large industrial users	= NCB proceeds
Coal price for domestic or commercial consumers	= NCB proceeds × 1.5
Coke price for domestic or commercial consumers	= Domestic coal price × 1.67

12.6   Technological developments

In this study it is possible to give only a brief review of technological developments in the extraction and use of coal. For more information, the reader is referred to Grainger and Gibson (1981).

Coal extraction

There has been considerable advance in conventional deep-mining techniques in recent decades. At the time of nationalisation (1947) almost all coal was mined by 'pick and shovel' methods, but these have been almost entirely replaced by advancing or retreating longwall methods, with mechanical shearing and loading of the coal and advancing hydraulic roof supports. Technical progress is taking place continually, aiming at greater automation, more powerful machinery (power loaders up to 600 kW are in use, and the machinery for a single face may cost up to £4.5 million), improved worker safety and better environmental conditions. New mine developments give much greater scope for such progress than is feasible in existing mines. Increased computer control can both increase efficiency and reduce the number of men required underground. Output per day and output per underground man-shift are approximately doubled by a move from conventional mechanised longwall mining to advanced technology mining (ATM) or heavy-duty systems. Dust suppression (e.g. by means of water sprays) is built into most new coal-cutting plant, contributing to improving health and safety (see below). Progress in exploration, tunnelling and underground transport is also substantial; as at the coalface, new mine developments represent an opportunity for major improvements over more traditional methods.

In-situ processing

In-situ processing of coal, particularly underground gasification, has been studied for more than a century as a technique for producing a premium quality fuel and avoiding or reducing underground labour. It is possible that the use of such techniques would considerably extend the total quantity of energy recoverable from coal, by bringing into use reserves which are not accessible by conventional mining.

The basic principle of underground coal gasification (UCG) is straightforward. Air is pumped through a borehole into the coal seam, and combustion is initiated. The combustion products – carbon dioxide and water – are reduced to carbon monoxide and hydrogen before being extracted through a second borehole. The product is a mixture of carbon monoxide, hydrogen, nitrogen and other contaminants, requiring considerable cleaning and possibly chemical treatment (e.g. methanation) before use.

The practical application of this principle is complex, and very dependent on the nature of the coal and the geological structure involved. Key issues are access to the seam, coal permeability (which may be enhanced by hydrofracturing or directional drilling), control of the flame front to optimise efficiency and control of gases leaking from the seam. In total, taking into account the use of energy above ground, some 40 to 50 per cent of the energy in the coal may be recovered. Research into UCG is at present concentrated in the US and USSR. There is substantial interest in the technique in the UK, but no practical programme since 1959.

Economic analysis indicates, as expected, that UCG is most likely to be viable for shallow, thick seams, so that energy obtained in this way from otherwise inaccessible deposits is likely to be expensive. The process cannot compete economically with open-cast mining, but the cost ranges for UCG and deep-mined coal overlap. Whereas international deep-mined coal costs escalate rapidly as depth increases towards 1 km, UCG costs show more gradual escalation and the technique seems viable, in principle, at greater depths. The labour intensity of UCG is also far less than that of deep-mining (around 15 per cent of total costs compared with around 50 per cent at present for deep-mining).

The environmental impact of UCG may be significant. Leakage from the seam may be around 10 per cent, and will include toxic carbon monoxide as well as sulphur compounds and a range of organic chemicals. These pollutants may reach the surface directly, or may affect underground water. Gas cleaning and processing, and other surface activities, would have environmental effects, but these are likely to be controllable at a cost.

In conclusion, the role of UCG in the UK is unlikely to be significant in the period covered by this study. In the world as a whole, it could well be used to gain access to (probably thick) seams at depths below 1 km.

Coal use

Technological developments relating to coal use are discussed in chapters 7, 10 and 14. Coal gasification and liquefaction are considered in chapter 11.

The other potential use for coal is as a chemical feedstock. Many process routes are available, depending on the mix of products required and the economic environment. A very substantial price advantage for coal (perhaps a ratio to oil price of less than one-third) would be necessary to justify the use of coal in this market. It is probable that the use of coal as a chemical feedstock will occur initially as a subsidiary activity associated with gasification or liquefaction.

12.7   Environmental and social issues

Coal mining is generally regarded as a dangerous and unpleasant occupation, and coal is widely considered to be a smoky and inconvenient fuel. However, this image is based on historical risks which are not necessarily representative of current or future practice. Also, the hazards involved are known from past

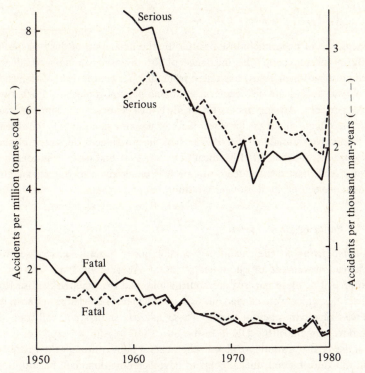

12.10 Accident statistics for the UK coal industry, 1950–80

experience and are tangible, so that the 'fear of the unknown' which may be associated with, for example, nuclear energy is not felt for coal. Flowers (1981) provides an authoritative analysis of all aspects of coal and the environment.

Worker safety

The hazardous nature of coal mining is indicated by the fact that the number of fatal accidents per man-year in 1975 was about nine times the figure for manufacturing industry as a whole, and 1.7 times the figure for the construction industry (Central Statistical Office, 1982). A miner has about a 1 per cent chance of dying as a result of an accident at work during a forty-year working life (about twice the probability of being killed in a road accident in the same period), and an 8 per cent chance of suffering an injury classified as serious. Accident rates have fallen significantly over recent decades (see figure 12.10), though they have been stable through the 1970s. It is hoped that greater attention to safety in the design of new pits will lead to a further fall in accident rates.

Worker health

The incidence of pneumoconiosis, caused by the inhalation of dust, has fallen steadily in recent years. The incidence of the disease in miners of all ages (including sub-clinical cases) has fallen from 10.2 per cent in 1961/2 to 3.6 per cent in 1980/1, and the incidence of certifiable pneumoconiosis in 1980/1 was only 0.9 per cent. Among miners under thirty-five years (an appropriate group to test the effects of recent improvements in working conditions), the disease was effectively eliminated from 1977, when more stringent dust control standards were introduced (NCB Medical Services, 1981 and earlier editions). As problems from dust are reduced, attention is being given to other problems, such as those caused by noise and vibration.

Public health and safety

For people living in the vicinity of a coal mine, hazards may arise from subsidence, movement of spoil heaps (as at Aberfan in 1966) and water pollution. All of these hazards are controllable, and the main risks arise from past activities which were carried out with less technical knowledge and with less awareness of environmental issues. These hazards should not constrain the future development of the UK industry.

Coal use is also a source of risk to the general public through the release of sulphur dioxide. Indeed, this appears to have been the dominant hazard in the past. It is convenient to identify two routes for the release of sulphur dioxide. One is the use of coal in densely-populated areas, particularly in households, which releases the gas at a low level. This can result in the formation of smog, and is a potent health hazard particularly for those prone to bronchial trouble. However, the establishment of smokeless zones, and the substantial move to gas in the domestic sector, has effectively eliminated this risk. The possible return to coal by domestic and small industrial users could re-introduce this problem in the longer term, though it should be noted that the sulphur content of UK coal is often less than that of the fuel oil currently used by industry.

The second route is the release of sulphur dioxide from power stations. At present, tall stacks are used to disperse the gas over a wide area, but it is alleged that this gives rise to 'acid rain' both in the UK and in Scandinavia, with consequent ecological damage. This is still a matter of research; if the magnitude of the problem is such that the 'tall stacks' policy is considered inadequate, it will be necessary to remove sulphur, for example by flue gas desulphurisation or by the use of suitable additives in a fluidised bed boiler. These options are expensive, and may influence the economics of coal use for electricity generation and industry. From a technological point of view, however, they are fairly straightforward.

The release of carbon dioxide from the combustion of coal may also be a hazard through its effects on the climate. Because carbon dioxide is opaque to infra-red radiation, an increase in the concentration of the gas in the atmosphere reduces the amount of heat lost by the earth to space, so leading to an increase in global temperature. Both the global carbon dioxide balance and the effect of increased carbon dioxide on climate are subjects of current research, but the present indications are that this effect could be important within the period covered by this study (e.g. Jäger, 1983). The climatic changes concerned could affect weather patterns in ways which would have profound social and political implications. How the world should respond to this possibility is by no means clear; we note it in the context of coal because coal is the fuel whose combustion releases the largest quantity of carbon dioxide per unit of energy.

Other pollutants associated with coal include particulates, oxides of nitrogen, organic compounds and radioactive elements present in the coal. These are all probably less important than sulphur, though oxides of nitrogen may also affect rainfall acidity. For a review of these and related topics from a UK perspective, see Robinson (1980).

Social issues

Coal mining is, of necessity, confined to specific areas, and in these areas it is often the dominant activity. As pits become uneconomic or are exhausted, their closure can severely dislocate the local community. This is particularly so in periods of high unemployment, which are also characterised by low demand for coal and pressure to improve the industry's efficiency by concentrating production in high productivity areas. The closure programme which is needed over the next two decades will affect the South Wales area in particular (where operating losses in 1981/2 were £13.2/tonne compared with a national average of £2.6/tonne), with Scotland and the North-East also substantially affected.

The 'correct' point at which to close a mine depends on the marginal cost of production (i.e. the element of costs which will actually be saved if production ceases) in relation to average costs and costs from new mines. Delay beyond this point may be justified if energy price rises are anticipated which would make a particular pit viable in the fairly near future, and this situation can readily be accommodated in the economic analysis. There is, however, no realistic basis for the view that pits should always be worked to exhaustion; this would merely be a subsidy from coal users to miners. The social problems resulting from pit closures are, nonetheless, real and important. In some cases it may be possible to site new mining developments, with higher productivity, in the same areas, as at Betws in South Wales, and this will ameliorate the impact of pit closures. Other possible measures include incentives to other industries in the areas concerned, and help to miners to move elsewhere. As with many other issues, satisfactory growth in the economy as a whole is likely to be as important as specific measures.

New coal mining developments may also be opposed because they are expected to change the character of the area concerned. Though this fear may be justified in some cases, it is likely that it owes much to an outdated image of coal, and modern mining developments need be no more obtrusive than any modern factory or office buildings.

13

UK energy conservation

Energy conservation has been discussed in other chapters for different sectors of final demand and in the energy industries, and expected levels of achievement are built in to our illustrative forecasts for future energy demand in the UK. In this chapter we shall be concerned with the role of government, or more specifically with the relations between government, other institutions and the public, since it is the actions of consumers that ultimately determine how much energy is used or saved. We shall include some discussion of the meaning of energy conservation and its measurement: how otherwise can progress and achievement be observed? We shall also consider obstacles to progress and how they might be overcome or modified. Finally, we shall review the needs and policies for energy conservation.

13.1 The role of government

Prior to the energy crisis of 1973 there was almost no involvement by the UK government in energy conservation, except for fuel rationing in wartime and petrol rationing following the 1956 Suez crisis. The idea that government could have an important role was put forward by the Central Policy Review Staff (CPRS, 1974) and independently by the National Economic Development Office (NEDO, 1974). It is true that building regulations already required minimum standards of insulation for dwellings, but the latter derived from health considerations, and were stimulated more by the need to reduce damp and condensation than by a desire to save energy. There had been no mention of energy conservation in the 1967 White Paper on Fuel Policy (Cmnd 3438, Ministry of Power, 1967).

However, in particular situations, through the nationalised industries, government had encouraged technical progress which sometimes led to spectacular energy savings. For example, the average efficiency of electricity generation improved from 22 per cent in the 1940s to over 30 per cent in the 1970s, and the conversion from coal-fired steam engines to diesels on the railways led to a fivefold reduction in energy consumption between 1960 and 1972 with only a relatively small reduction in passenger and freight traffic. Again, the rapid introduction of natural gas into the domestic sector encouraged the use of new and more efficient heating systems for dwellings and held their total consumption nearly constant whilst standards of heating were greatly improved. In the iron and steel industry new investment plans approved by government in the 1960s led to new technologies, such as basic oxygen steel-making, that reduced energy consumption per unit of output in addition to savings on other costs. Such developments as these were achieved without any specific dedication by government to energy conservation and without the added incentive of higher energy prices that began in 1973.

The two 1974 reports on energy conservation (by the CPRS and by NEDO) were in the form of recommendations to government rather than statements of government policy. The most urgent need was for coordination and exploration of options. At that time there was almost no general expertise on conservation either inside or outside government, nor was there adequate support for research and development. The first response by government came in 1974 with the appointment of the Advisory Council on Energy Conservation (ACEC) to advise the Secretary of State in the newly named Department of Energy, and the establishment of the Energy Technology Support Unit (ETSU) at Harwell under contract to the Department. The ACEC, chaired by a distinguished engineer, Professor Sir William Hawthorne, Master of Churchill College, Cambridge, included the chairmen (or deputy chairmen) of major energy supply industries, representatives of industrial and other consumers and the TUC, and some academics, with the chief scientists of the Department of Energy, Industry and the Environment as assessors. A separate initiative from the Department of Industry, also in 1974, set in progress two programmes to study (jointly with the Department of Energy) the industrial use of energy – the Audit Scheme, designed to evaluate the technologies of energy use in particular industries and identify opportunities for improved energy use through technological development, and the Thrift Scheme, which provided subsidised one-day energy surveys to identify energy-saving measures that could be immediately adopted with very little cost.

At the end of 1974 Mr Eric Varley, Secretary of State for Energy, announced a twelve-point interim programme of measures to save energy. This included a loan scheme for energy-saving investment in industry, a request to management and unions to include energy savings as a regular item in their joint consultation, a proposal for higher petrol prices, deferral of further reductions in the lead content of petrol to prevent further increases in the oil import bill, lower speed limits for road vehicles and a doubling of the standards required for insulation of new dwellings. The government would also back a publicity campaign to inform and advise consumers on energy savings – the 'Save-It' campaign.

Political and public pressure undoubtedly contributed to the government initiative in the twelve-point interim programme. The House of Commons Select Committee on Science and Technology was about to begin a study of energy conservation and would be taking evidence from the Secretary of State for Energy early in 1975. When their report appeared in July of that year (Select Committee on Science and Technology, 1975) it was apparent that the interim measures did not satisfy the Select Committee, who had expected to see a second package at an earlier date, and stated: 'We are deeply concerned at the general lack of urgency.' Their main recommendation was for an energy conservation 'Task Force' of ministers, officials and a few outside experts. This was accompanied by thirty or forty more detailed recommendations including: the use of targets for energy savings, compulsory use of heating control systems in some buildings, statutory controls on thermal insulation standards for offices, shops and commercial premises, extended information and advice services, inverted tariff structures for electricity and gas, grants to local authorities for energy conservation measures, test studies severely restricting private car use in one or two selected cities, statutory checks on fuel efficiencies of older cars. Amongst the targets was a proposed remit for the Task Force to aim at 15 per cent energy savings within two to three years. Although such a target might have been a useful persuader to show the need and the urgency, it was, at least with hindsight, quite unrealistic. The required measures were not identified in sufficient detail, the factors influencing market penetration of energy conservation measures were not understood, the government machinery and expertise was inadequate to identify – let alone manage – a massive conservation programme, necessarily involving many decentralised decisions.

However, one of the important features of a Select Committee Report is that the government is obliged to publish a reply. The preparation of the reply to the report on conservation reinforced other pressures on government to strengthen their teams of officials concerned with energy conservation, and added to the learning process on what could be done to improve the efficiency with which energy is used. The Departments of Energy, Industry and the Environment all began to develop a core of officials able and willing to assess or initiate proposals on energy conservation, and to defend necessary expenditure or other measures against officials or others supporting different causes.

The government's reply (Cmnd 6575, Department of Energy, 1976) to the Select Committee rejected some of the more draconian proposals: 'There are limits on how active a part Government can play without getting into a situation where it is taking consumers' decisions for them in a way that overlooks or undervalues factors to which they attach weight.' Conservation is important, they stated, but it should not pre-empt resources that would more profitably be devoted to other aspects of efficiency. The idea of a Task Force was deflected by appointing a minister in the Department of Energy with special responsibility for energy conservation, and making similar appointments in other departments. These ministers would provide overall coordination of governmental activities on energy conservation, and would have advice from the ACEC and from the Department of Energy's Conservation Unit, which was established in the summer of 1975. Similar arrangements were made for coordinating research and development on energy conservation including a strengthening of ETSU.

The coordinating committee of ministers functioned intermittently for two or three years, but the corresponding links between officials were probably more useful in the long run. The increasing responsibilities of the Conservation Unit led to its promotion to become a division of the Department of Energy. By 1983 it was evident that management and coordination of the conservation activities in different departments could be carried out more effectively if more of them were brought together in the Department of Energy in the form of an 'Energy Efficiency Office'. This would include the energy unit from the Department of Industry and would have more direct control over energy conservation activities in other departments.

13.2   Action by government

The gestation period for the government's second package of energy conservation measures turned out to be three years rather than the three months expected by the parliamentary Select Committee. This was due partly to the sheer lack of information both in government and elsewhere about energy-using activities and the potential or options for energy conservation, particularly in industry. For example, if grants were to be given for insulation or improved equipment, what were the best options, how would they be de-limited, how much would they cost and what would be the resultant energy savings? The resources made available to seek answers to these questions were inadequate and there was a lack of direction, notwithstanding the ministerial committee. Ministers changed too quickly to develop both knowledge and commitment on energy conservation. Public and parliamentary pressures for action were weakened and diffused by pressures for action on new and renewable energy sources. Government technologists and financial support were allocated to work on the next century's problems of energy from the sun, wind, waves and hot rocks, rather than the more substantial and immediate potential of energy conservation.

The key political incentive for a new initiative on energy conservation came with the visit to London in May 1977 by President Carter following his announcement of a major conservation programme in the US. The British prime minister, Mr Callaghan, joined him in including energy conservation amongst the priorities for new initiatives. The ACEC were asked in June 1977 to propose action areas (Energy Paper 31, Annex B, ACEC, 1978), and the government machine began to move. With a prime ministerial commitment, the Department of Energy was able to obtain support from other departments in the preparation of a substantial package of measures.

This package was approved by government and announced in December 1977. Some four years into the new era of high oil prices, it represented the first real evidence of a major commitment to a national energy conservation programme. This was designed to achieve energy savings that would amount to 11 MTOE (484 PJ, about 5 per cent of total use) after ten years, and expenditure of some £470 million was allocated for the first four years of the programme (1978/9 to 1980/1). Details are given in Energy Paper 33 (Annex B, Inter-Departmental officials, 1979) and 41 (Annex 4, Department of Energy, 1979). The aim was to:

- bring both private and public sector houses up to a basic level of insulation;
- improve the efficiency with which energy is used in the public sector, both for its own sake and as an example to private consumers;
- promote energy-saving investment in industry, commerce and agriculture;
- demonstrate the value of new or adapted technology to industry, commerce and agriculture, and, through research, development and demonstration (RD&D), to put the UK in a position to take advantage of new technology as it becomes cost-effective;
- reduce the rate of growth in demand for oil in transport;
- develop a national awareness of the need for energy conservation.

Details of the programme included a loan sanction to local authorities of over £100 million in the four years to 1982 to provide basic insulation in public sector housing. In a corresponding procedure for private dwellings, grants of 66 per cent up to a maximum of £50 were made available for basic insulation, with a total of £25 million allocated for use in the first year. Improved standards for insulation of hot water tanks were approved. Proposals for better insulation for dwellings, beyond the improved standards introduced in 1975, were set in progress. A series of leaflets on home insulation was introduced. An additional expenditure of over £100 million was announced for improved insulation and heating controls in central government buildings, in hospitals and other NHS buildings and in schools.

The approach by government to energy conservation in transport, whilst taking account of personal preferences and the realities of the market place, was shown by the introduction of compulsory fuel consumption testing and labelling of new petrol driven cars, and a voluntary agreement by the Society of Motor Manufacturers and Traders on an improvement target of 10 per cent for average petrol consumption of new cars by 1985. These may seem modest objectives, but they provided a valuable incentive towards recognition and awareness by the public of the value of improved efficiency of cars and, in a highly competitive market, the manufacturers will need to go considerably beyond the initial modest target.

Measures for energy conservation in industry approved in 1977 included £25 million over two years for selective grants to replace or improve inefficient boiler plant and insulate premises. A tax allowance was introduced which also covered insulation of heating systems in existing buildings. Grants were made available for one-day energy surveys and for more detailed energy audits. The voluntary development of effective energy management in industry was given an important boost by the provision of national energy management courses, and the formation of energy managers' groups. Finally the 'Save-It' campaign of national advertising and publicity was maintained and nearly £2 million was allocated for 1980.

In 1979, the Labour government was replaced by a Conservative one, dedicated to a reduction in state intervention and expenditure, and with greater conviction on the role of market forces. Those measures introduced in 1977 where definite commitments had been made were maintained, but extensions and renewals became rare. The selective insulation grants for industry came to an end in 1980, but a new scheme was introduced to encourage conversion from oil-fired boilers to coal-fired boilers for steam-raising (Energy Paper 49, ACEC, 1982). New building regulations with higher standards of insulation were approved. The insulation grants allowed to owner-occupiers and tenants of private dwellings were extended to tenants of local authorities, but the separation of capital allowances to local authorities for basic insulation of their dwellings from other capital allowances was discontinued, on the grounds that, within their own expenditure limits, they should be free to decide their own spending priorities.

The reduced intervention on energy conservation by the Conservative government compared with their Labour predecessors was compensated, at least in part, by their approach to energy pricing. The price of natural gas, particularly to domestic consumers, had been allowed by the Labour government to fall in real terms, and it was not only priced too low either to encourage conservation or for equity between consumers of different fuels, but its price did not take proper account of the long-run costs represented by new contracts to purchase Norwegian gas. At the risk of courting unpopularity with the electorate, the government imposed a real price increase for gas of 10 per cent per annum for three years – in money terms this meant a doubling of the price over the period.

As we noted above, not all of the governmental activities on energy conservation disappeared under the Conservatives. The ACEC remained in being, despite the widespread culling of similar publicly-appointed bodies, and it continued to exhort both government and others. The department's Conservation Unit became first a division and then the Energy Efficiency Office, despite general reductions in Civil Service numbers. Much of the credit for the modest degree of continuity in the active programme, and the development of institutional arrangements, should go to the increasing number of senior officials who were convinced of its importance and value. The evidence of such commitment can be seen in the inter-departmental report by officials (Energy Paper 33, 1979, cited above) on 'Energy conservation: scope for new measures and long-term strategy'. This review took place after the second (1977) package of conservation measures involving an initial commitment of £450 million. Their report stressed the importance of economic pricing, 'energy prices should reinforce [other] energy conservation measures and not work against them'; no doubt this observation was designed to remind ministers of the long-term perils of pleasing their electors unduly on energy prices. They recommended a continuation of information services on energy conservation, and emphasised the need for both government and the nationalised industries to set a good example. The report also gave support to training schemes on energy efficiency, to research, development and demonstration projects, and to improved energy-efficiency standards and codes of practice. However, it came out against mandatory regulations, except for those relating to a progressive improvement of standards for energy conservation in buildings. With regard to further financial incentives, the report said, in effect, wait and see the results of the schemes already in progress. In conclusion the report stated:

> Energy conservation is not a once and for all activity and cannot be achieved overnight. Policy and measures will need to be developed in the light of changing circumstances. Progress should be reviewed regularly and reported to ministers.

13.3   Progress and measurement

A functional definition

Before we can describe progress in energy conservation we need to say what it means – what it is that we are measuring. In their fifth report, the ACEC (1983) define energy conservation as *the adoption of any measure that cost-effectively increases benefits relative to the amount of energy consumed* – in other words 'the more cost-efficient use of energy'. They continue:

Switching from scarce to more plentiful fuels, and improvements in energy efficiency resulting from technical change, would be included in the definition, provided the benefits were not outweighed by costs. It is important also that the notion of benefits should include factors such as increased comfort . . . [thus] improvements in standards of living without any increase in energy consumption represent a benefit from energy conservation in the same way as energy saving . . . This functional definition represents an approach rather than a precise formula, and it is likely that additional more specific definitions will prove useful for individual sectors.

The energy ratio

One well-known measure of improvements in national energy efficiency is provided by reductions in the 'energy ratio' – the ratio between total primary energy consumption and GDP. In the UK this ratio has been decreasing since about 1880, though not at a uniform rate. Between 1950 and 1973, when energy prices were nearly constant, the energy ratio decreased at an average annual rate of 1.0 per cent, but between 1973 and 1982 the decrease averaged 2.0 per cent per annum. It is tempting, but misleading, to identify the additional 1 per cent per annum decrease as energy conservation. Much of it was due to structural change within the UK economy, notably the relative decline of manufacturing industry and the disproportionate decline of energy-intensive industries, particularly iron and steel.

Some of these structural effects will be reversed, or at least moderated, by economic recovery following the recession. Some are partly due to the increase in energy prices, finally tipping the balance against older industries in the UK which had for long been losing their comparative advantage over competitors in other countries. The Department of Energy have estimated that energy savings totalling some 6 per cent (aggregating all sectors except transport) over the period 1973–80 are attributable to the effects of rising real prices for energy (evidence for Sizewell Inquiry, Department of Energy, 1982) – though they warn that estimates of this kind are subject to considerable uncertainty.

Work by Jenne and Cattell (1983), discussed earlier in chapter 7, shows that structural change accounted for about half the 18 per cent reduction in the energy/output ratio for industry in the period 1973–82. The residual of 9 per cent represents an average annual energy-efficiency improvement of 1.0 per cent, similar to that experienced during 1968–73 before the increase in energy prices. However, during this earlier period industry was expanding, and investment in new equipment would have given a natural technological gain in energy efficiency. Conversely, during the period 1973–82, industry contracted and there were cash-flow problems that inhibited the purchase of new equipment. It is therefore not unreasonable to suppose that the higher energy prices and the increasing awareness of energy conservation options, aided by government publicity and support, contributed to the maintenance of efficiency improvements during 1973–82 at pre-crisis levels despite the recession. However, many industrialists will be aware of situations where cost-effective measures for energy conservation have been postponed because of low industrial activity and cash-flow problems, so it is probable that more would have been achieved if the government grants had been more generous or had continued over a longer period. More may be achieved also when industrial activity picks up after the recession.

In the domestic sector, discussed in chapter 6, we have seen that there was a steady improvement in energy efficiency through the 1960s and 1970s, with relatively small changes in total energy consumption, whilst living standards improved through the installation of central heating and other household equipment. This comes firmly within the ACEC's definition of energy conservation, though it would have ben less readily accepted in the mid-1970s when 'Save It' was the conservation slogan. During the period 1973–82 energy consumption in the domestic sector increased by nearly 5 per cent; however, there was an increase in the number of households and a rise in ownership of appliances using electricity (colour TV, freezers, dishwashers), and energy consumption for space and water heating per household showed a decline. But the limited response to energy-saving measures such as cavity-wall insulation, discussed in chapter 6, indicates that the potential for energy conservation is being realised only slowly.

The measurement of energy conservation in the transport sector displays even greater difficulties. The increase in car ownership represents, for most people, an improved standard of living, and this has been reflected in the continuing increase in energy consumption for transport – up by 8 per cent during 1973–82. Estimates of energy conservation can be made only by detailed modelling, based primarily on improved technical efficiencies of transport vehicles, modal changes and changes in load factors, as discussed in chapter 8. No clear conclusions emerge for the period 1973–82, though it may be noted that, although pricing signals were erratic due to fluctuating government policies on taxation, the concept of energy-efficient vehicles has become an important selling-point.

We conclude that estimates of overall progress on energy conservation may be misleading when expressed in terms of simple totals for energy use and economic activity. It is of greater value if a variety of indices are used that indicate the take-up of specific conservation measures, such as dwellings with

100 mm loft insulation, or with cavity-wall insulation, or motor cars with specific improvements in technology for energy efficiency. For industry also there are some specific technical measures, of heat recovery and insulation for example, that can be similarly identified, but often the greatest savings will come from new products or new product design. In their fifth report the ACEC (1983) took the view that the take-up of energy conservation measures identified in this way was poor and concluded that UK progress on energy conservation had been unsatisfactory, even though in terms of national aggregates it appeared to have been better than in some other industrialised countries.

13.4   Obstacles to energy conservation

The first and perhaps the greatest obstacle to energy conservation is its insubstantial nature – it cannot be packaged and sold in supermarkets, nor displayed in the front parlour. Its benefits are not here and now – they are a promise for the future: fuel bills will be lower, we shall be warmer and, because energy efficiency promotes industrial efficiency, we should be more prosperous in the future. These are hard concepts to sell, particularly when there is often significant uncertainty about the magnitude of the benefits even in specific cases.

The second great obstacle to energy conservation is its diversity and the third is its decentralised nature. Its diversity means that in particular situations, in a factory, or an office, or a dwelling or a vehicle, the factors that influence energy efficiency are many and various, ranging from the technology, processes or equipment, to the behaviour of the operators or occupants. The wide dispersion of energy-using equipment makes it difficult for centralised decisions or policies to be effective: at best their consequences will be uncertain, at worst they could divert resources from more useful projects.

The fourth great obstacle to energy conservation is that energy costs rarely dominate over other costs, whether in factories, homes or transport, and the benefits from improved energy efficiency may not be justified in isolation but may depend on some associated benefit, for example from new equipment, new dwellings or new vehicles.

The moral to be drawn from these difficulties is *not* that the government should abandon intervention except through energy-pricing policies and leave conservation to market forces. The moral is that the market for selling energy conservation is highly imperfect and even though effective central intervention may be difficult it is highly desirable if national benefits are to be reaped from improving energy efficiencies. The four great obstacles observed above give rise to many more detailed problems that present barriers to energy conservation:

- In the UK the replacement of equipment tends to be slower than in countries with higher economic growth, and it is particularly slow during economic recession. This increases the importance of energy-conserving modifications or retrofit alongside other measures to improve the competitive position of manufacturing industry.

- The wide diversity and dispersion of energy use creates institutional obstacles to energy conservation. Action needed from government overlaps many different departments, particularly Energy, Industry, Environment and Transport. Some of the resulting difficulties will be ameliorated by the creation of the Energy Efficiency Office, but others are bound to remain, not only because the major spending departments have other priorities than energy conservation, but also because the Treasury is reluctant to make capital grants where the benefit (through energy conservation) goes to the recipient and only indirectly benefits national finances.

- This division between expenditure and benefit creates barriers to energy conservation elsewhere. In dwellings or other buildings the landlord perceives the cost of conservation falling on him and the benefit in fuel savings or greater comfort going to the tenant. The tenant perceives the capital stock improvement going to the landlord, and, if the benefit is taken in greater comfort, the tenant does not end up with lower fuel bills so he would be reluctant to pay increased rent.

- Time horizons vary widely between different users of energy. A factory owner or manager may be concerned during a recession with financial viability from month to month – a three-year payback from energy conservation measures could then be way outside his time horizon. Similarly, a householder may expect to move within a few years, say two to seven, and would be reluctant to invest in conservation that is unlikely to make an identifiable difference to the value of his house. For many older buildings the cost of retrofit to provide good thermal insulation and draughtproofing is high and, even in national terms, the financial return is likely to be less than for other projects.

- The competition between investment capital for energy supply and for energy conservation undoubtedly is an obstacle to greater energy efficiency. The national discount rate of 5 per cent applied to investment for the generation of electric power would seem to justify a vast range of measures for energy conservation. However, the centralised decisions for electric power production are executively simpler than the multitude of decentralised decisions on conservation, and the provision of an electricity supply to ensure that demand can be met is an important element of freedom of choice.

13.5   Energy conservation policy and options

It is useful to remind ourselves of the reasons for energy conservation since these determine objectives and should influence policy and options. These are well summarised in paragraph 5.2 of the Green Paper on Energy Policy (Cmnd 7101, Department of Energy, 1978a):

> Improving the efficiency with which energy is used brings benefits both to the individual user and to the nation. The efficient use of energy resources saves money for the individual and the firm, increases industrial competitiveness and reduces the proportion of our national resources that has to be put into supplying energy. It reduces the rate at which finite reserves of energy such as oil, natural gas and coal are being used, postponing the time when they can no longer meet an expanding demand and the date of their ultimate exhaustion, and providing more time to develop and introduce the technologies that must ultimately replace them. It makes less formidable the worldwide problem of meeting, expensively and with difficulty, an expanding demand for energy. Reducing the production and use of energy through greater efficiency lessens the impact of energy on the environment. For all these reasons energy conservation is now seen by almost all countries as an integral part of energy policy.

To these reasons we would add that, for the UK, energy conservation can provide an important element of energy policy to avoid an excessive future dependence on energy imports. The risk from this, to which we shall return in chapter 15, is that a high level of energy imports creates a high exposure to fluctuating world energy prices – a likely future, as we have seen in chapter 2.

The main components of an energy conservation strategy recommended to government by the (1979) inter-department report on energy conservation by officials, cited earlier, are:

- Energy pricing.
- Information and motivation.
- Setting a good example.
- Specialised advice and training.
- Standards.
- Research, development and demonstration.
- Mandatory measures.
- Financial incentives.

To these we would add that government should always take account of the energy implications of its overall economic, industrial and social policies. They should bear in mind that energy costs are expected to increase, that industries that were once viable in the UK may lose their comparative advantage and that housing policy should allow flexibility so that future generations are not saddled with inefficient buildings as we are today. We consider the main elements of strategy in turn.

Energy pricing

Unless energy prices reflect the long-run cost of energy, they will give the wrong signals to energy consumers. Economic pricing in this sense needs to play a central role in energy conservation policy. However, the slow take-up of many conservation measures that give a good economic return at current prices shows that a correct policy on energy prices is not sufficient by itself – it needs to be reinforced by other measures.

Information and motivation

For many consumers, the use of energy represents only a small part of their activities and costs. Its diversity of use even for a single establishment means that consumers are rarely aware of the best way to use energy efficiently or to make investments to improve its effective use. To help him save energy the consumer needs adequate information about energy costs and ways in which energy can be used more efficiently.

Setting a good example

Public administration accounts for about 6 per cent of energy consumption in the UK and it is important that this use should be efficient. In addition, through local authorities, government is responsible as a landlord for over six million dwellings. It was planned in 1978 to bring them up to a minimum standard of (loft) insulation, but other improvements are also needed.

Advice and training

The main need here is to maintain and extend existing schemes, and in particular to see that they are adequately financed so that employers are not discouraged from using them by the expense involved.

Standards

It is likely that the best progress on improved standards in energy efficiency will come from public demand – for energy-efficient heating equipment, for better-insulated houses, for cars with lower petrol consumption. However, government can encourage such public demand through its influence on trade associations and other bodies concerned with standards. In housing it is clearly necessary to set mandatory standards (see below), but in other areas improved public awareness and trade response is likely to provide more versatility. For example, improved designs can often reduce energy needs by saving materials – this would be very difficult to achieve through mandatory standards on energy efficiency.

Research, development and demonstration

There has been a successful programme for identification of new technologies for energy conservation that are capable of replication but require operating experience to establish their reliability and their costs and benefits. Credit should go to the industrial companies involved and to the ETSU and NEL management teams. There has been less satisfactory support for work not directly related to conventional engineering, for example research on the market penetration or take-up of established energy conservation technologies, where the factors that influence decision-making and the potential for improvement through government aid on particular technologies are not well understood. Interdisciplinary in character, but central to policy on energy conservation, this area of research seems to fall in the chasm between the two cultures of engineering science and social studies – it is a good example of institutional failure to cope with the diversity of energy conservation.

Mandatory measures

By far the most important of these are the insulation standards for new buildings, where standards should be progressively raised in line with the technical capabilities of the building industry and the skills of the workforce. Elsewhere, particularly in industry, mandatory measures could have adverse effects on overall industrial efficiency. In other sectors, such as transport, mandatory standards could aid progress in energy efficiency, but, for example, restrictions on transport modes could begin to infringe on individual preferences and personal freedom.

Financial incentives

The slow take-up of conservation measures shows that both companies and private householders are unlikely to take full advantage of cost-effective investment opportunities unless they are given some inducement to do so. As a result the level of conservation investment that is desirable on policy grounds may not be achieved, or the required adjustment may not take place until too late. It is therefore of great importance for (properly researched) government aid to be provided to improve energy efficiencies or to aid substitution from oil or gas to lower-cost fuels.

14

The UK energy outlook

14.1 Introduction

In this chapter, we bring together the results of the demand sector analyses and the assessments of fuel supply to outline the prospects for energy in the UK as a whole. The resulting pictures are not intended as quantitative forecasts, but as a framework for the discussion of energy policy issues here and in chapter 15. We examine first the overall primary energy balance, and the change in aggregate energy efficiency over the period of the study. We then consider the changing structure of final energy consumption before analysing the prospects for each major primary fuel and for electricity.

14.2 Primary energy balance

At present, the UK enjoys a net energy surplus. Imports of gas from the Norwegian sector of the North Sea (414 PJ in 1982) are more than offset, in energy and in financial terms, by net exports of oil (1284 PJ in 1982). Figure 14.1 shows the future energy balance for the central economic growth case, together with the structure of indigenous fuel supply. It may be seen that the period of UK self-sufficiency is short-lived, and that from around 1990 onwards we would once again be dependent on imports. We note several features of this picture:

(a) Coal production (see section 14.5) remains nearly constant, with new investment offsetting the fall in capacity resulting from the closure of uneconomic pits.

(b) Oil supply falls sharply through the 1990s, and gas a little later, so that the total contribution of these fuels, which peaks at some 65 per cent of UK primary fuel production around 1985, has fallen to 50 and 27 per cent by 2000 and 2020 respectively.

(c) The contribution from nuclear energy, hydro-electric power and other renewable electricity sources (within which nuclear energy is by far the most important) does not rise substantially until the early years of the next century, allowing a substantial energy import requirement to

253

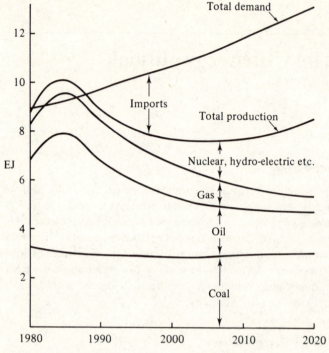

14.1 UK primary energy balance, central case, 1980–2020

develop. By the end of the period, the rate of increase of nuclear capacity (see section 14.8) is sufficient to stabilise the import requirement.

The pattern for the other economic growth scenarios is summarised in table 14.1. Some adjustment of energy supply takes place in response to economic growth, but it is not sufficient to match the change in demand, so that import requirements are higher under high economic growth, and conversely.

The structure of imports is shown for the central case in figure 14.2. Exports, when they occur, are almost wholly in the form of oil. However, oil demand exceeds supply from some time in the 1990s, creating a growing import requirement. The major import, however, is of coal, which is used to fuel the growing demand for electricity (see section 14.8) during the period when nuclear power expansion is limited. Gas imports rise initially (these could be in the form of pipeline gas from the Norwegian North Sea or continental Europe, or as LNG), but fall later as world gas supplies start to decline.

Both the scale and structure of fuel imports are very uncertain, and will be

Table 14.1. *UK primary energy balance to 2020*

	Energy demand[a]	Indigenous energy supply	Import requirement	Import dependence[b]
	EJ	EJ	EJ	%
1980	8.9	8.7	0.2[c]	2
High economic growth:				
2000	11.3	7.9	3.4	30
2020	15.4	9.5	5.9	38
Central economic growth:				
2000	10.6	7.6	3.0	28
2020	13.1	8.5	4.6	35
Low economic growth:				
2000	9.5	7.2	2.3	24
2020	10.1	7.4	2.7	27

Notes:[a] Energy demand includes ships' bunkers.
[b] Import dependence is defined as the ratio of imports to total demand × 100 per cent.
[c] 1980 import requirement does not take stock adjustment or statistical errors into account.

sensitive to change both within and outside the UK. For example, higher world gas prices could prompt a switch from imported gas to coal-based SNG, increasing coal imports. Conversely, high world coal prices would encourage gas imports, and could substantially reduce coal imports by increasing electricity costs and thereby reducing electricity demand.

Are these high levels of imports sustainable? If we make the simplifying assumption that import costs are equal to average UK costs (where costs include taxes levied on oil and gas producers), then net energy import costs become positive (for the central case) just before 1990, and rise to nearly 3 per cent of GDP by 2000, stabilising at just under 4 per cent (though note that small changes in assumptions may lead to significant changes in this figure). Comparison with the historical pattern in the UK and elsewhere suggests that such a level of import costs is high, but probably sustainable given the generally optimistic climate for industrial output which is implicit in this scenario.

Seen in a world context, however, the picture appears less consistent. In comparison with many developed economies, the UK is in a strong energy supply position. If our energy import dependence approaches 30 per cent by the end of the century (see table 14.1), then it is likely that many industrialised

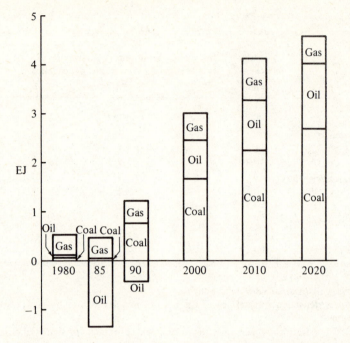

14.2 The structure of UK energy imports, central case, 1980–2020

countries will be in a similar, or a worse, situation. Such a view of the world is unlikely to be internally consistent, which implies that the relatively modest assumptions we have made for world energy prices (particularly for coal later in the period) are unrealistic, and that import costs would therefore be higher. Furthermore, the decline of the UK as an oil-producing country, together with increasing energy imports, will exert a downward pressure on the exchange rate (which we have assumed remains constant at around $1.5 in 1980 terms), which would increase the sterling cost of energy imports. It should also be noted that for an energy-importing country, exchange rates effects amplify the impact of changes in world fuel prices, which is a very unwelcome source of instability. We therefore conclude that the projected level of imports is a major area of concern in long-term energy policy.

14.3   Energy efficiency

It might be argued that the level of import dependence discussed in the previous section is the result of an over-cautious view of the prospects for aggregate energy efficiency. Figure 14.3 shows the ratios of primary energy and final

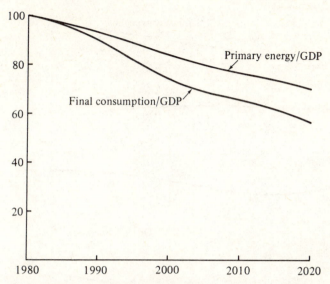

14.3 Projections of aggregate energy intensity, central case, 1980–2020. (Scaled to 1980 = 100.0.) Includes ships' bunkers

consumption to GDP for the central case. Final consumption per unit of GDP falls by 26 per cent between 1980 and 2000, and by 44 per cent over the period as a whole. The reduction in primary energy intensity is smaller (30 per cent over the whole period), owing to the shift to greater use of electricity. Aggregate conservation is greater in the high growth case and less in the low growth case (31 and 27 per cent respectively for primary energy intensity); this is mainly the result of saturation, especially in the household sector.

These substantial improvements in energy efficiency are, of course, the result of structural change as well as energy conservation. There is no doubt that, in many sectors, the technical potential for energy conservation is larger than is implicit in figure 14.3. Nevertheless, the obstacles to the achievement of that potential are considerable, as the discussions in the consumption sector chapters (6–9) and in chapter 13 have shown. It would not be prudent therefore to 'assume away' the future energy problem by postulating more rapid gains in aggregate energy efficiency.

14.4 Final consumption

The mix of fuels in final consumption, shown for the central case in figure 14.4, changes substantially over the period. From 13 per cent in 1980, solid fuels rise to 17 per cent in 2000 and 24 per cent in 2020, with most of the rise occurring in

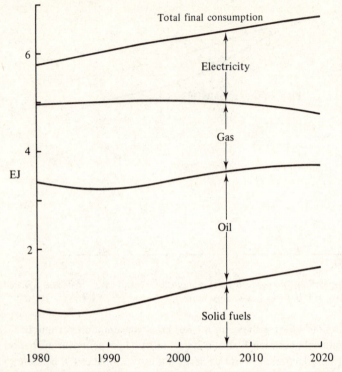

14.4 Projections of fuel shares in final consumption, central case, 1980–2020

industry. Electricity also makes great gains, increasing its share from 14 per cent in 1980 to 20 and 30 per cent in 2000 and 2020 respectively, a factor increase in electricity demand of 2.5 over the whole period (see section 14.8). Oil, on the other hand, falls from 45 per cent to 31 per cent, and is increasingly confined to the transport sector. Gas (including manufactured gas) accounts for 15 per cent in 2020, compared with 27 per cent in 1980.

Table 14.2 shows the split of final consumption between sectors. The household sector falls in importance, since its energy demand is only weakly linked to economic growth. Conversely, both industry and services grow in importance, while transport retains a nearly constant share in final consumption.

14.5   Coal supply and demand

Table 14.3 shows the demand for coal in the three economic growth scenarios, indicating that a very large increase in coal supply may be needed. The projected coal demand in the central case is consistent with output targets for

Table 14.2 *Sectoral structure of final energy consumption, central case (PJ; percentages in brackets)*

	1980	1990	2000	2020
Households	1665 (29)	1561 (26)	1473 (23)	1221 (18)
Iron and steel	302 (5)	380 (6)	391 (6)	444 (7)
Other industry	1537 (27)	1610 (27)	1773 (28)	2336 (34)
Transport	1489 (26)	1673 (28)	1763 (28)	1707 (25)
Services	789 (13)	827 (14)	908 (14)	1074 (16)
Total	5783 (100)	6051 (100)	6308 (100)	6782 (100)

Note: Summations may not be exact due to round-off.

Table 14.3. *UK coal demand to 2020 (PJ; million tonnes in brackets)*

	High case	Central case	Low case
1980	3140 (122)	3140 (122)	3140 (122)
1990	3772 (147)	3702 (144)	3457 (135)
2000	4782 (187)	4487 (175)	3996 (156)
2020	6885 (269)	5776 (225)	4126 (161)

the coal industry published in 1977 (see chapter 12), but it is now generally recognised that the supply of capital, together with environmental and planning constraints, make the previously forecast high levels of output very unlikely. A more realistic view (as shown in figure 14.1) is that new investment will do little more than offset the decline in capacity resulting from the closure of uneconomic pits, giving a level of production in 2020 of somewhere between 100 and 140 million tonnes. The demand projections therefore imply massive coal imports.

As noted earlier, the price at which coal imports will be available to the UK in the long term is of key importance for energy policy, and is extremely difficult to predict. The implied high levels of coal imports therefore represent a source of risk, the management of which is an important long-term problem.

Coal use in the central case is portrayed in figure 14.5. Electricity generation remains the major application, accounting for 63 per cent of coal use in 2020 compared with 68 per cent in 1980. Industry is a growing market, reaching 18 per cent by 2020. Solid-fuel manufacture is tied to the output of the iron and steel industry, and remains fairly stable. Gas manufacture becomes significant

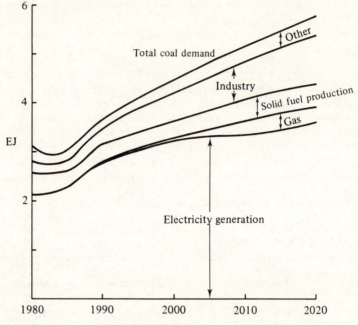

14.5 The structure of coal demand, central case, 1980–2020

beyond 2000, but its growth is limited by the competition which gas is by this time experiencing from electricity. The fall in demand between 1980 and 1985 is the result of stock-building by users in the early 1980s, and is not significant in a planning context.

The pattern of coal demand indicates that the most important influences on the scale of coal imports will be the demand for electricity and the rate of expansion of nuclear capacity; we note that 1 GW of nuclear capacity replaces annually some 2.7 million tonnes of coal (about 64 PJ).

14.6   Oil supply and demand

The balance between oil demand for the three economic growth cases and indigenous oil production is shown in figure 14.6. The range of oil production is the result of uncertainty about reserves on the UK Continental Shelf (see chapter 11); for any given level of reserves, the timing of production can be varied to some extent as a matter of depletion policy. On a central view of reserves, self-sufficiency lasts from now until between 1992 and 1996; with high reserves and low growth it could last into the early years of the next century. By

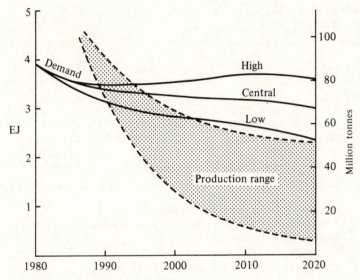

14.6 Oil demand and production in the UK, 1980–2020

the end of the period, imports (against a central view of reserves) are between 30 and 54 per cent of demand. Because of the high price of oil in comparison with other fuels, and the petro-currency status which is likely to be enjoyed by sterling during the early part of the period, the oil balance is particularly important to the development of the economy as a whole.

The split of oil use between sectors is shown in figure 14.7. Transport (including ships' bunkers) is dominant throughout, increasing its share from 58 per cent in 1980 to 81 per cent in 2020. Oil use in electricity generation and industry, where there is substantial scope for substitution to coal, falls sharply, whereas the fall in households and services is more gradual. Non-energy uses increase somewhat due to the growth in industrial output and the output of the chemicals industry; the feedstock component in non-energy use of oil is limited by continuing substitution to gas and, in the next century, by some use of coal as a chemical feedstock.

The changing shape of the oil demand barrel is shown for the central case in table 14.4. Note firstly the rapid decline in fuel oil use, due principally to replacement by gas and, later, coal in the industry sector. This is complemented by a substantial increase in the share of kerosene and gas oil, mainly due to the limited scope for improving the efficiency with which these fuels are used in the transport sector and to the growth of air transport. On the other hand, gasoline use remains fairly stable at first as efficiency gains cancel out the continuing growth in car use (see chapter 8), and later falls as the private car market is

Table 14.4.   *The changing structure of oil demand, central case (PJ; percentages in brackets)*

	1980	2000	2020
Naphtha[a] etc.	324 (9.7)	353 (11.7)	435 (15.7)
Gasoline	899 (27.0)	891 (29.5)	743 (26.9)
Kerosene[b]	374 (11.2)	453 (15.0)	436 (15.8)
Gas/diesel oil[c]	836 (25.1)	779 (25.8)	826 (29.9)
Fuel oil[c]	897 (26.9)	544 (18.0)	323 (11.7)
Total	3330 (100.0)	3020 (100.0)	2763 (100.0)

Notes: Summations may not be exact due to round-off.
[a] All products used for non-energy purposes, including chemical feedstocks.
[b] Including aviation turbine fuel.
[c] Ships' bunkers included.

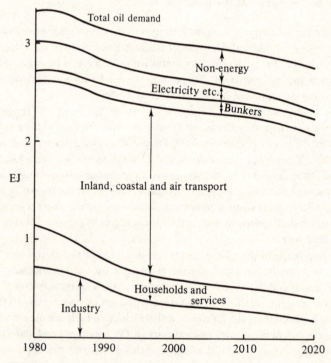

14.7 The structure of oil demand, central case, 1980–2020

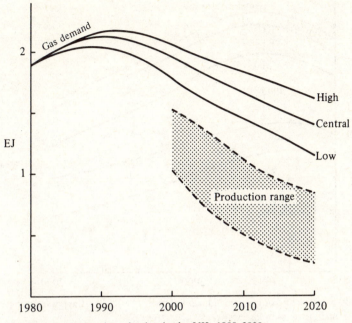

14.8 Gas demand and production in the UK, 1980–2020

affected by saturation. Oil products used as chemical feedstocks take an increasing share of the product barrel.

14.7 Gas supply and demand

In the short and medium term, the rate of depletion of gas resources is dependent on UK demand, since imports are relatively inflexible. Thus high demand in the early part of the period will, for a given level of reserves, imply low production at a later date. Figure 14.8 shows the demand profiles for the three economic growth cases, together with the probable range of UK production beyond the end of the century. The deficit between supply and demand must be made up from increased imports and/or coal-based manufactured gas. In the central case, SNG becomes significant at some time in the first decade of the next century: by 2020, 44 per cent of gas demand is met from indigenous production, 39 per cent from imports and the remainder from coal. The balance between coal and imported gas will, in practice, depend on relative prices and the availability of imports; we should note the possibility of pipeline gas from Europe, and of seaborne LNG, as well as increased purchase of Norwegian gas.

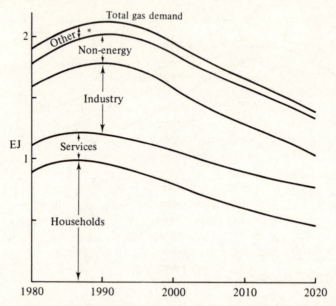

14.9 The structure of gas demand, central case, 1980–2020. *Energy sector own use and distribution losses

The split of gas demand between sectors is shown for the central case in figure 14.9. The overall pattern is one of increasing demand in all sectors in the short term, as gas remains the cheapest fuel for many purposes. From around 1990, however, several mechanisms combine to reduce gas use:

(a) A growing price advantage for coal over gas (reinforced by the withdrawal of interruptible tariffs in industry) prompts substitution to coal in non-premium markets; see the fuller discussion in chapter 7.
(b) Gas suffers from competition from electricity in the premium heat market, including much of the domestic sector, from around the end of the century. This depends on the price stability for electricity brought about by the growing role of nuclear power, and is discussed in section 14.8.
(c) Energy conservation reduces the size of some of the markets in which gas competes, especially in the household sector.

Exceptions to this general pattern are the services sector, where the prospects for coal are much more limited than in industry and where economic growth outpaces the effects of conservation on total energy demand, and gas use for feedstocks, which is largely related to growth in the chemicals sector.

14.8   Electricity and nuclear power

A very noticeable feature of the projections is the growing role envisaged for electricity. In the central case, electricity output grows by 2.3 per cent per annum, corresponding to an increase in the ratio of electricity to GDP of 0.45 per cent per annum. By historical standards, this is not unrealistic. Between 1960 and 1973 the electricity/GDP ratio grew by 2.9 per cent per annum (though since that date the ratio has fallen slightly). Nevertheless, most recent forecasts, including those by the electricity supply industry, have been much more pessimistic. The arguments on which our projections are based are given in chapters 6–9. In general terms, the case for low growth in electricity demand is based on the undoubtedly large scope for technical improvements in the efficiency of electricity use. Against this must be placed the a priori likelihood that long-run historical upward trends in electricity intensity will continue, and the observation that electricity prices are likely to rise fairly slowly, if at all, so that there will be little pressure for continuing conservation effort. This attractive price outlook for electricity is the result of the dilution of the fuel-cost element in electricity costs by the more stable capital-cost component, the dependence of electricity on coal (the price of which is likely to rise more slowly than those of oil or gas) and the growing role of nuclear energy.

A second result of the expected stability in electricity prices is that towards the end of the period, electricity will be increasingly able to compete with gas in premium heat markets, including the domestic sector. This is reinforced by the availability of off-peak nuclear electricity at prices substantially below the average price, and represents a largely new market for electricity which helps to create the projected growth in electricity demand.

Since growth in electricity use is the result of several conflicting pressures, the uncertainties involved are considerable and the problem of forecasting is far from being solved. It is unwise, however, to sidestep the problems of meeting future demand by assuming that very substantial improvements in technical efficiency will be achieved in practice.

The split of electricity use between sectors for the central case is shown in figure 14.10. Industry is the fastest-growing sector, rising from 36 to 50 per cent of electricity use over the period as a whole. Process heat uses are of key importance in this sector (see chapter 7). Electricity use in the services sector doubles over the period of the study, representing a slight fall in electricity use per unit output. Growth in the household sector is lower, owing to the weak link with economic growth, to saturation in appliance ownership and to the reduction in heat requirements resulting from energy conservation.

The energy input to electricity generation in the central case is shown in table 14.5. Note that in spite of the major expansion of nuclear energy, coal still

Table 14.6.   *Primary energy and electricity demand, central case and the high gas case (EJ)*

	1980	1990	2000	2020
Coal	2142 (76.1)	2776 (79.1)	3221 (73.0)	3612 (52.6)
Oil[a]	298 (10.6)	245 (7.0)	200 (4.5)	91 (1.3)
Nuclear energy[b]	323 (11.5)	433 (12.3)	930 (21.1)	2981 (43.4)
Other[b,c]	50 (1.8)	55 (1.6)	61 (1.4)	182 (2.7)
Total	2813 (100.0)	3509 (100.0)	4412 (100.0)	6866 (100.0)

Notes: [a] Including a small amount of gas in 1980.
[b] Hydro-electric and nuclear energy are measured in terms of the primary fossil fuel which they replace.
[c] Hydro-electric power plus renewable electricity sources.

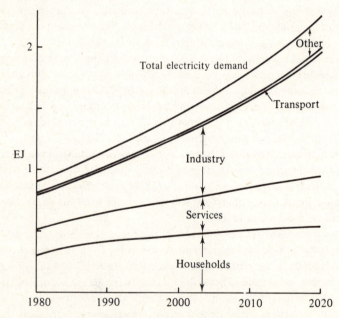

14.10 The structure of electricity demand, central case, 1980–2020

accounts for more than half the fuel use in 2020. The contribution from nuclear power corresponds to nuclear capacities of 15 GW in 2000 and 48 GW in 2020; these levels are mainly determined by the constraints on capacity expansion, though this rapidly becomes less important beyond the end of the century. A more detailed discussion of the role of nuclear energy is given in chapter 10. The category labelled 'other' in table 14.5 includes renewable sources of electricity (probably mainly wind energy), which show rapid expansion towards the end of the period, although they remain of minor importance to electricity generation as a whole. The table does not include the tidal barrage on the Severn estuary; if this is built it will represent an equivalent fuel input of some 135 PJ.

14.9   Scenarios with high demand for gas

In previous sections of this chapter we have described the results of scenarios under particular assumptions about the development of fuel prices. These include the assumption (chapter 11) that the price of gas increases towards a long-run marginal cost of around £5 per GJ derived from the cost of converting coal to SNG. In this section we explore the consequences of an alternative assumption that the large proven world reserves of natural gas lead to competitive pricing of gas in international trade so that imported gas to the UK remains much cheaper than synthetic gas, at least until 2020. This would lead to a different pattern of fuel demand in the UK, which provides an additional uncertainty to be compounded with results from differing levels of economic growth.

With central economic growth but significantly lower gas prices we would obtain a 'high gas' case differing from the central case discussed in previous sections mainly through higher demand for gas and lower demand for electricity but with small changes in other fuels also. There would be an additional effect in the fuel conversion sector since it would no longer be economic to manufacture SNG from coal. The changed pattern of fuel demand is illustrated in table 14.6, in which, since the high gas case requires less electricity generation, we have made proportionate reductions in nuclear energy.

We make no estimates of the relative probabilities of the central case and the high gas case (both have central economic growth). They depend on world economic conditions, on the resolution of international problems for natural gas distribution and on whether social resistance to nuclear power remains an important factor in the world energy balance. Qualitatively, we would expect low world economic growth (and correspondingly low growth in the UK) to favour the high gas case with low gas prices, whereas a high growth future would tend to move the price of gas more rapidly towards the cost of SNG.

Table 14.6.   *Primary energy and electricity demand, central case and the high gas case (EJ)*

	1980	2000 central	2000 high gas	2020 central	2020 high gas
Coal	3.14	4.49	4.07	5.78	5.53
Oil	3.90	3.24	3.11	2.99	2.94
Gas	1.86	1.90	2.15	1.17	1.70
Nuclear	0.32	0.93	0.77	2.98	2.16
Other	0.05	0.06	0.06	0.18	0.15
Total primary energy	9.27	10.61	10.16	13.10	12.48
Electricity demand[a]	0.81	1.29	1.11	2.01	1.51

Note: [a] Demand in final consumption sectors.

Table 14.7.   *Energy costs: central projection (1980 £ billion, percentages of GDP in brackets)*

	1980	2000	2020
Fuel costs:			
imported	0.5 (0.2)	8.3 (2.6)	17.3 (3.7)
indigenous	13.5 (6.0)	20.2 (6.3)	20.5 (4.3)
Conversion and distribution costs[a]:			
electricity	4.8 (2.1)	8.4 (2.6)	10.6 (2.6)
other	4.4 (1.9)	6.3 (1.9)	8.2 (1.4)
Total energy costs	23.2 (10.2)	43.2 (13.4)	56.6 (12.0)

Notes: Non-energy uses of fuels are included. Consumer taxes (e.g. on transport fuel) are excluded; oil and gas production taxes are included as part of indigenous fuel costs.
[a] All costs associated with nuclear power, hydro-electric power and renewable electricity sources are included under conversion costs.

14.10   Risks and uncertainties

The picture that emerges from the quantitative analysis is summarised in table 14.7. This shows, for the central projection, that the present period of energy self-sufficiency is likely to be followed by a period of rising energy imports and an increasing percentage of GDP will be required to pay for them. In addition, it is expected that the costs of indigenous energy production will rise, though more slowly than GDP over the period as a whole. Conversion costs rise rapidly in this projection, largely through the increasing role of electricity, though as a fraction of GDP they are fairly stable. Conversion costs would be lower for the high gas scenario discussed in the last section, where electricity growth is slower, but energy import costs would be higher. There is a trade-off here, to which we shall return in the next chapter, but it is not a simple policy choice since table 14.7 does not show user costs and benefits, which vary considerably between different fossil fuels and electricity.

We shall discuss risks associated with different policies or scenarios more fully in the next chapter, but the quantitative results which we have noted in this chapter point particularly to the possibility of economic risks from rising import costs. Earlier in this chapter (section 14.2), we expressed the view that the central projection, with energy imports increasing but dominated by fairly low-cost coal, could just be sustainable with import costs stabilising at a little under 4 per cent of GDP. We ask now: How robust is this figure of 4 per cent for energy import costs? If it were to become much greater, this would undoubtedly have a large (and probably adverse) effect on the UK economy – and the relatively optimistic economic growth (nearly 2 per cent per annum) of the central scenario might not be sustained.

The particular risk that we associate with energy import costs at nearly 4 per cent of GDP or higher is not so much the absolute level but the fact that energy price fluctuations in world boom or slump would probably be in phase with the energy import needs of the UK, and together these could produce quite a large increase in import costs over a short period. This would tend to weaken sterling, thus producing a third multiplicative factor to increase energy import costs. The importance of the average level of energy import costs is that it provides the base from which short-term variations could develop – thus its magnitude is a measure of the risk of economic exposure to energy price fluctuations.

We conclude this section by noting some of the uncertain factors that could affect the average cost of energy imports as a percentage of GDP.

(a) Higher world oil prices, or (probably more important in the long run) higher coal prices, which could substantially raise import costs.
(b) Falling sterling exchange rate, which would increase import costs and is likely to be correlated with higher world fuel prices.
(c) Changes in world gas prices – the risk comes from uncertainty and timing: if gas prices were to remain low, so that a high gas scenario developed in the UK (section 14.9), and then increased sharply to long-run costs of SNG (perhaps inducing an increase in the coal price),

the UK could develop a pattern of fuel demand that suddenly became non-optimal.

(d) Lower oil or gas reserves than expected for the UK, leading to more rapid depletion and higher import needs.

(e) Less nuclear power development, due either to delays in planning, or excessive capital requirements, or to social opposition. This would raise energy import needs, though this effect could be ameliorated by increased coal production.

(f) Energy conservation could be lower than in our central case giving a greater need for energy imports, or it could be greater than expected, giving rise to some wasteful investment in excess electricity capacity, but also reducing import needs.

(g) Economic growth will undoubtedly fluctuate, and it may have a lower long-term trend than our central case. A temporary slump could be interpreted as part of a long-term trend, leading to inadequate investment in energy supply or complacency on energy conservation, that could frustrate any possible economic recovery by increasing the risk of high energy import costs.

These uncertainties and risks provide an important part of the background for energy policy which we discuss in chapter 15.

15

Policy

15.1   Aims and options

Energy policy is concerned with the performance of the economy, with social welfare and with environmental protection. Some objectives in these three areas conflict with each other, so energy policy involves choice and compromise. The options are affected also by other issues such as national security or international cooperation. Decisions and objectives for energy policy may be changed by world events where UK influence may be small – by world recession or a higher price for oil, by a nuclear accident or climatic change. Thus uncertainty is unavoidable and risk reduction becomes an important factor. Some objectives are not feasible or become increasingly costly because of physical limits, lead-times for change or new social priorities. Economic choice of a least-cost energy system may be changed through social or institutional opposition – not necessarily because of persuasion to a new consensus but because the opposition itself alters the factors that determine relative costs, for example, through the protection of employment in high-cost coal mines, through new controls on sulphur emissions or through additional safety measures in nuclear power stations.

We have seen in earlier chapters that the long-term needs of the UK energy economy are likely to be radically different from those existing today, but in some respects the long term may be measured in a few decades and is all too short for many of the changes that might be desired. Whatever routes and objectives are chosen, whether on the supply side or in energy consumption, or from the left or the right in politics, a degree of consistency is desirable. Even in the face of acknowledged uncertainty about the future, long-term planning can be crippled by short-term expediency. Political consistency requires public understanding, so there is a need for explanation – not all desirable objectives are feasible, some are mutually incompatible, hard choices have to be made, an apparent benefit now may mean greater problems later. The reader will recall from our discussion in chapter 3 that British governments since the war have have had singular difficulty in maintaining consistent energy policy objectives –

indeed they have become expert in facing uncertainty. It has to be recognised however that these uncertainties have in the main originated outside the energy sector itself: in the macro economy and especially in its international trading position. As long as Britain remains a relatively open economy these influences are likely to remain critically important and therefore the balance between indigenous and imported energy supplies will remain a constant source of concern. This concern will be a function not only of the economics of the energy sector but also of the trading performance of the rest of the economy.

Energy policy requires a statement of objectives, to which we turn next, but these do not by themselves define a policy. Policy involves strategies and pathways towards these objectives, and an institutional framework within which choices and priorities can be assessed; it involves alternative options and new routes when circumstances change – as they most certainly will. A policy does not imply a plan in any simple sense nor is it solely a matter for the government; many decisions will inevitably be taken by those outside the government system, by other institutions and by consumers. It implies an awareness of how decisions may be taken and priorities determined by all those involved, of whether coordination is desirable and of the circumstances in which government intervention may be either necessary or desirable.

Before we discuss these issues further it is useful to distinguish between the main objectives of energy policy and other objectives that are subsidiary from the energy viewpoint, but arise from other policy considerations and may modify or constrain the pathways towards the main objectives.

Main objectives of energy policy

The *traditional objectives* are that there should be adequate and secure energy supplies, that these should be efficiently used, and that these two objectives should be achieved at least cost to the nation. This highly compressed statement implies economic aims for proper resource allocation, risk reduction and the encouragement of efficiency:

- *Economic aims.* These seek to encourage proper resource allocation both within the energy sector and other sectors. In aiming for least cost overall, account needs to be taken of the costs of production, distribution and use, the merits of alternative fuels and the comparative benefits of energy imports or indigenous supplies. It also raises the issue of resource conservation and the balance between today's needs and needs in the future.
- *Risk reduction.* Uncertainty about future energy demand, prices and sources of supply requires that risk reduction must be an important

objective of energy policy. This objective impacts on all other areas from national security to social welfare, but, as with all insurance, there is a cost in risk reduction which must be weighed against its benefits. It raises issues of the diversity of fuels and sources, the degree of energy self-sufficiency that may be desirable and the amount of spare supply capacity that it is prudent to have available.

- *Improved efficiencies*. This includes improvements in the efficiency of energy supply as well as in its distribution and use. Energy conservation, or reduced energy consumption without any loss of benefit from its use, is an important aspect of cost reduction, but it also helps other aims by lowering the social and environmental costs of energy as well as preserving resources for future needs.

Other policy considerations

The Green Paper on Energy Policy (Cmnd 7101, Department of Energy, 1978a) observed that the traditional economic objectives of energy policy cannot be pursued in isolation from other policy considerations – industrial, social, political, macroeconomic, environmental and so on. From the viewpoint of energy policy these may give rise to subsidiary objectives, but their importance may be so great as to impose constraints on how the main objectives of energy policy may be pursued. They include:

- *Social welfare*. There is a need to ensure that everyone has access to heat and light in their own home, and freedom of choice between fuels as far as this is practicable. Social policies or anti-inflation policies may moderate the rigid pursuit of economic energy pricing but in the long run they should not dominate decisions on energy pricing policies.
- *Environmental protection*. All systems of energy production and use have environmental drawbacks, and it is the duty of government to ensure that the cost of making these systems environmentally acceptable is equitably shared between producers, users and the public at large. It is also the duty of government to encourage reasonable moderation in the response to risks so that resources are not excessively used to reduce a particular type of risk at the expense of other objectives for national or individual welfare.
- *National security and foreign policy*. Energy choices should ensure a basic level of security of supply so that national policies, including economic growth and social welfare, are not placed at risk through the threat of interruption of energy supplies, either from overseas sources or from internal pressures. This does not imply that energy self-

sufficiency is either necessary or desirable, but it points to a need for diversity of supply including both imports and indigenous production.

- *International cooperation*. The economic turbulence caused by energy crises in the 1970s is proof enough of the importance to the nation of international cooperation to help towards a more stable world energy regime. In addition to economic self-interest and cooperation with trading partners, the UK has a responsibility with other developed countries to assist less developed countries, both through direct aid and through helping to avoid undue pressure of demand for limited energy resources.

Implementation – a key objective

- *Implementation of energy policy*. There is little value in having a magnificent energy policy if it is not implemented. For this reason, we list implementation as a key objective, and also because the need for timely implementation may be in conflict with other objectives. The frustration of a feasible development by those who seek an impossible dream is a notable feature of planning in the UK, but it imposes its own costs on the nation – the best is often the enemy of the good.

15.2   Energy futures: world and UK

Uncertainty about energy prospects is an important feature of energy planning. However, there are limits to what is reasonable in taking account of uncertainty – the idea that everything is so uncertain that planning is impossible is as much beyond these limits as is the idea that all can be left to market forces. There are underlying features of energy prospects, both for the world and for the UK, that are so near to certainty that no prudent government can ignore them. The idea that market forces will recognise these features, and respond accordingly, ignores the fact that government is directly involved in much of the market – through the nationalised industries, through licensing and taxation and through price regulations.

The prospects for world oil supplies strongly suggest that there will be an almost constant production ceiling for two or three decades, not very far above current demand. After that, production will decline unless there is an increasing supplement to conventional oil from high-cost sources such as heavy oil, tar sands, shale or synthetic oil from coal. Thus, in the early part of the next century, when UK oil production is declining, world oil prices will be higher in real terms than in recent years, except perhaps during periods of economic depression. Indigenous production will be more costly and increasing payments for oil imports may adversely affect the exchange rate.

The firm conclusion to be drawn is that energy policy should aim for a long-term reduction in the consumption of oil in the UK. Some areas of oil consumption cannot readily change to other fuels and others have long lead-times for change. The question for energy policy is whether market forces will be adequate to encourage the full potential for improved efficiencies or substitution to other fuels. Doubts about this may be raised by the expectation that, although world oil prices will rise in the longer term, there will certainly be periods of oil glut when prices will fall in real terms.

Prospects for natural gas are more uncertain, and this is reflected in the alternative scenarios that were discussed in section 14.9. The production of natural gas in the UK will decline – perhaps quite rapidly – during the early part of the next century. However, increased imports of gas by pipeline from Norway and from the USSR are possible, as well as LNG from Africa and the Middle East. The uncertainty about traded gas is in the price that would need to be paid and the terms of contracts that could be negotiated, as well as their robustness if world trade conditions were to change substantially, for example during an economic cycle.

The international price of natural gas is already approaching more than twice the average cost of North Sea gas. If it were to rise further towards the cost of SNG made from coal, the price could double again by the early part of the next century. Under these conditions, our detailed calculations of final energy demand reported in earlier chapters show that there could be an increasing use of electricity for heating leading to a decline in the UK use of gas. Alternatively, since world resources of natural gas are believed to be comparable in magnitude with world oil resources, there may be increasing competition for world gas markets so that the price in international trade remains well below that of SNG – at least for a number of decades. With gas imports at such prices, UK demand could be maintained, or even increased, and this would cause significantly lower growth in electricity demand.

The demand for coal in the UK will continue to be dominated by its use for electricity generation for several decades. World coal prices are expected to remain well below the cost of oil and gas, with competition continuing for several decades between coal from different parts of the US and coal from South Africa and Australia. The price of coal delivered to coastal sites in the UK could provide severe competition for indigenous coal and, because of inland transport costs, the future pattern of UK coal production and imports will increasingly depend on the location of power stations and other large users through the choice of coastal sites or sites near to mining areas.

At present the only credible supplement or alternative to fossil fuels for electricity generation is nuclear power. We expect world coal prices to increase in real terms, so that the costs of nuclear power would become more favourable compared with power from coal-fired stations, particularly in Europe but also in some parts of North America and elsewhere, for sufficiently large and developed electricity systems. If the development of nuclear power is further delayed in many countries through social opposition, then the world price of coal will increase earlier than would otherwise be the case. It is still unclear whether the increased use of nuclear power already in place will lead to public familiarity and confidence, or whether opposition will continue.

New forms of renewable energy are unlikely to make a large contribution to energy supply for several decades. However, hydro-electricity will see a major expansion, particularly in developing countries. Woodfuel is likely to retain its importance in many countries, though woodfuel scarcity will continue to create serious problems in some regions. The UK, with other developed countries, will have a responsibility as well as an enlightened self-interest to provide assistance to poorer developing countries in the improvement of their energy resources. More rapidly growing developing countries provide an opportunity to the UK for increased trade, and their increased needs for energy technology could be an important factor in such trade.

For several decades, oil supply and demand are expected to dominate the world energy maket and sudden changes in the oil price will disturb economic growth. In many respects, oil will remain the marginal fuel, and therefore liable to greater swings in supply, demand, and prices than other fuels, and OPEC will remain the marginal supplier. There will continue to be a conflict of interest between the UK (and other similar producers), wishing to maintain full production from high-cost oil production platforms already in place, and members of OPEC, concerned with fluctuating revenues from their shares of a changing world oil market. The shadow of Middle East instability will continue to affect the world oil market – the risk of closure of the Straits of Hormuz may turn into reality. Such a contingency, implying actual scarcity of oil for a period, creates responsibilities for the UK, both as an oil producer and as an oil consumer. The IEA, formed for just such an emergency, is a club for developed countries, yet we expect to see oil demand growing much faster in the group of developing countries than in present IEA members. The balance of world oil demand will change, and one might question whether our projections in chapter 14 for UK oil demand show an adequate decline in relation to the overall world picture. Energy policy would be well advised to prepare for difficulties over future imports of oil.

15.3   Implementing energy policy

The implementation of energy policy has two related but distinct components:
(i) the formulation of strategies and decisions and (ii) the instruments of policy
through which these strategies and decisions are carried out. The relation
between these components arises because the available instruments both limit
the choice of strategies and influence decisions.

Formulation

The formulation of strategies is the process by which energy policy objectives
are translated into decisions. It is at this stage that compromises between
conflicting interests have to be derived, and the results expressed as feasible
decisions. The decisions will often need to be carried out by others than
government, and this requires a degree of consensus amongst those involved,
since otherwise the decisions may be frustrated, or resistance may introduce
unwanted side effects. Thus the formulation of strategies becomes, in part, the
shaping of opinion – directed towards 'the establishment', but with contributions
from interest groups of all sorts. Some of these procedures, and attempts to
formalise new ones, were described in chapter 3.

The nationalised energy industries and the major oil companies form an
essential part of the decision-making process. Their existence, their initiatives
and their needs provide both the framework for many decisions and the
machinery for carrying them out. The Working Group on Energy Strategy,
chaired by a deputy secretary in the Department of Energy, plays an important
role in reaching a consensus, or at least in providing a perspective where
disagreements remain. This group brings together officials from the department
and corporate planners or economists from the nationalised industries and
major oil companies. Energy conservation is inevitably under-represented in
such a group – not by design but because supply decisions are structurally
simpler compared with the diversity and dispersed character of decisions on
energy demand.

There are periodic suggestions, in the media and elsewhere, for a more open
forum, such as an 'Energy Commission', to formulate and oversee energy
policy. In practice, the proponents appear to be seeking a plan rather than a
policy, as such a commission would be a public version of the energy strategy
group. The failure of past attempts at such an organisation was described in
chapter 3. One reason for failure is that important energy decisions have to be
made at a political level, by ministers or possibly by the Cabinet. These cannot
be delegated to a commission. The liaison aspects of the strategy group meet
some needs of the energy sector, but they do not fully meet the needs of

government, where the impact of energy decisions on other policy objectives requires a link to other departments, through an inter-departmental group of officials, or through ministerial discussions. Neither of these needs could be met by a commission.

However, there is a gap here, there is a lack of communication and insufficient 'open government'. The publication of occasional Green Papers or speeches on energy policy by ministers or officials is not sufficient to meet a justified public concern. Nor is this satisfied by the legal complexities and the extended procedures involved in current methods of public inquiry. More could be done by way of departmental publications, or seminars, stating the problems and options that are under discussion – not the solutions in White Papers, nor the suggested solutions in Green Papers, but the problems and possibilities, presented at a stage where public opinion may still be effective, or expressions of government concern may be educational. To some extent this is already achieved through publications of Advisory Councils and other publicly-appointed bodies, but these tend to be views of outsiders rather than those of government, and a central view on the changing problems to be met by energy policy is rarely perceived.

Universities could play a more useful role in providing both a means for raising the quality of the discussions on energy options and more opportunities for public participation by government in these discussions. No doubt the slowness of academia in responding to the educational opportunities and the challenge presented by energy problems since 1973 has been due, in part, to their financial difficulties and retrenchment in recent years. However, it remains surprising, if not deplorable, that interdisciplinary energy studies have not received more attention from economics and engineering departments of British universities.

Instruments

The methods available to government for implementing energy policy range from instruments that affect financial aspects of the energy economy such as energy prices or interest rates, to instruments involving more direct controls, such as mandatory standards or directives to nationalised industries. In practice, central government neither has full control over these instruments – they are affected also by the vagaries of the market place and by institutional factors – nor can it pre-determine the consequences of particular actions, such as new energy taxes or support for research and development. The options are further complicated in that many of them also involve important elements of government policies in areas other than energy.

The instruments that may be considered include:

- *Financial factors.* Controls on energy prices, taxes on fuels or on energy-using equipment, subsidies, investment controls and loan sanctions, the Bank rate, the Treasury discount rate.
- *Institutions.* Particularly the nationalised energy industries but also other energy companies with whom the government has a close involvement with opportunities for liaison and persuasion. Other institutions, whose role can be important on specific issues, include the National Economic Development Office, where liaison with trade unions during the 1970s led to major changes in forms of agreement and working practices on construction sites for power stations.
- *Specific powers.* The government has powers to issue licences for exploration and production from the UK Continental Shelf, and powers to delay the development of fields and order cut-backs in production. In addition to its general powers over capital investment in the electricity industry, the government has the power to control the construction and conversion of power stations that burn oil or gas. It also has powers to control the construction or extension of oil refineries. There are powers directly concerned with energy consumption, including building regulations and standards of thermal insulation.
- *Public Inquiries.* There are a variety of inquiry procedures that provide a degree of control on energy policy, including Royal Commissions, parliamentary inquiries, and planning inquiries. The 1983–4 Inquiry into the proposal to build a PWR nuclear power station at Sizewell is an important example. Such an inquiry leads to a report to the Secretary of State for Energy, who has then to make his decision on whether to grant planning permission. If planning approval is given, he would also have to give approval for the capital expenditure by the CEGB before construction could proceed.
- *Government's own energy use.* Central government has a major element of control over energy use in its own buildings through the Property Services Agency. In addition it can exert influence on energy used by local authorities and other parts of the public sector including schools and hospitals.
- *Education and publicity.* Government can provide encouragement and support for education in the diversity of energy use and technology and its relevance to daily life. Direct publicity is an important part of the government's programme on energy conservation and efficiency in use.

- *Research and development.* The R & D programmes of the nationalised energy industries are settled in consultation with the Department of Energy. In addition, government has influence (for example through officials on committees or through administration) over the emphasis given to energy research by such organisations as the Science and Engineering Research Council which supports research in universities. Government also provides some direct support to finance demonstration projects for improving energy efficiencies.

15.4   Energy demand and conservation

Government policies inevitably have a major influence on long-term trends in energy demand. Economic growth and interest rates affect the ability of industry and consumers to invest in new equipment, allowing better efficiencies or the use of alternative fuels. Regional development grants, subsidies to nationalised industries (or their withdrawal), financial targets and the level of capital investment by nationalised industries, by central government or by local authorities, all have a major effect on the structure of the economy and the structure of industry. Government policies can accelerate or retard the decline of heavy industry. Policy on energy pricing can change the profitability or the viability of heavy industries such as chemicals, or aluminium smelting. Differential prices between various fuels and electricity can change the mix of fuel demand and different policies can accelerate or retard the rates of change.

Thus government influence on energy demand is pervasive and substantial throughout the national economy, mainly through actions that appear to be remote from energy planning. Energy policy should not play a passive role in these wider issues. Their energy implications may change the pattern of demand so that national energy assets are wasted or under-used, or they may cause the UK to become unduly exposed to costly changes in the price of energy imports. Such changes may frustrate industrial or regional planning by removing any comparative advantage that may have existed over industries in other countries.

We have seen in chapter 14 that energy costs form an important part (about 10 per cent) of total national expenditure. Whether this burden increases or decreases in the future, relative to the country's trading partners and competittors, may well depend more on structural change in the economy than on direct actions to improve the economic efficiency of energy use in each specific area of energy consumption. We do not argue that energy factors should be given undue importance in national planning, nor that government should seek to intervene excessively in the energy market. What we do argue is that government actions have a major effect on national trends in energy demand. Energy policy should not be determined by default – at the very least government should be aware of the energy implications of other policies. More generally energy policy should seek to promote actions that will increase national benefits in relation to energy costs. The implications for energy demand should be a recognised dimension in national planning.

Energy prices and uncertainty

Energy policy may have a direct effect on energy demand through its influence on energy prices or through other instruments. Government should seek to ensure that current prices encourage correct decisions by consumers in relation to future prices during the effective lifetime of equipment. However, the consumer needs to be aware that circumstances may change so that prices move unexpectedly; it may be worthwhile for him to ensure that his equipment includes an option for change if this can be done at a reasonable cost. Sometimes a prior decision, for example in the level of domestic house insulation or in building design, may be much cheaper than any option for subsequent change if energy prices should increase. Government has a role to play here: it is widely believed that energy prices to domestic consumers will increase in real terms, and mandatory standards on the thermal efficiency of new dwellings should take this into account, especially since subsequent improvements are often more costly, or are not undertaken because of social or institutional inertia.

Our projections of energy demand described in chapter 14 show a move towards an increased use of electricity compared with other fuels. This changing pattern of demand reflects our assumptions about the costs and prices of different fuels, though we note that there would be uncertainty about the rate of change even if future prices were known – industrial structure and economic structure in general could develop differently, or loyalty by consumers to particular fuels may be greater than we have supposed. Government could have an influence on a possible move from gas towards electricity, described in our central projection, by retaining lower gas prices for a longer period reflecting average costs rather than long-run costs. Alternatively, world prices for gas may be lower, leading to the same result, which is illustrated by our high gas scenario in chapter 14.

Energy prices and conflicting objectives

It is unlikely that government intervention and control of energy prices will be determined solely by energy policy objectives. The total national expenditure on energy makes it a prime target for use by the Treasury as one of the instruments for managing the national economy. Taxation imposed directly on energy includes taxes on fuels for transport, and other taxes designed to bring

North Sea oil prices to levels near to world prices. In addition, there is an increasing tendency for prices of electricity and gas to be set at levels that are convenient for macroeconomic targets. Whilst similar factors affect coal prices, they are also influenced by political and social factors in the coal industry. Energy policy should seek to ensure that short-term considerations of economic management or other influences do not deflect the long-term trends in energy prices too far from those needed for sensible management of energy demand and substitution between fuels.

Other factors that could arguably affect decisions on energy prices in the short term include industrial needs and social needs. An example of the former is that competition between energy suppliers to energy-intensive industries overseas may give a short-term advantage to foreign industries compared with those in the UK. Some 'market response' by energy suppliers in the UK might be expected in a free market – the monopoly control by government of the general level of energy prices does not absolve them from examining whether some relaxation of control is desirable for a period if, for example, survival of an important industry is at stake.

Social factors are recognised in energy policy objectives – 'to ensure that everyone can afford heat and light in their own home'. The best way to achieve this is not necessarily through low energy prices, inverted tariffs or fuel-cost grants on social security, though the latter, at least, may be essential as an interim measure. The provision of heating equipment that involves lower fuel costs to the user, gas heaters instead of electric fires for example, would generally involve a lower cost to the community and give greater benefit to those on low incomes. Capital expenditure on energy conservation may also be a more effective social benefit than current account payments towards high fuel costs. There is a need for re-assessment of the ground rules relating to capital and current expenditure for buildings, not least for those managed by the public sector, so that a better optimisation of energy use can be achieved.

Energy efficiency

The energy Efficiency Office created in October 1983 from the Conservation Division of the Department of Energy showed continuing support by government for encouraging energy saving and good energy management. The emphasis on market forces and energy efficiency was timely in that many cost-effective opportunities for energy conservation had been identified but not put into practice. The improving economic climate at that time would also permit more willing investment for energy saving, particularly since many projects in industry could give a payback in less than two years.

Obstacles to improving energy efficiency

Reliance on market forces is not sufficient to achieve all worthwhile energy savings. There are well recognised areas where institutional or social obstacles prevent improvements in energy use that should be high on the list of national priorities, both in the short run and in the long run. Such obstacles were reviewed in section 13.4. They include the diversity and dispersed nature of energy conservation – it is not readily packaged and sold, and savings are a promise for the future rather than an immediate tangible benefit. Encouragement from government, correct pricing signals and companies making profits by selling energy conservation services can all contribute towards overcoming this type of obstacle.

Further obstacles arise from the fact that energy costs rarely dominate other costs. In local-authority housing, for example, the most efficient overall use of resources may require that benefits from energy conservation measures must wait until they can be obtained in conjunction with other benefits from renovation and modernisation of property. This example illustrates also the institutional obstacle where the landlord controls the decision and the capital expenditure for energy-saving measures, whereas the tenant suffers high energy costs or a cold house until such time as improvements are made. The separation of capital expenditure from running costs in government buildings creates obstacles to energy efficiency. In the final analysis, public opinion would ensure that hospitals were adequately heated, but it can be hard to persuade authorities to spend £100 this year to save £200 next year. Social mobility of owner-occupiers discourages capital expenditure to save energy, just as cost minimisation by builders may not give a best value to home buyers who have to meet unnecessarily large heating bills. There is, of course, an important market response to higher energy prices even in these areas, but it is imperfect and government has a duty to intervene, particularly where, as with local authorities or its own buildings, the institutional obstacles to improved energy efficiency have been created by government itself. The instruments of intervention could include the setting of standards for energy-efficient equipment and buildings, loan schemes or other incentives, persuasion of local authorities and some changes in the procedures for relating controls on capital expenditure to ongoing costs – this might also have beneficial effects in areas other than energy conservation.

Research and development

There is an uneasy division of responsibility for research on energy conservation between government, industry and universities. Expenditure on coal research is limited because of financial difficulties in the industry, but, if coal could be marketed and used with the convenience of oil or gas, its prospects would be greatly enhanced. In contrast to coal, research to improve the efficiency of the use of gas is clearly enhanced by the prosperity of the industry. Government support for demonstration schemes to establish new energy-efficient technologies provides a useful contribution, but the potential benefits are small compared with those that could be derived if existing established technologies were more widely adopted. Research into the factors that influence improvements in energy efficiency and the market for energy conservation has received remarkably little support. It is amazing that ten years since the onset of the energy crisis the fifth ACEC report (ACEC, 1983) should need to emphasise how little is understood about the structure of energy conservation and the measurement of progress. Perhaps the concept is a chimera, whose pursuit will reveal only its mythical character, but there may be something more substantial and rewarding, and one would like to see a greater effort by universities on research into this important aspect of energy policy.

15.5   Energy supply

The dominant objectives for UK policy on energy supply are to ensure that fuels and electricity are available to meet demand at the lowest cost to the nation, taking account of economic, social and environmental factors. In this section we shall consider the strategies that are available to meet these objectives for different fuels and electricity.

We do not consider in any detail the issue of privatisation of the national coal, gas or electricity industries, though there has been some political and public discussion of this possibility in recent years, and small moves towards competition in gas and electricity. The disruption that would be caused to these industries by a major re-organisation resulting from privatisation, and the uncertainty about possible renationalisation by a future government, would take management resources away from the urgent matters of energy strategy noted in this chapter. The coal industry is already making progress towards reducing its costs; the gas industry is already examining options for replacing North Sea production; and the electricity industry is moving towards a major construction programme to replace old plant. Peripheral questions such as showrooms and customer service are a different matter but, for the mainstream production and distribution, we doubt whether possible benefits of major institutional changes would outweigh the losses from disturbance and uncertainty. In particular, safety of the public and reliability of supply are of particular importance in the supply of gas and electricity, and the good record of the nationalised industries has established public confidence which one would wish to see maintained in the future.

Coal

The future of the coal industry in the UK is critically dependent on its ability to produce coal at costs that customers are willing to pay. If this is not achieved, potential customers in industry and elsewhere will be reluctant to convert to coal, and power stations will be increasingly sited on coastal sites so that they can burn imported coal. The alternative of continuing high subsidies and imposing restrictions on coal imports would raise costs to the nation as a whole and reduce the competitiveness of industry.

There are two key factors in the strategy of the NCB to reduce their costs and produce cheaper coal (see chapter 12): closure of uneconomic high-cost mines, and investment in new and more efficient production. The opportunity to invest is likely to be withheld or reduced by government unless there is a large measure of success in reducing the financial burden imposed by high-cost mines. The regional and social difficulties that would arise from a rapid closure programme are considerable, but they are no more severe than those that have arisen from the decline of other industries, where, unlike coal mining, there was little prospect of revival in other parts of the country.

Our projections, described in chapter 14, show an increasing demand for coal in the longer term. In our central case (figure 14.5), admittedly slightly optimistic for economic growth, coal demand begins to pick up by 1990 and reaches over 200 million tonnes by 2020. Although it may be technically possible and reserves are sufficient, it is unlikely that coal production could approach this level by that year – delays must be expected from uncertainty (demand could be much less so the necessary prior investment would not be authorised), from institutional problems (resistance to mine closures would delay investments), from cash-flow problems limiting growth rates for new investment and from limits on the skilled personnel available for planning new mining developments.

Strategies for coal should therefore envisage the possibility of substantial coal imports, although it should be recognised that these could be subject to balance of payments constraints. Because of the high cost of inland transport, some coal-fired power stations will need to be located on the coast, particularly in the South-East. The way in which coal demand is developing should be clearer by the time coal is required for the production of SNG (which may be several decades in the future), but it is probable that this also would be on coastal sites. Our expectation is that UK coal production is likely to remain in the range of 100 to 140 million tonnes, and that the very uncertain margin of demand above this range would be met from imports. The price of world traded coal is expected to set limits on the price of coal in the UK. These limits will be close to the world price at coastal sites, but at some inland sites they would be higher because of transport and handling charges for moving imported coal inland.

Oil

We expect the world price of oil to increase by the end of the century to between $40 and $60 per barrel at 1980 values. Although there are bound to be fluctuations, the price is likely to be near the top of this range – perhaps higher – by 2020. This would provide opportunities for the development of more costly fields in the North Sea, probably including both heavy oil that requires advanced recovery methods and smaller fields of conventional oil. The timing and extent of these opportunities will depend not only on world oil prices but also on the issue of licences for further exploration and development. It will also depend critically on the taxation regimes that are adopted in the future and on the track-record of the UK government in the fairness and stability of past tax regimes.

Our discussion of future UK oil production in chapter 11 shows a wide range of uncertainty due to the range of estimates of oil yet to be discovered. By the end of the century production will almost certainly be well below the peak levels of 120 million tonnes per year in the early 1980s, probably within the range 30 to 65 million tonnes, falling to between 10 and 50 million tonnes by 2020. It is clear that energy policy should not be based on particular expectations about production levels, but higher costs are inevitable and there will be a substantial fall in production.

The projections of UK energy imports discussed in chapter 14 shows a rapid increase near the year 2000 in their costs as a percentage of GDP (section 14.10). With lower growth this rapid change would come slightly later. The resulting disturbance to the economy could be accentuated by a simultaneous fall in the value of sterling consequent on increasing payments for these oil imports. The decline in production from existing oil-fields is inevitable, but the rate of decline overall could be moderated by new developments in the 1990s. The extent of these developments depends on the willingness of government to allow the possibility that companies may obtain large rewards for the high-cost, high-risk ventures that would be necessary.

Gas

The production of UK natural gas is expected to fall after the year 2000 (figure 14.8) but probably less rapidly than for oil production. By 2020 gas production is likely to be in the range 5 to 20 MTOE compared with a possible peak of nearly

40 MTOE around 1990. Government has considerable control over exploration and development, not only through licences, but also through its influence on the price paid for gas by the BGC who will remain the major consumer.

Our central projection for UK energy suggests that by 2020 the demand for gas could be met by a mix of indigenous production (44 per cent), imports of pipeline gas and LNG (39 per cent), with the remainder (17 per cent) provided by synthetic gas from coal. There is considerable uncertainty about these percentages, partly because of the wide range of possible demand and indigenous production levels, and partly because the price of natural gas in world trade could remain below the cost of manufacturing SNG from coal until well into the next century.

Although the picture of future demand and supply of gas is very uncertain, the main features are clear. Additional facilities will be required for new UK production, and for additional imports from the Norwegian sector of the North Sea. It may be desirable to have a link to the European natural gas pipeline network so as to allow the possibility of importing gas from the European network including gas from the USSR. World trade in LNG will be set at prices that reflect the availability of pipeline gas to major markets, and on this basis LNG imports to the UK should be available at prices comparable with those of pipeline gas. The eventual need for synthetic gas made from coal suggests that some commercial production should commence near to the year 2000. Its manufacture might be based on imported coal if this had a price advantage at coastal sites over UK coal. Again the balance of payments burden of possible coal imports would need to be kept in mind.

Electricity, nuclear power and renewable power

Our central projection shows electricity demand increasing faster than GDP and reaching more than twice the 1980 demand by 2020. Even with our alternative high gas scenario (section 14.9) there is considerable growth in electricity demand. By 2020 in our central case the energy required for electricity generation reaches more than half the total UK primary energy demand. This case shows nuclear power providing 43 per cent of electricity in that year and coal 53 per cent, compared with values of 11 per cent and 76 per cent respectively in 1980.

The levels of nuclear power production in our central case (48 MW capacity by 2020) are determined by our assumptions about the time required for construction and the capacity of the nuclear construction industry. Although faster production could be possible, this would probably raise costs and it might lead to an over-large nuclear construction industry if electricity demand was much lower than our central case. However, the more immediate problem, from the viewpoint of cost-minimisation, is that, on almost any sensible projection of electricity demand, the nuclear power component of electricity generation will be below its optimal economic value until well beyond the year 2000. It is clear that no decisions can be taken until the results of the Sizewell Inquiry are known, but, if this leads to an approval for the PWR power station, there would be a strong case for series ordering on a clearly stated programme. This is one area where the advantages to government of flexible planning are outweighed by the disadvantages of the uncertainty caused to industry. The need for new power station capacity from the mid-1990s onwards is inevitable because of the increasing age of existing stations, many of which are due for retirement near the turn of the century.

If the Sizewell decision should be unfavourable to PWR nuclear power, the need for new capacity would presumably be met mainly by a mix of coal and AGR nuclear power stations, though possibly also with some additional use of existing oil-fired power stations as a temporary measure. Wind, waves and geothermal energy could make a small contribution, and there might be a decision to develop the Severn barrage for tidal power. There is relatively little scope for expansion of hydro-electric power. One option, which might become attractive if the UK nuclear programme proceeds only slowly or at high cost, would be to take imports of nuclear electricity from France on a firm power basis. Initially this could be based on the 2 GW link that is under construction, though much more would be required if links to France were to have a substantial effect on the need for power production in Britain.

15.6   Environmental factors

We have remarked on the impact of environmental factors on energy use and production in earlier chapters. Concern about the environment and public health due to emissions from coal fires was a major factor in the development of smokeless zones in cities during the 1950s. This concern now seeks to grapple with less obvious pollution than the black fogs of earlier years. Some of these environmental problems are so complicated, or so enmeshed in background effects, that appropriate courses of action are difficult to identify. There may be strong public demand for change (or resistance to change), based on imperfect information, for example, concerning 'acid rain' and emissions from the use of coal, or radiation from nuclear power production or nuclear waste.

The problem for energy policy caused by concern about risks from energy production or use is that these risks are generally small compared with other risks that are widely accepted, such as smoking or travelling by road transport. The comparative risks of different energy sources are not widely understood, and the idea of a trade-off between the cost of risk reduction and alternative forms of expenditure is rarely appreciated. Perhaps more work needs to be done on multi-attribute decision analysis in order to understand better the importance attached by different groups to such attributes as public risk and private choice, economic costs, health risks, unfamiliarity or dread of a serious accident, which may be associated with various forms of energy. A complementary approach would be to seek to enlarge the public appreciation of comparative risks and safety – nothing can be made completely safe. From the narrower viewpoint of ensuring energy supplies at a reasonable cost, a change in public attitude to a particular form of energy could radically change the form of an optimum policy, or in some circumstances it could lead to an actual shortage or to an under-capacity in the case of electricity supply.

15.7   Strategies

What then are the major issues which the government and the energy industries should be thinking about during the next few years? What should they bring to the attention of ministers and what actions and priorities should they recommend? We consider these questions under three headings:

- Decisions that must be taken and commitments that must be made at an early date, simply to keep the country's energy infra-structure functioning.
- Creation of a business environment in which sensible decisions can be made by other participants in the energy industries.
- Options that need to be opened, either because they will be required or because they may be required in the future.

In the near future

There is an increasingly urgent need for an orderly expansion of the electric power construction industry so that it can provide replacement power stations during the 1990s and beyond, as existing stock is retired. If decisions – on power station types and sites – are further delayed, there will be higher costs and less chance of an orderly development. Decisions on a nuclear power programme depend on the outcome of the Sizewell Inquiry. However, even if this led to permission for a PWR station to be built, an adequate programme based on nuclear power will still not be feasible unless future sites are given approval more quickly.

Decisions on future coal-fired power stations will depend on the ability of the coal industry to show that it can modernise sufficiently to compete with internationally traded coal. Without a reduction in the number of high-cost pits, it is unlikely that the industry will obtain adequate investment for new mines and other new developments. Under such conditions new coal-fired power stations could be placed on coastal sites. With modern practices of redundancy pay, resettlement allowances and early retirement, the social problems created by the closure of coal mines are less formidable than in earlier years though they are still serious, and are likely to take some years to resolve.

The problem of reducing coal costs is pressing and immediate, particularly since it is very likely that with lower costs demand for UK coal could begin to rise. In particular, this would encourage renewed construction of coal-fired power stations at inland sites and, by opening an option for smaller units (at slightly higher cost), there could be additional flexibility and improved construction rates for power stations if this proved to be necessary.

The business environment

The creation by government of a business environment suitable for long-term energy needs requires increasingly favourable tax treatment of oil and gas exploration and development, as their costs rise and financial risks increase. We have drawn attention to the possibility, clearly shown by our central projection in chapter 14, that oil imports could increase quite quickly near the turn of the century. Further discoveries from exploration made within the next few years will be an important factor in helping to moderate the rise in oil imports.

One important consequence of the decline of North Sea oil production in the 1990s and the increased costs of production from new fields is that there will be a major fall in government revenues from the North Sea. This fall will take place during a period when capital investment needs for the national energy industries are likely to be both substantial and increasing. It is clear that government should take these factors into account in its long-term financial planning. For example, institutional changes might be helpful so that the nationalised energy supply industries have greater freedom in raising the capital that will be required. The need for a steady programme of orders for electric power stations noted above is also an important factor in the business environment for the electric power construction industry. Regular orders would assist both management and labour in developing the necessary organisation and skills that are needed for an efficient programme. Energy conservation will continue to require encouragement from government, and regulations or subsidies will be required in situations where the market is unable to operate effectively (ACEC, 1983). Recovery in the economy as a whole will also provide conditions in which industrial and commercial fuel users will more readily invest to save energy, or switch to more cost-effective fuels.

The longer term

For the longer term, energy imports will almost inevitably continue to increase unless there is substantially increased investment in low-cost coal production and in nuclear power. Energy conservation can make a very large contribution, and this is a key factor in our central projection in chapter 14 which suggests that a vigorous development of coal, conservation and nuclear power could stabilise UK energy import costs by 2020 at a manageable level.

In this period it is unlikely that new renewable forms of energy would make a large contribution to UK production, though some development of windpower is likely to prove economic. Solar energy will contribute primarily through passive solar systems, improving solar gain by better design and siting of buildings. Fusion power is not likely to be commercially relevant before the middle of the next century, if then, and the involvement of the UK could proceed adequately through a share in an international programme. FBR power stations would be needed within a worldwide nuclear programme, but probably not until well into the next century. Thus, although the UK was in the vanguard of their early development, it would now seem a better policy to join an international collaboration.

The most important message that comes from work in recent years on new renewable forms of energy is that they do not provide an easy or economic solution to future energy problems. More could be achieved over the next few decades by concentrating on energy conservation, in the widest possible sense of better design and materials conservation as well as improved energy efficiencies.

15.8   Concluding remarks

In our detailed analysis of energy prospects for the UK we have used a central scenario whose long-term average economic growth is nearly 2 per cent per annum. This may seem optimistic when judged against other contemporary long-term energy studies, but we argue that it is wrong for investment for the future to be based on pessimism because such policies are likely to be self-fulfilling, and because the risks of over-provision and under-provision are not symmetrical. We accept that economic growth may be lower and lifestyles may change so that future energy demand is less than even in our low economic growth scenario, but we do not accept the view, sometimes expressed by opponents of energy projects, that energy planning can be sensibly based on the likelihood of such a future. However, even in a future where growth was so low that total electricity demand remained nearly constant, almost all existing power stations would need to be replaced before 2020, and nearly 80 million tonnes of new coal production capacity would be required to maintain production at present levels. These needs alone would require firm decisions to be made and construction to be completed with fewer delays than have been experienced in the past decade. A better performance will be necessary if there is to be renewed growth, and recent industrial achievements in the production and distribution of North Sea oil and gas show that this can be done.

It may be suggested that environmental concern in the Vale of Belvoir presents a more formidable obstacle to coal development than storms in the North Sea present to oil and gas production. Also, government approval for investment in coal is not encouraged by bad industrial relations, whilst new customers for coal will hesitate so long as prices are held high in order to support losses in uneconomic pits. Opposition to nuclear power is not as widespread in the UK as in some other countries, though unease about the problem of waste disposal and the possibility of nuclear accidents has been increasing. This has contributed to delays and to higher costs. If would be helpful if information about comparative risks from different forms of energy supply was more widely available, and if the cost of investment to reduce risk in energy supply was more frequently compared with the resulting loss of benefits from equal investments in other areas.

The wider appreciation of comparative risks of accidents or other losses, and the costs and benefits of reducing them, is one of many areas in energy studies where the academic contribution has been less than satisfactory. Neither the economic assessment of energy options and policies, nor the engineering assessment of energy projects, has attracted mainstream attention from economics or engineering faculties in the UK. No doubt this failure by British universities to respond adequately to a major problem of our time can be attributed to the interdisciplinary character of energy studies and the difficulty of fitting it into existing institutional structures. Government and the research councils could assist more effectively than in the past, but the main need is for the relevant university departments to do more, primarily in teaching but also in research.

In previous sections of this chapter we have observed that government involvement in UK energy prospects goes beyond decisions on energy investment, for example, through fuel taxation, through taxes on oil companies and financial targets for nationalised industries, through housing policies and regulations, and through their influence on structural change in the economy as a whole. Government's most obvious and urgent task is to ensure that investment decisions for energy production are not unduly delayed, whether by financial constraints on companies due to the taxation of production in the North Sea, or by excessively long inquiries before planning permission is granted for new coal mines or for electric power production. Any major improvement in the process of making decisions on energy investment will require cooperation from the public and from the media. The effective and timely completion of energy projects will require cooperation of management and labour. None of us should suppose that government alone can change the social environment in which energy decisions are made and projects carried out. Economic growth and social welfare for present and future generations depends on the effective and timely development of the energy supply system in the UK, and on the efficient use of energy by all. If these objectives are to be achieved we shall need both cooperation and tolerance from different parts of our community, and a willingness to accept change. An understanding of future needs is an essential step towards such achievements, for which both academics and the media could make a helpful contribution.

Appendix: units and conversion factors

The international system of units (SI system) is used as standard throughout this book, alongside more familiar units of measurement where appropriate. In the SI system, the unit of energy is the joule (J) and the unit of power (i.e. the rate of use or production of energy) is the watt (W), equal to 1 joule per second. For practical purposes, multiples of these units are denoted by the prefixes shown in table A1.

Table A1   *Prefixes used with SI units*

Prefix	Symbol	Power	Examples
Exa	E	10^{18}	EJ (exajoule)
Peta	P	10^{15}	PJ (petajoule)
Tera	T	10^{12}	TJ (terajoule)
Giga	G	10^{9}	GJ (gigajoule)
Mega	M	10^{6}	MW (megawatt)
kilo	k	10^{3}	kW (kilowatt)

The relationship of other commonly used units to the SI units and to one another are as follows:

1 British thermal unit (btu)	$= 1.055\,\text{kJ}$
1 therm $= 10^{5}\,\text{btu}$	$= 0.1055\,\text{GJ}$
1 calorie	$= 4.186\,\text{J}$
1 kilowatt hour (kWh)	$= 3.6\,\text{MJ}$
1 Terawatt hour (TWh)	$= 3.6\,\text{PJ}$
1 horse power hour	$= 2.685\,\text{MJ}$
1 therm	$= 29.3\,\text{kWh}$
1 kWh	$= 3412\,\text{btu}$
1 btu/hr	$= 0.293\,\text{W}$
1 horse power	$= 746\,\text{W}$
1 EJ/year	$= 31.7\,\text{GW}$

Quantities of fuels are often measured in other units, such as tonnes (coal or oil), barrels (oil) or cubic feet or metres (gas). The energy equivalent of these units depends on the grade of fuel, and also on the measurement convention. Thermal content may be measured in gross (or higher calorific value) terms, in which case it includes the heat content of the water vapour produced in combustion, or in net (lower calorific value) terms, in which case it excludes the heat content of the water vapour. For gas the lower calorific value is about 10 per cent less than the higher calorific value, about 5 per cent less for oil and about 1 per cent less for coal. Some approximate thermal equivalents, based on higher calorific values, are given in table A2.

Table A2   *Approximate thermal equivalents*

Coal	1 tonne coal		29.3 GJ (UN convention)
			26.4 GJ (UK convention)
	1 tonne lignite		16 GJ
Oil	1 tonne crude oil		44 GJ = 7.3 barrels crude oil
	1 barrel crude oil		6 GJ
	1 million barrels per day oil equivalent (MBDOE or mbdoe)		50 million tonnes oil equivalent per year (MTOE or mtoe)
Gas	1000 cubic metres (m³)		38.2 GJ
	1000 cubic feet (ft³)		1.08 GJ

Statistics covering more than one fuel should preferably be expressed in terms of SI units. However, other conventions are often used, including the 'tonne of coal equivalent' (TCE or tce) or 'tonne of oil equivalent' (TOE or toe), and sometimes 'barrel of oil equivalent' (BOE or boe). These conventions vary from one source to another: 1 TCE (or tce) may range from around 26 GJ to around 29 GJ, while 1 TOE (or toe) may range from less than 42 GJ to over 45 GJ. UK statistics generally use gross calorific values, whereas most international bodies define energy equivalents in terms of net calorific values.

The conversion efficiency from thermal input to electricity output for a modern fossil fuel fired power station is about 0.35. Thus 1 kWh of electricity requires 2.86 kWh of energy input, approximately equal to 10 MJ. Differences of convention in the measurement of electricity output (e.g. inclusion or exclusion of electricity use within the power station) may hinder the comparison between statistics for different countries.

A power station of capacity 1 GWe (i.e. electrical output) at 70 per cent load factor gives 6136 GWh or 22 PJ of output per year. At a conversion efficiency of 0.35 this requires a thermal input of 63 PJ, equivalent to around 2.2 MTCE (or mtce) or 1.4 MTOE (or mtoe).

References

ACEC (1977a) *Freight transport: short and medium term considerations,* Department of Energy, Energy Paper 24, HMSO, London
— (1977b) *Road vehicle and engine design: short and medium term energy considerations,* Department of Energy, Energy Paper 18, HMSO, London
— (1978) *Report to the Secretary of State for Energy,* Department of Energy, Energy Paper 31, HMSO, London
— (1979) *Civil aviation: energy considerations,* Department of Energy, Energy Paper 36, HMSO, London
— (1981a) *Review of the UK transport energy outlook and policy recommendations,* Department of Energy, Energy Paper 47, HMSO, London
— (1981b) *Energy conservation in the production of domestic hot water,* Department of Energy, Energy Paper 48, HMSO, London
— (1982) *Report to the Secretary of State for Energy,* Department of Energy, Energy Paper 49, HMSO, London
— (1983) *Fifth Report to the Secretary of State for Energy,* Department of Energy, Energy Paper 52, HMSO, London
Adelman, M. A. (1972) *The world petroleum market,* Johns Hopkins University Press, Baltimore and London
Akins, J. (1973) 'The oil crisis: this time the wolf is here' in *Foreign Affairs,* Vol. 51, No. 3, pp. 462–90.
Armitage Norton Consultants (1982) *Energy conservation investment in industry,* Department of Energy, Energy Paper 50, HMSO, London
Atkinson, F. J., Brooks, S. J. and Hall, S. G. F. (1983) 'The economic effects of North Sea oil' in *NIESR Review,* No. 104, pp. 38–44, NIESR, London
Barber, H. (1983) *Electroheat,* Granada Publishing Ltd, London
Barker, T. S. and Brailovsky, V. (eds.) (1981) *Oil or industry? Energy, industrialisation and economic policy in Canada, Mexico, the Netherlands, Norway and the United Kingdom,* Academic Press, London
Bending, R. C. (1982) *A revised simulation model of UK industrial energy use,* Report EDP 20, Cambridge Energy Research Group, Cambridge, UK
Berrie, T. W. (1983) *Power system economics,* Peter Peregrinus Ltd, London
Berrie, T. W., Mallalieu, B. D. and Mylon, K. R. D. (1983) 'Interactive load control and energy management' in *Energy economics in Britain* (ed. P. Tempest), Graham and Trotman, London
Blackaby, F. (ed.) (1979) *De-industrialisation,* Heinemann, London
British Gas Corporation (1981) *Annual report and accounts 1980–81,* BGC, London

British Railways Board (1981) *Review of main line electrification (final report)*, British Rail, London

Building Research Establishment (1976) *Heat losses from dwellings*, BRE, Watford

Burn, D. (1978) *Nuclear power and the energy crisis: politics and the atomic industry*, Macmillan, London

Bush, R. P. and Matthews, B. J. (1979) *The pattern of energy use in the UK: 1976* Report R7, Energy Technology Support Unit, Harwell

CACI (1981) *Diesel potential to 1985: Vol. 1 – Automobile markets in Europe and the United States*, International Business Reports, London

Cattell, R. K. (1983) *The market for coal in UK industrial boilers*, Report EDP 25, Cambridge Energy Research Group, Cambridge, UK

CEGB (1982) *Sizewell B power station public inquiry: CEGB statement of case*, 2 volumes + appendices, CEGB, London

(1983a) *CEGB statistical yearbook 1982–83*, CEGB, London

(1983b) *Annual report and accounts 1982–83*, CEGB, London

Central Statistical Office (1981) *National income and expenditure*, HMSO, London

(1983 and earlier editions) *Annual abstract of statistics*, HMSO, London

Chem Systems International Ltd (1976) *Reducing pollution from selected energy transformation sources*, Graham and Trotman, London

Chesshire, J. and Robson, M. (1983) *UK industrial energy demand: economic and technical change in the steam boiler stock*, Report 19, Science Policy Research Unit, University of Sussex

CIBS (1980) *Guide A3: Thermal properties of building structures*, Chartered Institution of Building Services, London

Clarke, P. T. (1977) *A preliminary analysis of the potential for energy conservation in industry*, Department of Industry, HMSO, London

Combined Heat and Power Group (1977) *District heating combined with electricity generation in the UK*, Department of Energy, Energy Paper 20, HMSO, London

(1979) *Combined heat and electrical power generation in the United Kingdom*, Department of Energy, Energy Paper 35, HMSO, London

Cottrell, A. (1981) *How safe is nuclear energy?*, Heinemann, London

Cousins, S. and Potter, S. (1982) *Annual vehicle taxation policies in Europe*, The Open University, Milton Keynes

CPRS (1974) *Energy conservation*, HMSO, London

Crisp, V. H. C. (1983) 'Lighting controls to save energy' in *International Lighting Review*, Vol. 34, No. 1, pp. 16–21

Department of Employment (1980) *Family expenditure survey, 1979*, HMSO, London

Department of Energy (1974) *Coal industry examination, final report 1974*, Department of Energy, HMSO London

(1976) *Energy conservation (reply to Select Committee)*, Cmnd 6575, HMSO, London

(1977) *Coal for the future*, Department of Energy, HMSO, London

(1978a) *Energy policy: a consultative document*, Green Paper Cmnd 7101, HMSO, London

(1978b) *A North Sea gas-gathering system*, Department of Energy, Energy
   Paper 44, HMSO, London
(1979) *National energy policy*, Department of Energy, Energy Paper 41,
   HMSO, London
(1982) *Proof of evidence for the Sizewell B public inquiry*, Department of
   Energy, HMSO, London
(1983a and earlier editions) *Digest of United Kingdom energy statistics*,
   HMSO, London
(1983b) *Development of the oil and gas resources of the United Kingdom 1983*,
   HMSO, London
Department of Environment (1980) *National travel survey 1978/9*, HMSO,
   London
Department of Environment, Scottish Development Department, Welsh Office
   (1981) *Housing and construction statistics*, HMSO, London
Department of Trade (1978) *Airports policy*, White Paper Cmnd 7084, HMSO,
   London
Department of Transport (1980) *National road traffic forecasts, Great Britain*,
   HMSO, London
(1981) *Transport statistics: Great Britain 1970–1980*, HMSO, London
Drake, E. (1974) 'Oil reserves and production' in *Energy in the 1980s*, Royal
   Society, London
Eckbo, P. L., Jacoby, H. D. and Smith, J. L. (1978) 'Oil supply forecasting:
   a disaggregated process approach' in *Bell Journal of Economics*, Vol. 9,
   No. 1, pp. 218–35
Eden, R. J. (1983) *World energy outlook to 2020*, Report EDP 27, Cambridge
   Energy Research Group, Cambridge, UK
Eden, R. J., Posner, M. V. et al. (1981) *Energy economics: growth, resources
   and policies*, Cambridge University Press, Cambridge
Electricity Council (1983) *Handbook of electricity supply statistics 1983*, Electric-
   ity Council, London
ETSU (1976) *Solar energy: its potential contribution within the United Kingdom*,
   Department of Energy, Energy Paper 16, HMSO, London
(1984) *Contribution of renewable energy technologies to future energy require-
   ments*, Report ETSU R14, HMSO, London
Evans, N. L. (1981) *Electricity supply modelling: theory and case study*, Report
   EDP 14, Cambridge Energy Research Group, Cambridge, UK
(1983) *Nuclear power in the western world to 2020*, Report EDP 29,
   Cambridge Energy Research Group, Cambridge, UK
(1984) 'The Sizewell decision: a sensitivity analysis' in *Energy Economics*,
   Vol. 6, No. 1, Butterworth Scientific Ltd, Guildford
Evans, N. L. and Hope, C. W. (1984) *Nuclear power: futures, costs and benefits*,
   Cambridge University Press, Cambridge
Fisk, D. J. (1979) *Microprocessors in building services*, Report CP 12/79, BRE,
   Watford
(1981) *Thermal control of buildings*, Applied Science Publishers, London
Flood, M. (1983) *Solar prospects: the potential for renewable energy*, Wildwood
   House, London
Flowers, Sir B. (1976) *Royal Commission on Environmental Pollution – sixth
   report: nuclear power and the environment*, HMSO, London

Flowers, Lord (1981) *Coal and the environment*, Report of the Commission on Energy and the Environment, HMSO, London

Forsyth, P. J. and Kay, J. A. (1980) *The economic implications of North Sea oil revenues*, Institute of Fiscal Studies, London

Francis, R. J. and Woollacott, P. N. (1980) *Prospects for improved fuel economy and fuel flexibility in road vehicles*, Energy Technology Support Unit, Harwell

Grainger, K. and Gibson, L. (1981) *Coal utilisation: technology, economics and policy*, Graham and Trotman, London

Green, M. B. and Pattison, J. R. (1981) *Saving gas in home heating: a review of developments*, Communication 1158, Institution of Gas Engineers, London

Hamilton, A. (1978) *North Sea impact: offshore oil and the British economy*, International Institute for Economic Research, London

Handy, L. J. (1981) *Wages policy in the British coal mining industry*, University of Cambridge, Department of Applied Economics, Monograph 27, Cambridge University Press, Cambridge

Hankinson, G. A. and Rhys, J. M. W. (1983) 'Electricity consumption, electricity intensity and industrial structure' in *Energy Economics*, Vol. 5, No. 3, pp. 146–52, Butterworth Scientific Ltd, Guildford

Hannah, L. (1982) *Engineers, managers and politicians: the first fifteen years of nationalised electricity supply in Britain*, Macmillan, London

Heap, R. D. (1979) *Heat pumps*, Spon, London

Humphrey, W. S. and Stanislaw, J. (1979) 'Economic growth and energy consumption in the UK, 1700 to 1975' in *Energy Policy*, Vol. 7, No. 1, pp. 29–42, IPC Science and Technology Press Ltd, Guildford

Inter-Departmental Officials (1979) *Energy conservation: scope for new measures and long term strategy*, Department of Energy, Energy Paper 33, HMSO, London

International Energy Agency (1982) *Coal prospects and policies in IEA countries: 1981 review*, OECD, Paris

Jäger, J. (1983) *Climate and energy systems: a review of their interactions*, John Wiley and Sons, Chichester

James, J. G. (1980) *Pipelines as a mode of freight transport*, Report SR 592, TRRL, Crowthorne

Jenne, C. and Cattell, R. K. (1983) 'Structural change and energy efficiency in industry' in *Energy Economics*, Vol. 5, No. 2, pp. 114–23, Butterworth Scientific Ltd, Guildford

Kaldor, N. (1966) *Causes of the slow rate of economic growth of the United Kingdom*, Cambridge University Press, Cambridge

Kemp, A. G. and Rose, D. (1983) 'Tax changes give new incentives' in *Petroleum Economist*, Vol. L, No. 5, pp. 163–65, Petroleum Press Bureau, London

Kilpatrick, A. and Lawson, T. (1980) 'On the nature of industrial decline in the UK' in *Cambridge Journal of Economics*, Vol. 4, pp. 85–102

Leach, G. (1975) *Energy and food production*, International Institute for Environment and Development, London

  (1979) *A low-energy strategy for the United Kingdom*, Science Reviews Ltd, London

Leach, G. and Pellew, S. (1982) *Energy conservation in housing*, International Institute for Environment and Development, London

MacKay, D. I. and Mackay, G. A. (1975) *The political economy of North Sea oil*, Martin Robertson, London

Ministry of Fuel and Power (1955) *A programme of nuclear power*, Cmnd 9389, HMSO, London

Ministry of Power (1964) *The second nuclear power programme*, Cmnd 2335, HMSO, London

(1965) *Fuel policy*, White Paper Cmnd 2798, HMSO, London

(1967) *Fuel policy*, White Paper Cmnd 3438, HMSO, London

MIT World Oil Project (1976) *Supply forecasting using disaggregated pool analysis*, Report 76-009, MIT Energy Laboratory, Mass.

Monopolies and Mergers Commission (1983) *A report on the efficiency and costs in the development, production and supply of coal by the NCB*, Vols. 1 and 2, Cmnd 8920, HMSO, London

Moses, K. (1981) 'Britain's coal resources and reserves: the current position' in *Assessment of energy resources*, Report 9, Watt Committee on Energy Ltd, London

National Coal Board (1974) *Plan for coal*, NCB, London

(1979a) *Statistical tables 1978/9*, NCB, London

(1979b) *Coal in South Wales* (leaflet), NCB, London

(1981) *Report and accounts 1980/1*, NCB, London

National Institute of Economic and Social Research (1981) *National Institute Economic Review*, No. 98, NIESR, London

NCB Medical Services (1981) *Annual report 1980/1*, NCB, London

NEDO (1974) *Energy conservation in the United Kingdom*, HMSO, London

NEPSG (1977) *Nuclear power issues and choices*, Ballinger, Cambridge, Mass.

NIES (1983) *Annual report and accounts 1983*, NIES, Belfast

Noreng, O. (1980) *The oil industry and government strategy in the North Sea*, Croom Helm, London

Nørgard, J. S. (1979) 'Improved efficiency in domestic electricity use' in *Energy Policy*, Vol. 7, No. 1, pp. 43–56, IPC Science and Technology Press Ltd, Guildford

NSHEB (1983) *Report and accounts 1982/3*, NSHEB, Edinburgh

O'Callaghan, P. W. (1978) *Building for energy conservation*, Pergamon Press, Oxford

Odell, P. R. and Rosing, K. E. (1980) *The future of oil*, Kogan Page, London

Office of Population Censuses and Surveys (1979) *General household survey*, HMSO, London

(1981) *Population trends*, HMSO, London

OPEC (1982) *OPEC review*, Vol. vi, No. 4, pp. 374–407, Pergamon Press, Oxford

Open University (1978) *Energy in the home*, Open University Press, Milton Keynes

Ormerod, R. J. (1980) *The factors affecting the future markets for coal*, NCB, London

Raiffa, H. (1970) *Decision analysis*, Addison-Wesley, Reading, Mass.

Ridley, Viscount (1952) *Report of the committee on a national policy for the use of fuel and power resources*, Cmnd 8647, HMSO, London

Roberts, L. E. J. (1984) *Nuclear power and public responsibility*, Cambridge University Press, Cambridge

Robinson, F. A. (ed.) (1980) *Environmental effects of utilising more coal,* Royal Society of Chemistry, London

Romig, F. and Leach, G. (1977) *Energy conservation in UK dwellings: domestic sector survey and insulation*, International Institute for Environment and Development, London

Select Committee on Energy (1982) *Energy conservation in buildings, Vol. I: report and minutes of proceedings,* HC 401–1, HMSO, London

Select Committee on Science and Technology (1975) *Energy conservation*, HMSO, London

Skea, J. F. (1981) *Modelling coal penetration in the industrial steam-raising markets: an engineering approach*, Report EDP 6, Cambridge Energy Research Group, Cambridge

Southern, J. R. (1981) 'External insulation of walls' in *BRE News*, No. 55, BRE, Watford

SSEB (1983) *Report and accounts 1982/3*, SSEB, Glasgow

Tanner, J. C. (1977) *Car ownership trends and forecasts,* Report LR 799, TRRL, Crowthorne

   (1981) *Saturation levels in car ownership models: some recent data*, Report SR 669, TRRL, Crowthorne

Taylor, R. H. (1983) *Alternative energy sources for the centralised generation of electricity*, Adam Hilger Ltd, Bristol

Thirring, H. (1954) *Power production*, Harrap, London

Treasury (1961) *The financial and economic obligations of the nationalised industries,* White Paper Cmnd 1337, HMSO, London

   (1967) *Nationalised industries: a review of economic and financial objectives,* White Paper Cmnd 3437, HMSO, London

   (1978) *The nationalised industries*, White Paper Cmnd 7131, HMSO, London

Turrent, D., Doggart, J. and Ferrano, R. (1980) *Passive solar housing in the UK,* Energy Conscious Design, London

Turvey, R. and Anderson, D. (1977) *Electricity economics: essays and case studies*, Johns Hopkins University Press, Baltimore and London

Watt Committee (1979) *A warmer house at lower cost: the national use of energy in the home*, Watt Committee on Energy Ltd, London

Whittle, G. E. and Warren, P. R. (1978) *Efficiency of domestic hot water production out of the heating season*, BRE Current Paper CP 44/78, BRE, Watford

Williams, R. (1980) *The nuclear power decisions: British policies 1953–78*, Croom Helm, London

Wilson, C. L. (1980) *Coal – bridge to the future: Report of the WOCOL coal study*, Ballinger, Cambridge, Mass.

World Energy Conference (1983) *UK national energy data*, National energy data report series, World Energy Conference, London

Index